HOPELESS SAVAGES

34

WRITTEN BY JEN VAN METER

ILLUSTRATED BY CHRISTINE NORRIE

LETTERED BY ANDY LISS

FLASHBACKS AND "STICKS AND STONES" ILLUSTRATED BY CHYNNA CLUGSTON-MAJOR

COVER, LOGO, CHAPTER BREAKS, AND "ROMANCE #1" COLORING BY ANDI WATSON

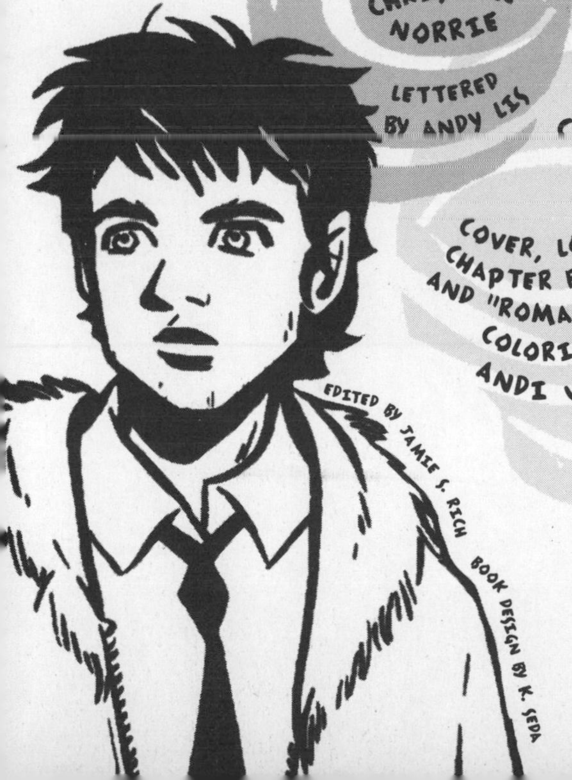

EDITED BY JAMIE S. RICH

BOOK DESIGN BY K. SEDA

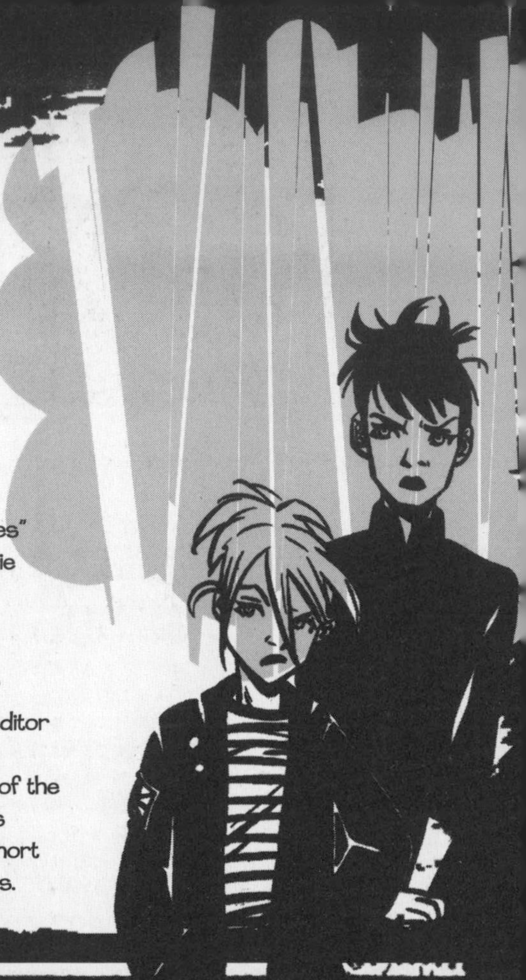

Cover colored by
Guy Major

Lettering font provided by
Larry Young

"Sticks and Stones"
gray tones by Guy Major
lettered by Amie Grenier

"Open House" and "Good Fences"
gray tones by Christine Norrie

Published by Oni Press, Inc.
Joe Nozemack, publisher
Jamie S. Rich, editor in chief
James Lucas Jones, associate editor

This book collects all four issues of the Oni Press comic book series Hopeless Savages, as well as short stories from various sources.

ONI PRESS, INC.
6336 SE Milwaukie Avenue, PMB30
Portland, OR 97202
USA

www.onipress.com
www.spookoo.com

Second Oni Press edition: September 2003
ISBN 1-929998-75-9

1 3 5 7 9 10 8 6 4 2

PRINTED IN CANADA.

PHOTO BY CHYNNA CLUGSTON-MAJOR '77

..IERE WAS RIOTING IN THE STREETS...OR SO WE LIKE TO THINK.

77 was a long time ago, and we all like to remember ourselves as a lot bigger
..an when we were. I know most of my stories have taken on legendary proportions.
..t only did I burgle the Louvre one Friday night, but my accomplices were Joe
..rummer and that guy who played Jimmy in *Quadrophenia* (you know, the "Parklife,"
..ves-a-bit-of-it guy). Winston Churchill drove the getaway car wearing a Mohican
..g so no one would recognize him. It was mental.

..s the sort of thing where, yeah, if you really remember it, you weren't there. If
..u have a pretty good idea of how dank and nasty a lot of it was—how much urine
..ere was in the street, the proliferation of gobs on the wall, the warmness of the
..er—you probably have seen it in picture books or watched one of the countless
..cumentaries meant to cash in on the occasional punk rock fever. You know, like
..en Green Day turned into Sum 41 and suddenly kids were putting chains on their
..llets again. Which, come to think of it, is the perfect fashion accessory to separate
..e real deal from the mallrat poseur. If you look like several feet of bad medicine
..th leather and studs and hair that airport security would be worried to let you
..ard with, do you really need to be concerned about some stupid pickpocket
..cking your wallet? Didn't think so.

.., yeah, most of you weren't there.

..t some of you were. I mean, somebody had to be there otherwise it would never
..ve happened, if you catch my drift. And like I said, it was mental. It may not be
.. crazy as they tell you, but it's as crazy as we pretend to recall.

..d I remember seeing Dirk Hopeless for the first time. It was around that period
..ere labels were snatching up anything that came on black plastic and was
..apped in a little paper sleeve. A lot of cack was getting signed, pressed, and
..ayed on BBC to scare the grandmothers while they chomped their biscuits—
..t it hadn't gotten so bad that you couldn't yet tell the true from the false. Dirk
..peless was no fake. Like those aliens in those movies that burn holes in metal
..en they bleed, Dirk's sweat was like acid to the opportunists who wanted to put
..e boot into good, old fashioned, we-hate-you rock-and-roll. Dirk on stage was
..e Neil Armstrong on the moon. A boy of seventeen couldn't help but let his jaw
..op and think, "This...this is better than anything anyone has ever done *ever*."

Keep in mind, this was the beginning of the set, even. Nikki Savage hadn't yet m
one of her amazing appearances. You know how she was—like Bowie wanted to
had he really needed to wear a bra. Their sexuality, their smolder, their passio
this wasn't some come-on, Mick Ronson letting Ziggy make sweet kisses to his fr
so the California surf jocks could be all, "Ewww, gross." It was all that swea
fumbling backseat stuff *rawk* was supposed to be about.

I was lost forever. I pierced my ear that night with a book of matches and
ballpoint pen. Thankfully, this was in the days before DNA testing, coz I left tr
of earlobe blood all over the museum while me and Joe and Jimmy went runn
through its halls…but that's not the point.

The point is, in big capital letters, DIRK HOPELESS AND NIKKI SAVAGE WERE T
SPONSORS OF MY TEENAGE REBELLION, AND NOW THEY HAVE FOUR FREAKIN' KI
A HOUSE IN THE SUBURBS, AND THEY DON'T EVEN DO DRUGS! WHAT IN GOD'S NA
HAPPENED?

Granted, as you'll find out when you read their story, they aren't exactly yo
regular society types. As far as I can tell, Dirk doesn't own a set of golf clubs
he did, I'd use them to brain him). But it's a bit freaky, no?

Then again, Nikki's 1998 album was her best to date. The production on it can m
you weep like George W. Bush when he opens the briefcase and finds piles
corporate hush money. So no one's fire has really gone dim. No one's burnt o
no one's faded away. And I bet the two of them still like to riot from time to ti

Anyone know where they're keeping the good museums these days?

> Chester Melville
> North of the equator,
> south of the pole
> May 2002

Chester Melville is an influential
rock writer and editor who helped
form *The Pants Pages* in the late
'70s, in a time when it was still
okay to be rude, offensive, and
non-corporate. Currently, he inhabits
similar havens on the world wide
web, but figures it's only a matter
of time before they find him there,
too. He urges you buy his book,
Spunk & Junk, a collection of some
of his best pieces, because he could
sure use a couple of royalty checks.

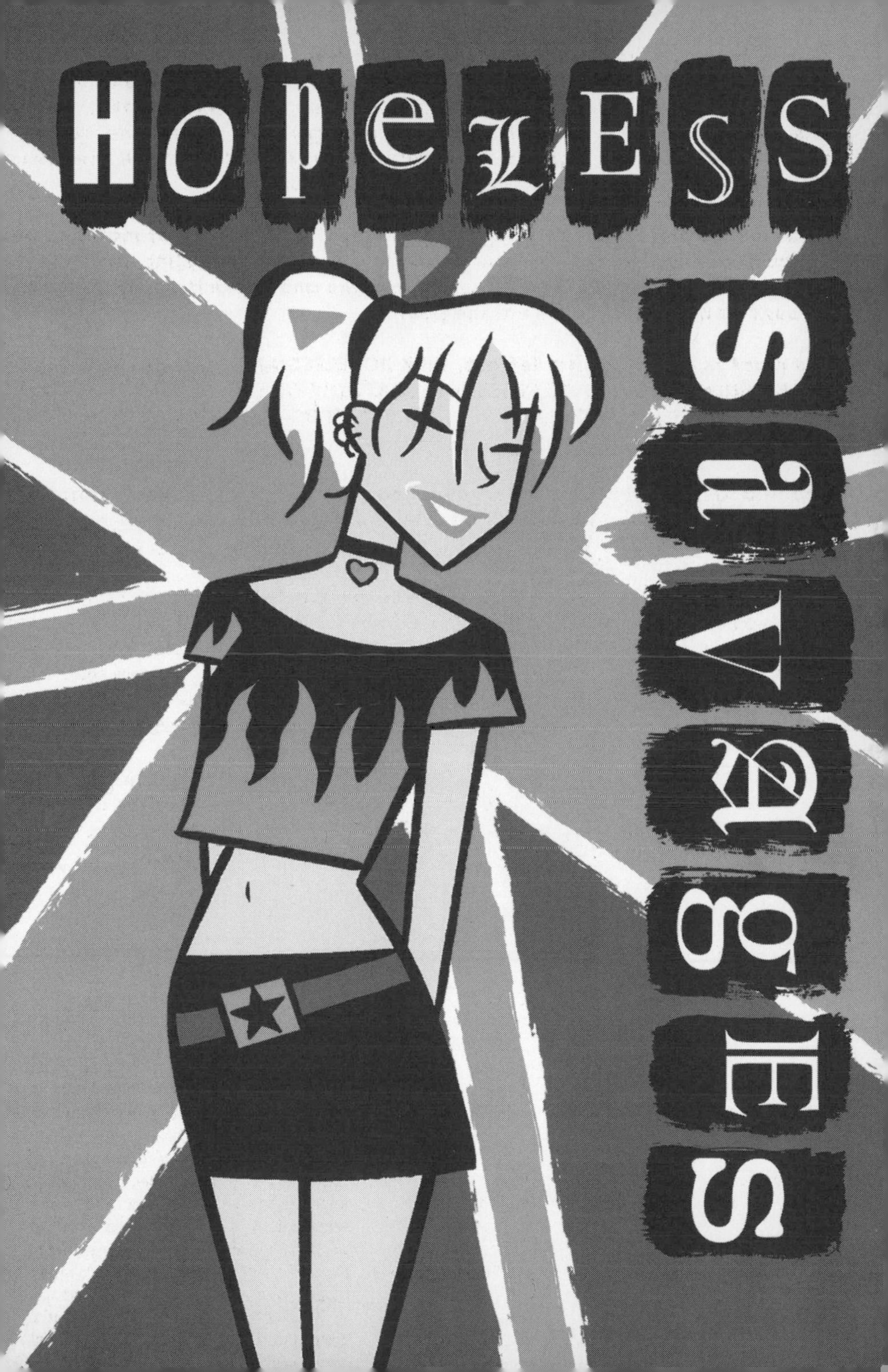
Hopeless
Savages

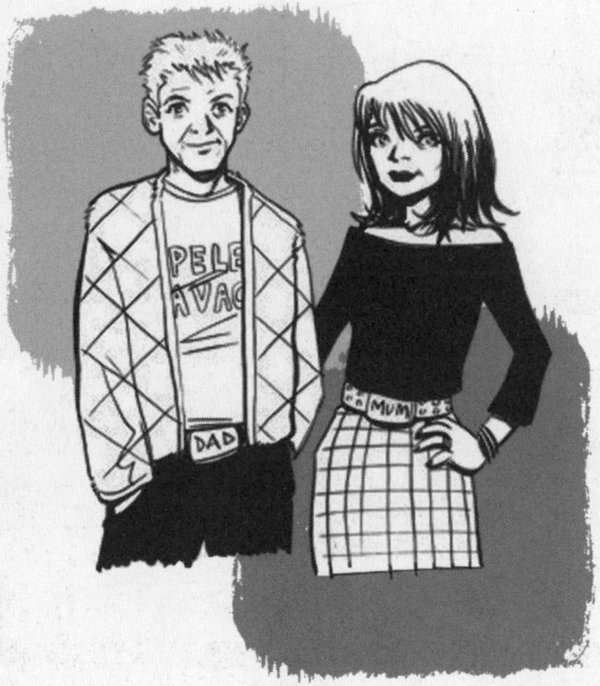
PELE
AVAC
DAD
MUM

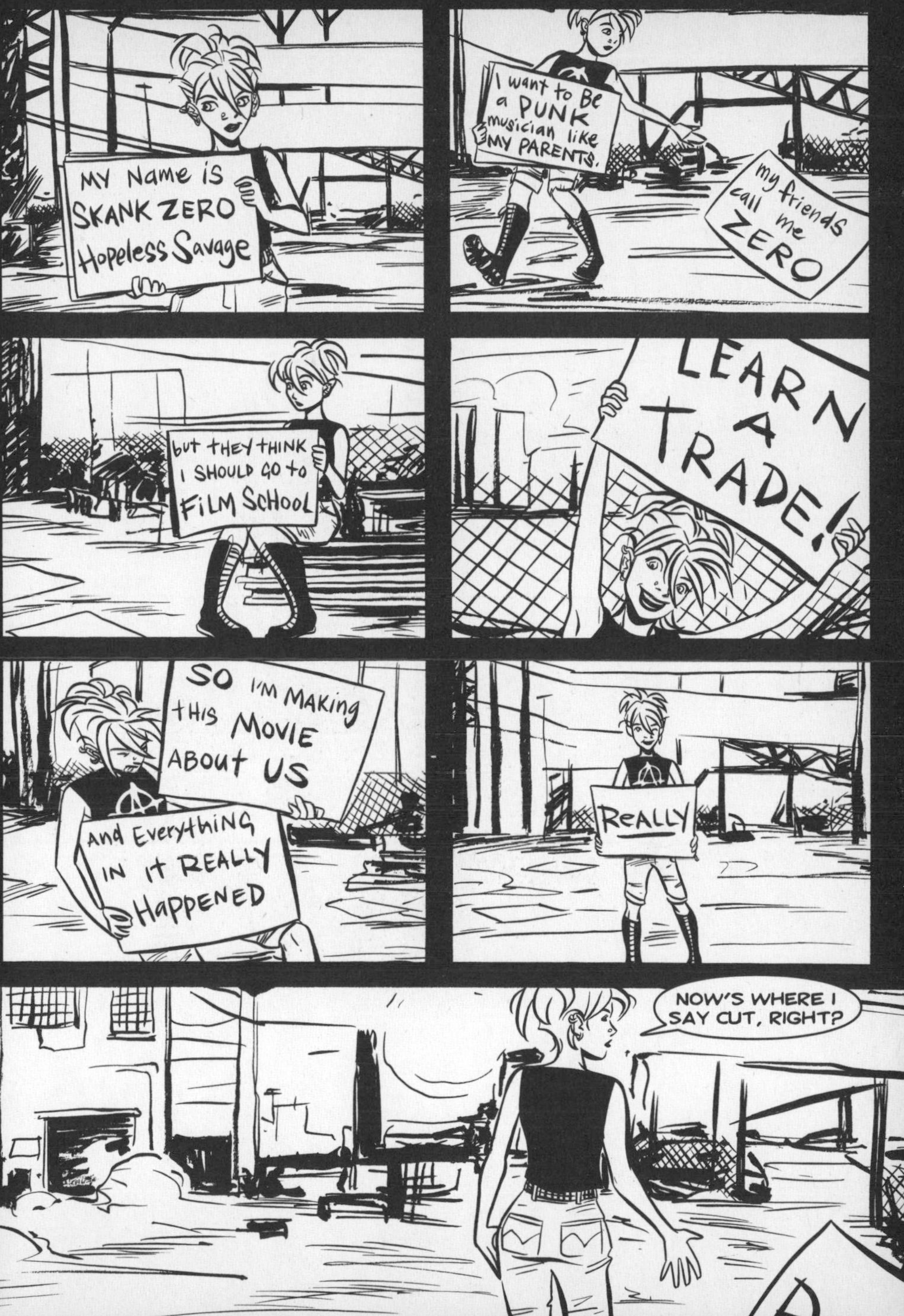
MY Name is
SKANK ZERO
Hopeless Savage
I want to Be a PUNK musician like MY PARENTS.
my friends call me ZERO
but THEY THINK I SHOULD GO to FiLM SCHOOL
LEARN A TRADE!
SO I'M MAKING tHIS MOVIE ABOUT US
AND EVERYTHING IN IT REALLY HAPPENED
REALLY
NOW'S WHERE I SAY CUT, RIGHT?

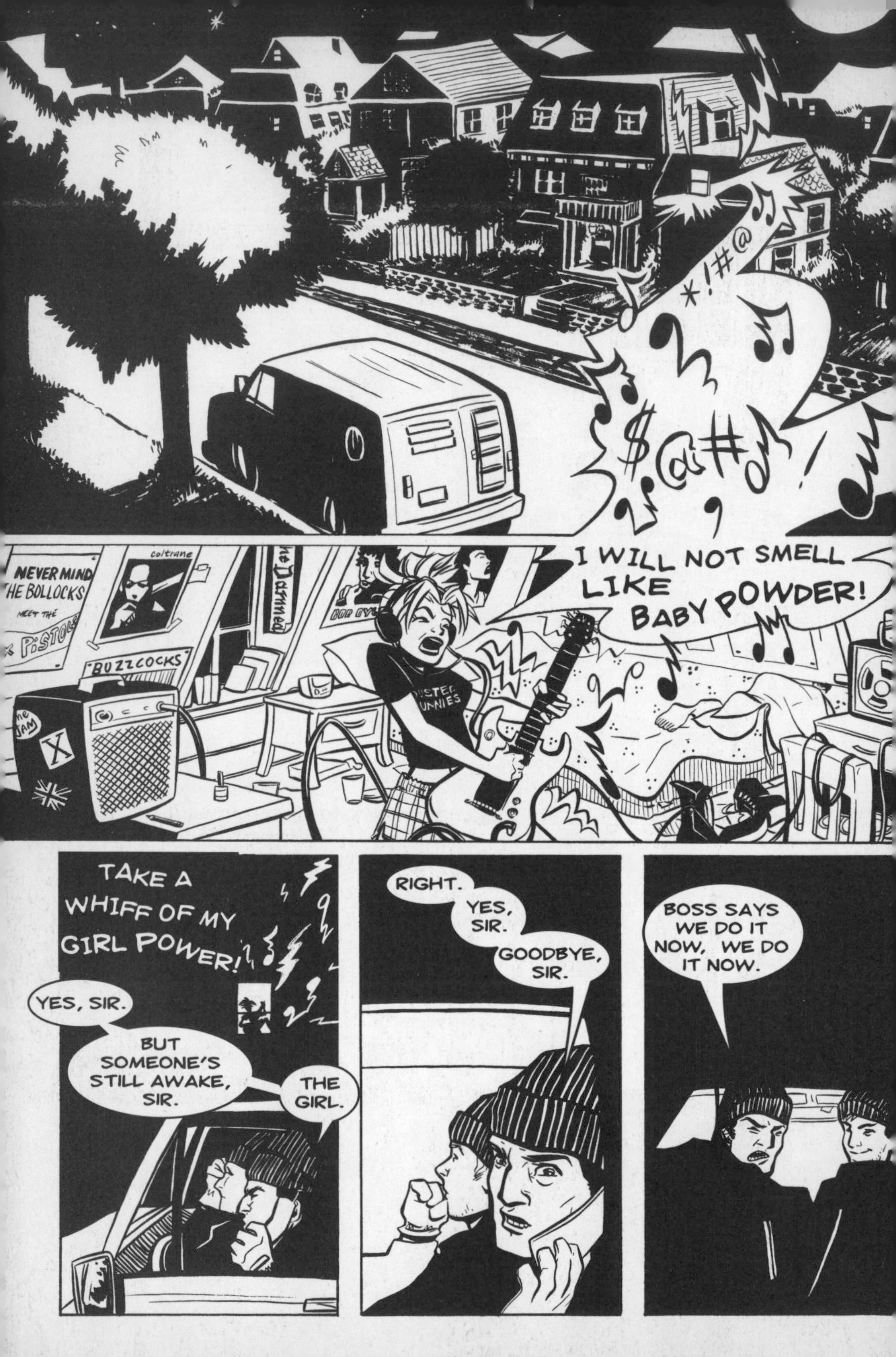
*!#@
$@#
I WILL NOT SMELL LIKE BABY POWDER!
NEVER MIND THE BOLLOCKS
coltrane
BUZZCOCKS
TAKE A WHIFF OF MY GIRL POWER!
YES, SIR.
BUT SOMEONE'S STILL AWAKE, SIR.
THE GIRL.
RIGHT.
YES, SIR.
GOODBYE, SIR.
BOSS SAYS WE DO IT NOW, WE DO IT NOW.

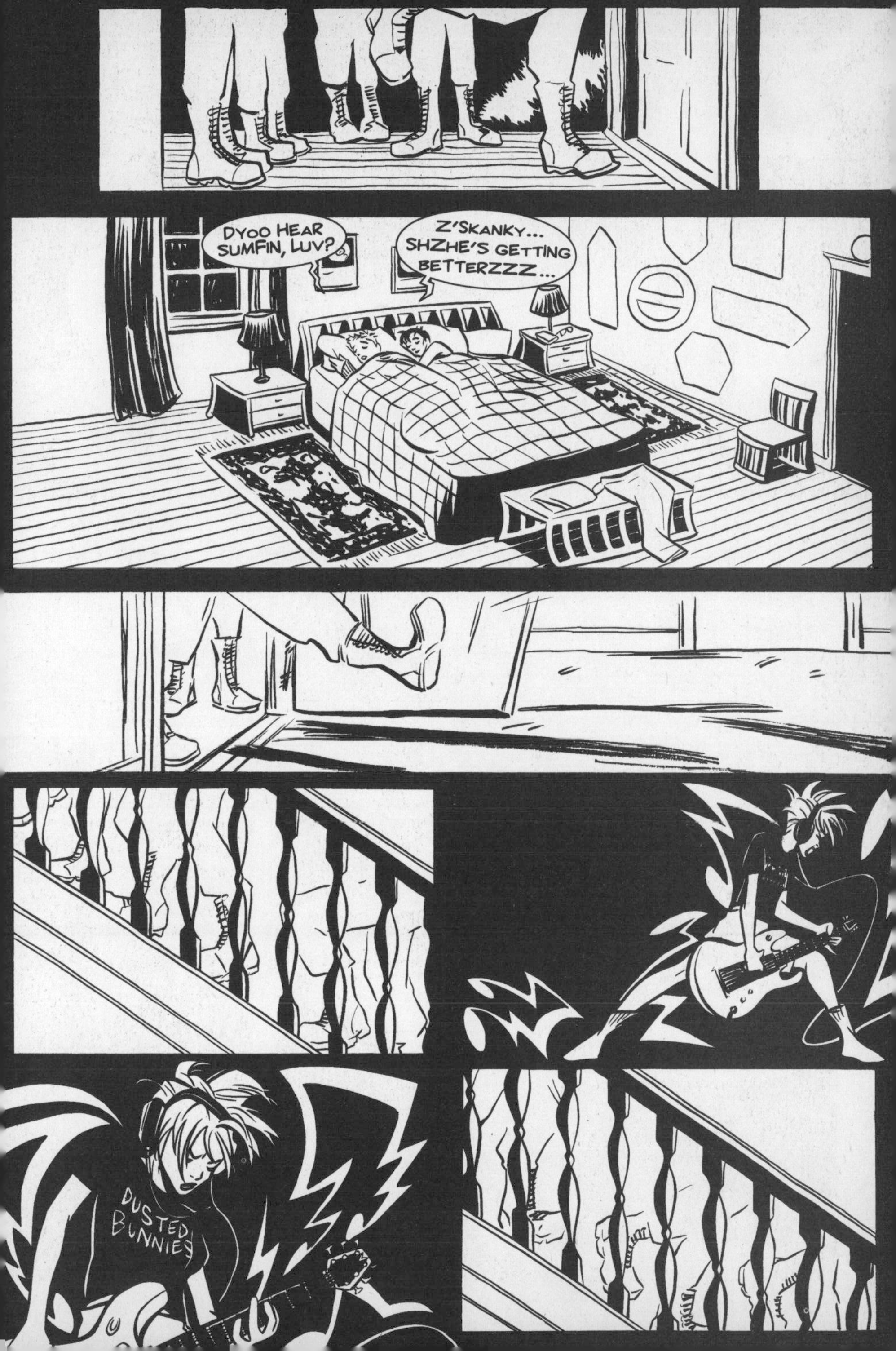
DYOO HEAR SUMFIN, LUV?
Z'SKANKY... SHZHE'S GETTING BETTERZZZ...
DUSTED BUNNIES

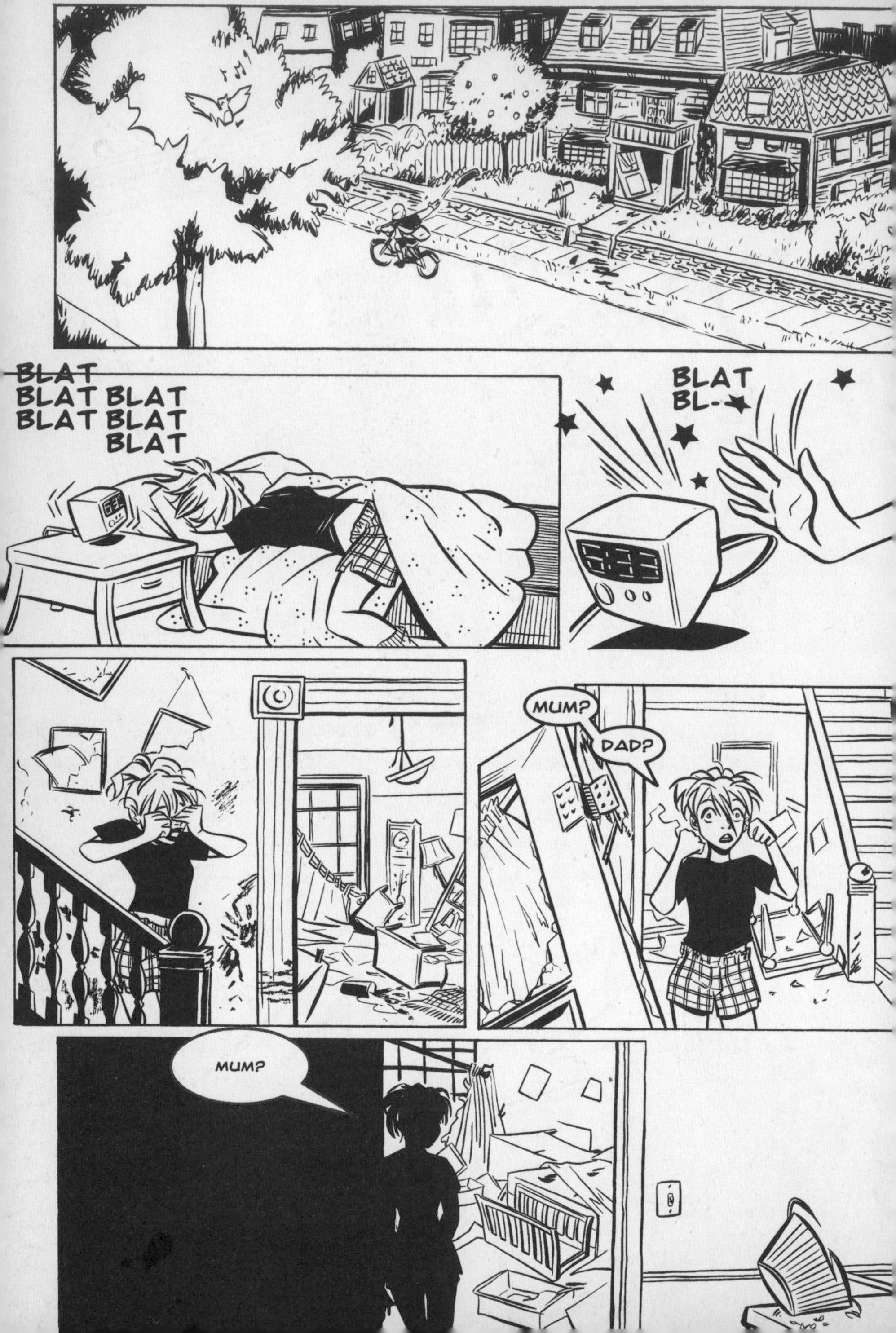
BLAT
BLAT BLAT
BLAT BLAT
BLAT
BLAT
BL-
MUM?
DAD?
MUM?

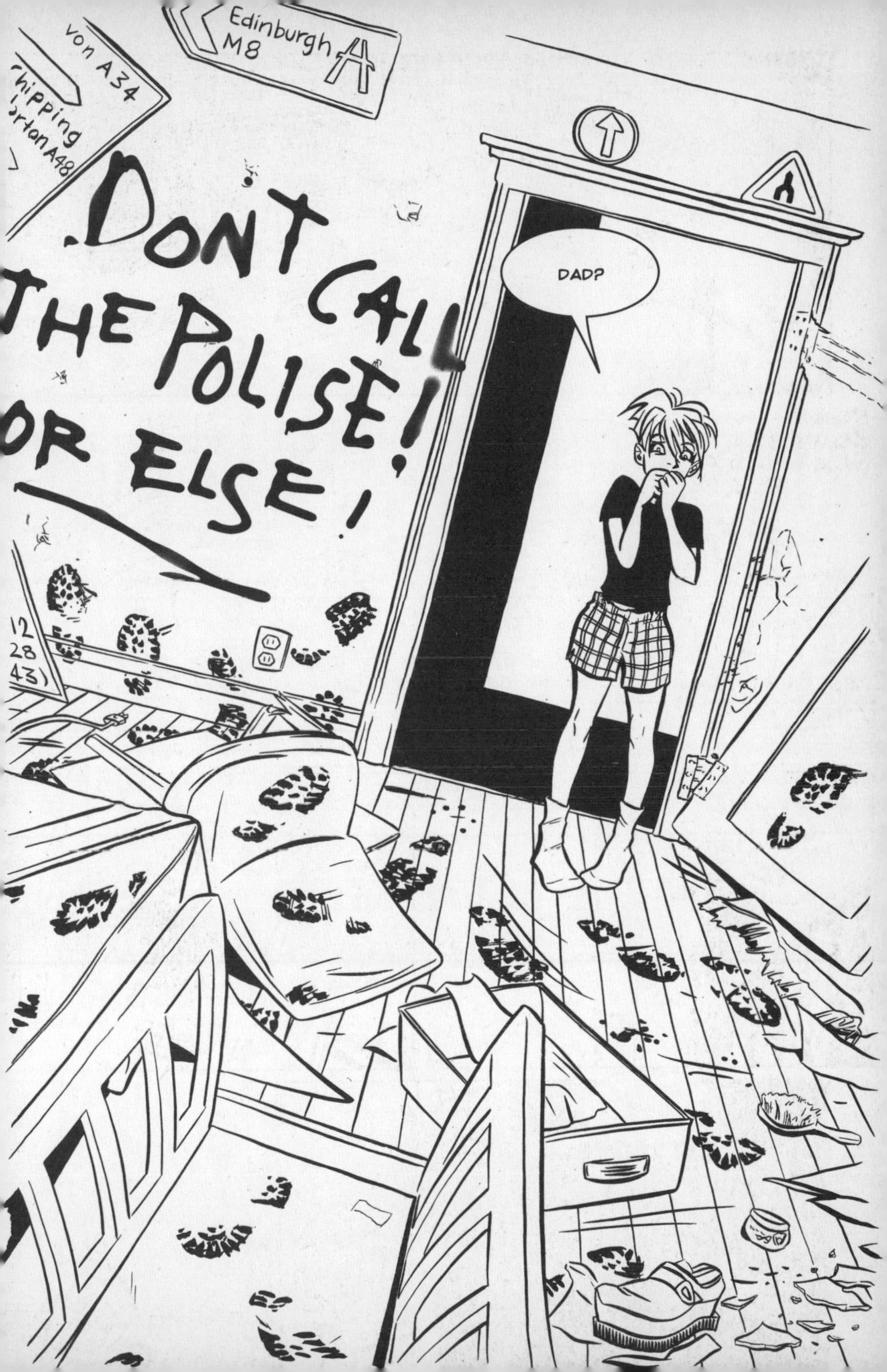

Edinburgh
M8
von A34
Chipping
Norton A48
DON'T CALL THE POLISE OR ELSE!
DAD?
12
28
43)

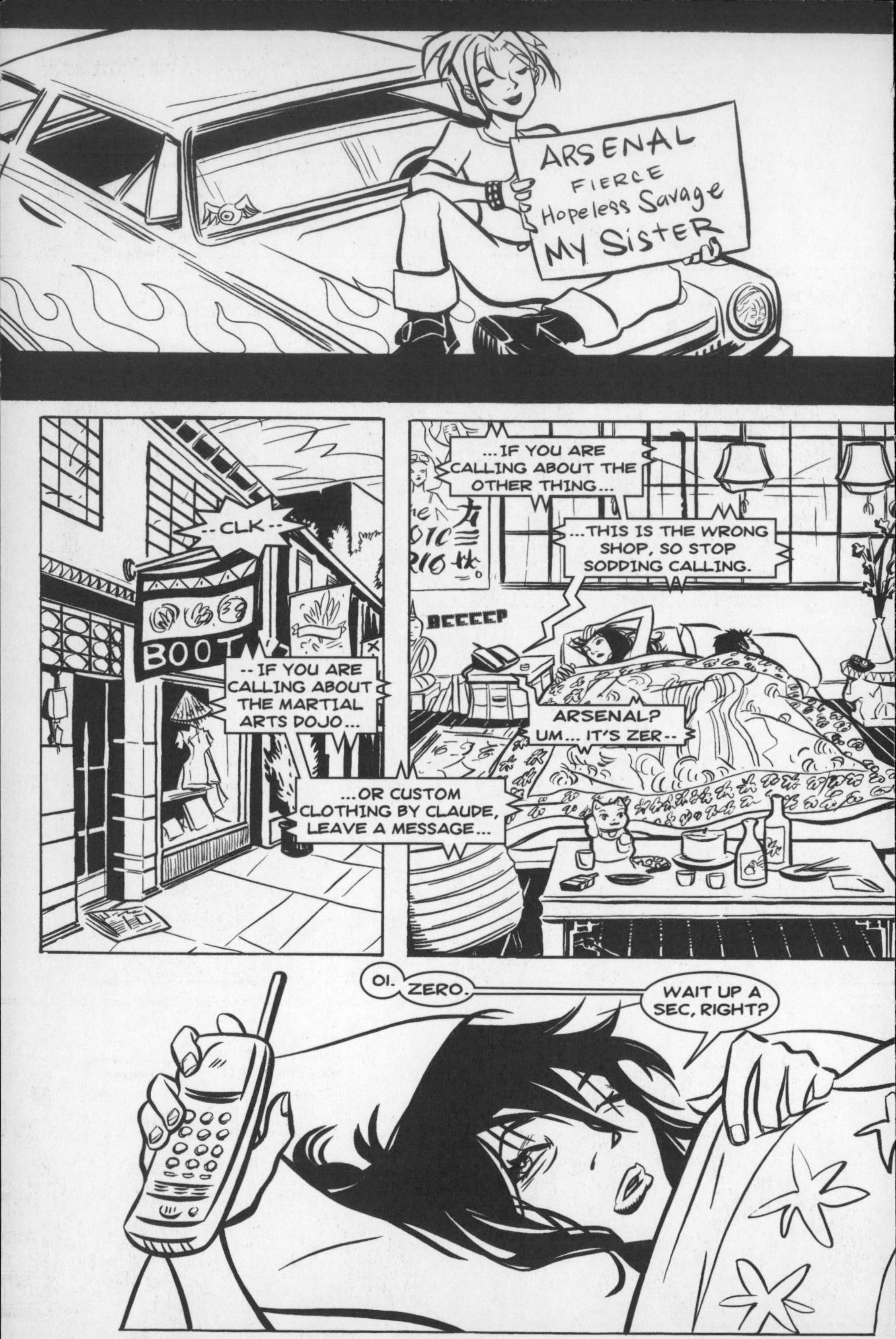
ARSENAL
FIERCE
Hopeless Savage
MY SISTER
BOOT
--CLK--
--IF YOU ARE CALLING ABOUT THE MARTIAL ARTS DOJO...
...IF YOU ARE CALLING ABOUT THE OTHER THING...
...THIS IS THE WRONG SHOP, SO STOP SODDING CALLING.
BEEEEP
ARSENAL? UM... IT'S ZER--
...OR CUSTOM CLOTHING BY CLAUDE, LEAVE A MESSAGE...
OI.
ZERO.
WAIT UP A SEC, RIGHT?

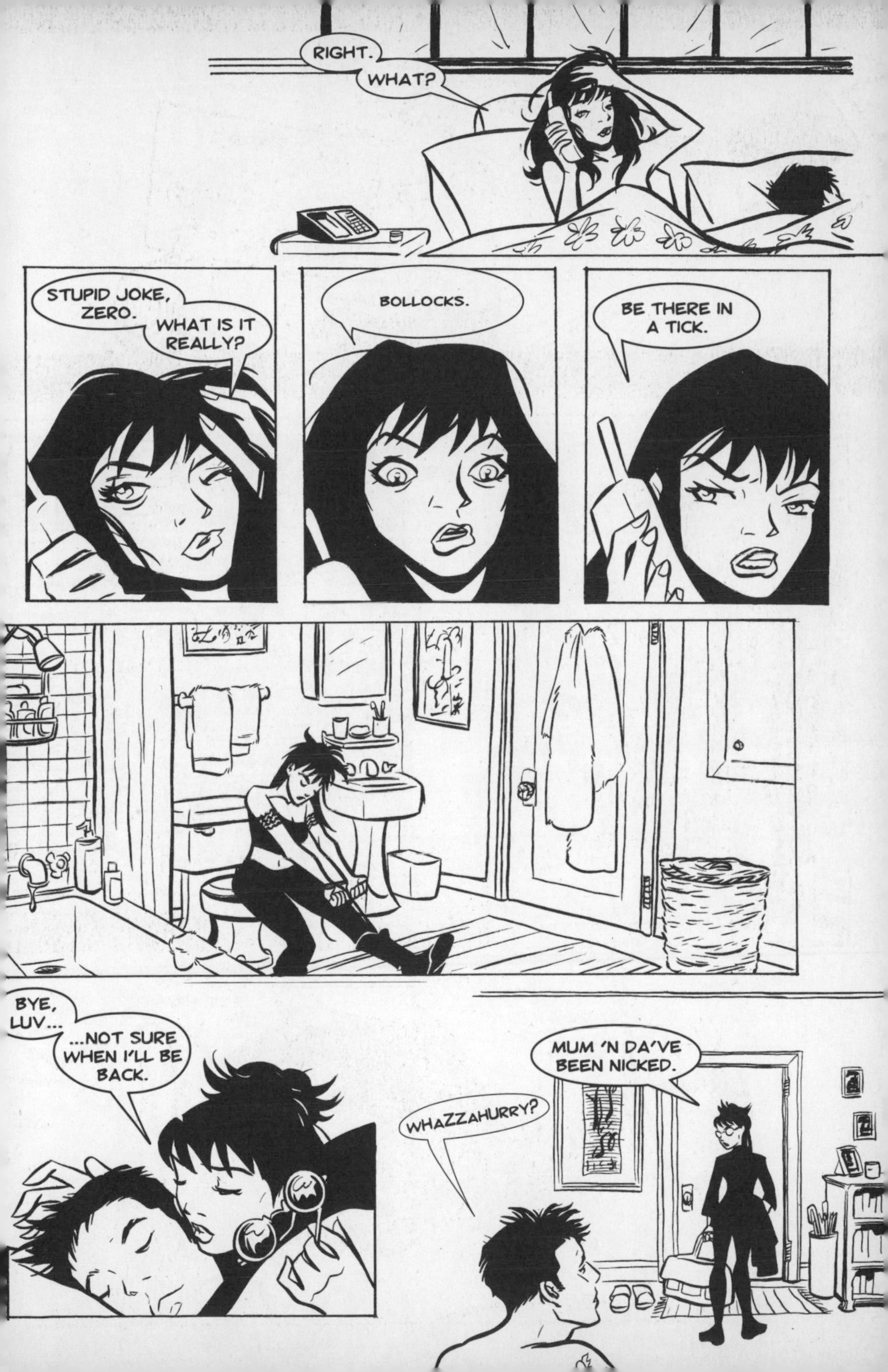
RIGHT.
WHAT?
STUPID JOKE, ZERO.
WHAT IS IT REALLY?
BOLLOCKS.
BE THERE IN A TICK.
BYE, LUV...
...NOT SURE WHEN I'LL BE BACK.
WHAZZAHURRY?
MUM 'N DA'VE BEEN NICKED.

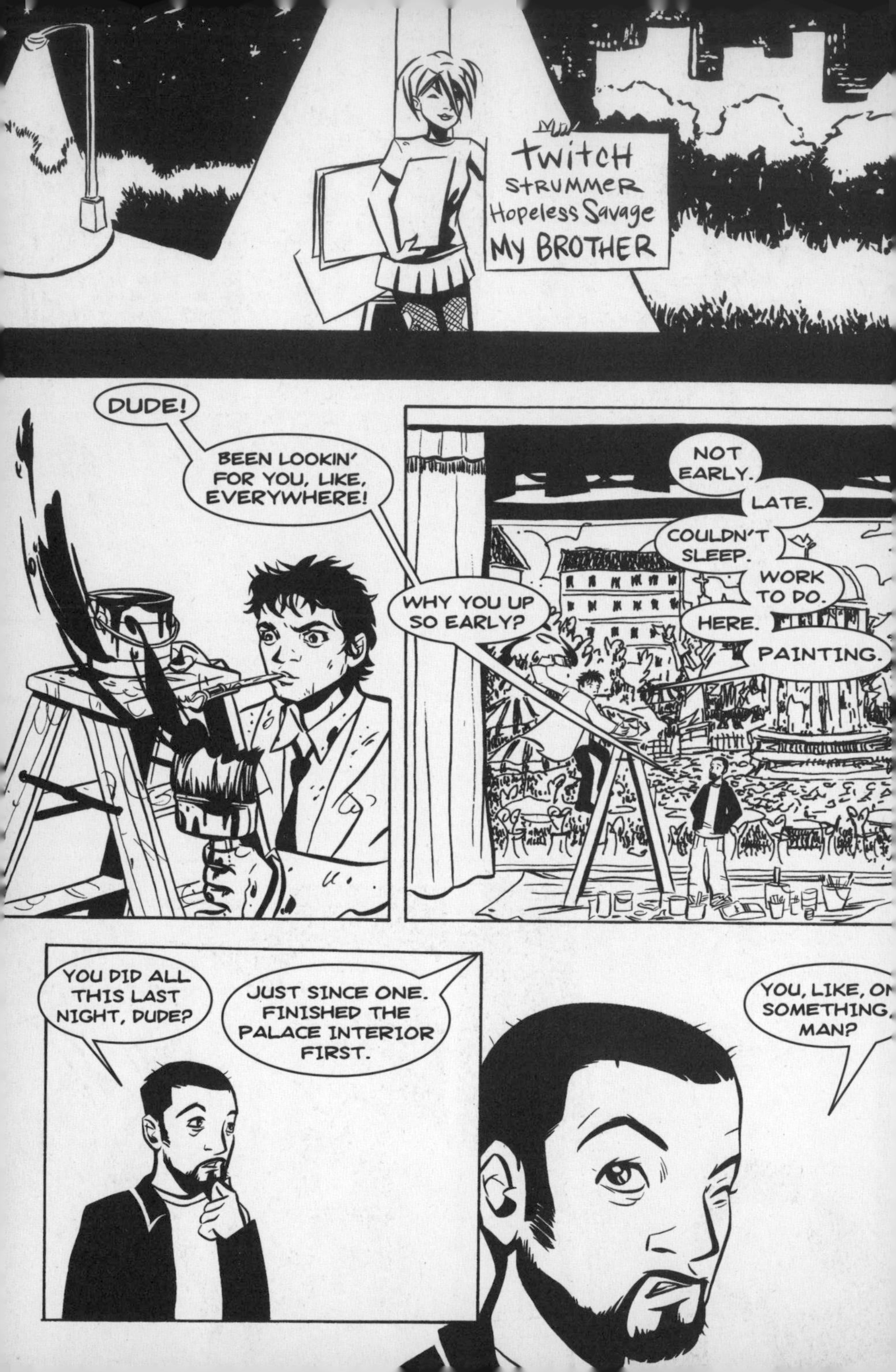
twitch
strummer
Hopeless Savage
My BROTHER
DUDE!
BEEN LOOKIN' FOR YOU, LIKE, EVERYWHERE!
WHY YOU UP SO EARLY?
NOT EARLY.
LATE.
COULDN'T SLEEP.
WORK TO DO.
HERE.
PAINTING.
YOU DID ALL THIS LAST NIGHT, DUDE?
JUST SINCE ONE. FINISHED THE PALACE INTERIOR FIRST.
YOU, LIKE, ON SOMETHING, MAN?

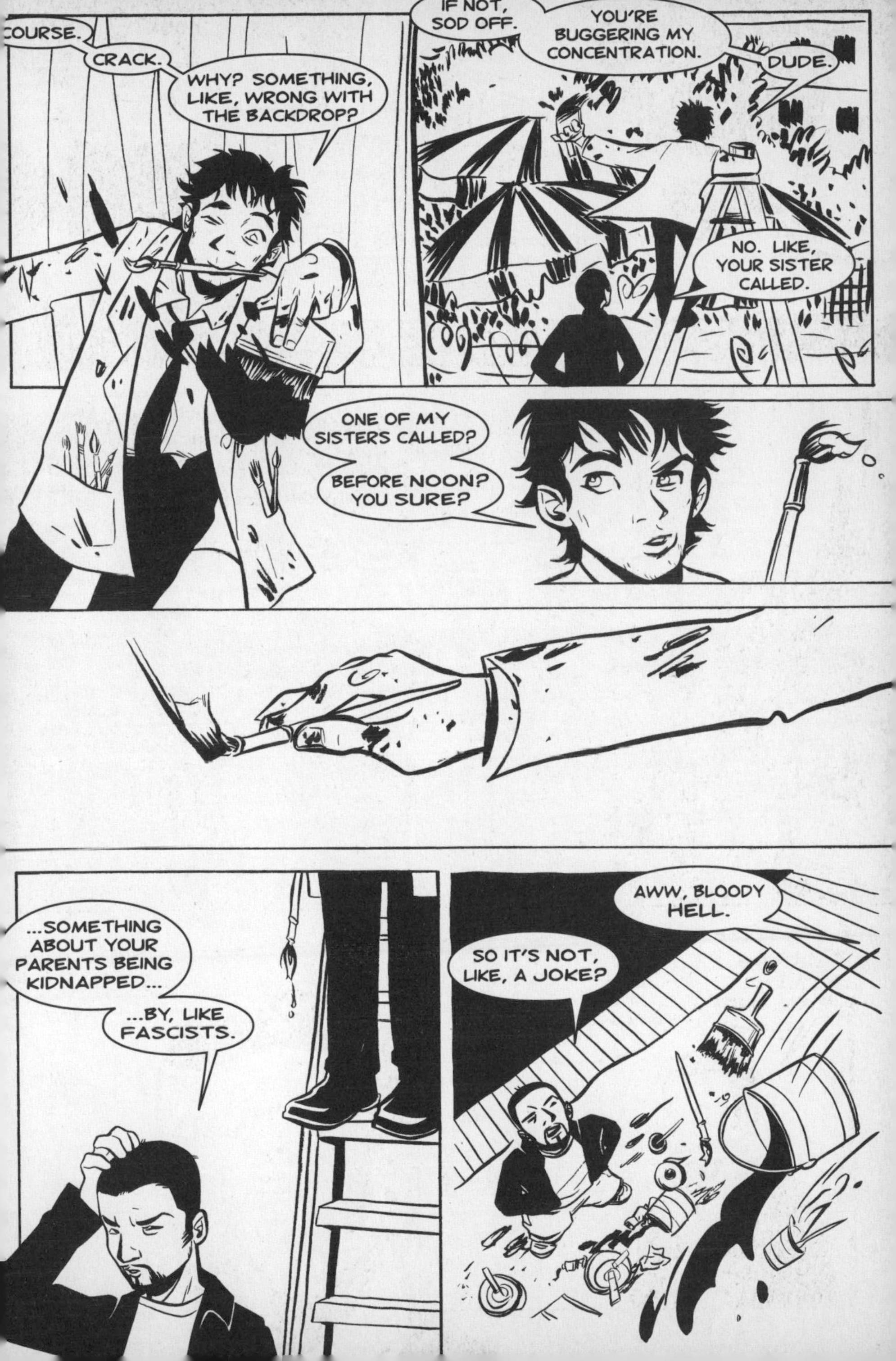
COURSE.
CRACK.
WHY? SOMETHING, LIKE, WRONG WITH THE BACKDROP?
IF NOT, SOD OFF.
YOU'RE BUGGERING MY CONCENTRATION.
DUDE.
NO. LIKE, YOUR SISTER CALLED.
ONE OF MY SISTERS CALLED?
BEFORE NOON? YOU SURE?
...SOMETHING ABOUT YOUR PARENTS BEING KIDNAPPED...
...BY, LIKE FASCISTS.
AWW, BLOODY HELL.
SO IT'S NOT, LIKE, A JOKE?

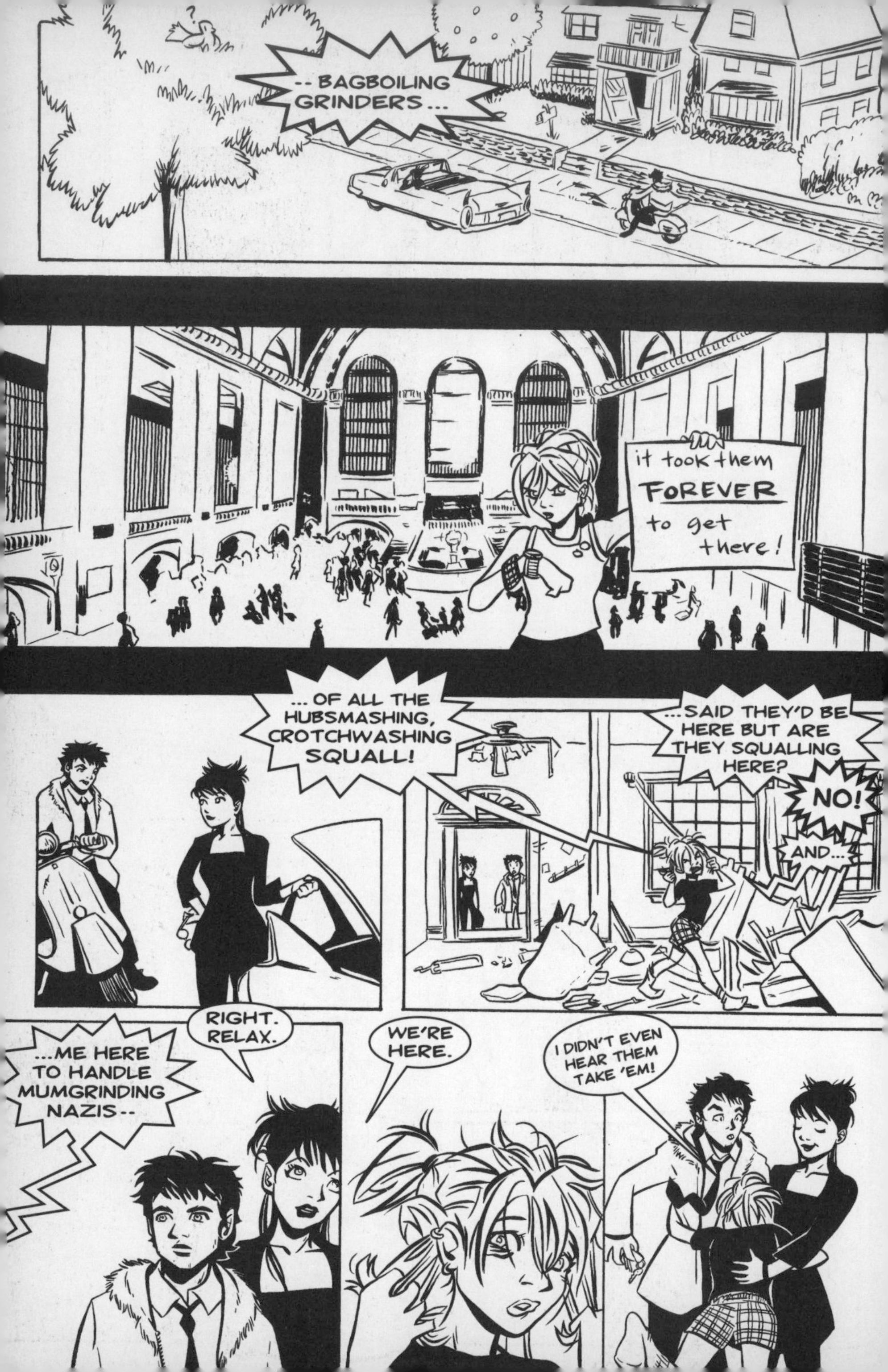

-- BAGBOILING GRINDERS...
it took them FOREVER to get there!
...OF ALL THE HUBSMASHING, CROTCHWASHING SQUALL!
...SAID THEY'D BE HERE BUT ARE THEY SQUALLING HERE?
NO!
AND...
...ME HERE TO HANDLE MUMGRINDING NAZIS--
RIGHT. RELAX.
WE'RE HERE.
I DIDN'T EVEN HEAR THEM TAKE 'EM!

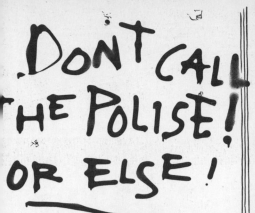

DON'T CALL THE POLISE! OR ELSE!

BLOODY UNPROFESSIONAL FOR A START.

PERSONAL, TOO.

OR ELSE WHAT, D'YA THINK?

ELSE THEY COME BACK AND SPELL BADLY S'MORE?

THIS IS UNBELIEVABLE!

YOU TWO STAND THERE SMATCHETING AROUND LIKE IT'S A JOKE--

--BUT IT'S NOT A SODDING JOKE. IT'S OUR PARENTS AND SOMEONE HAS THEM!

WHAT ARE WE SQUALLING GOING TO DO?!

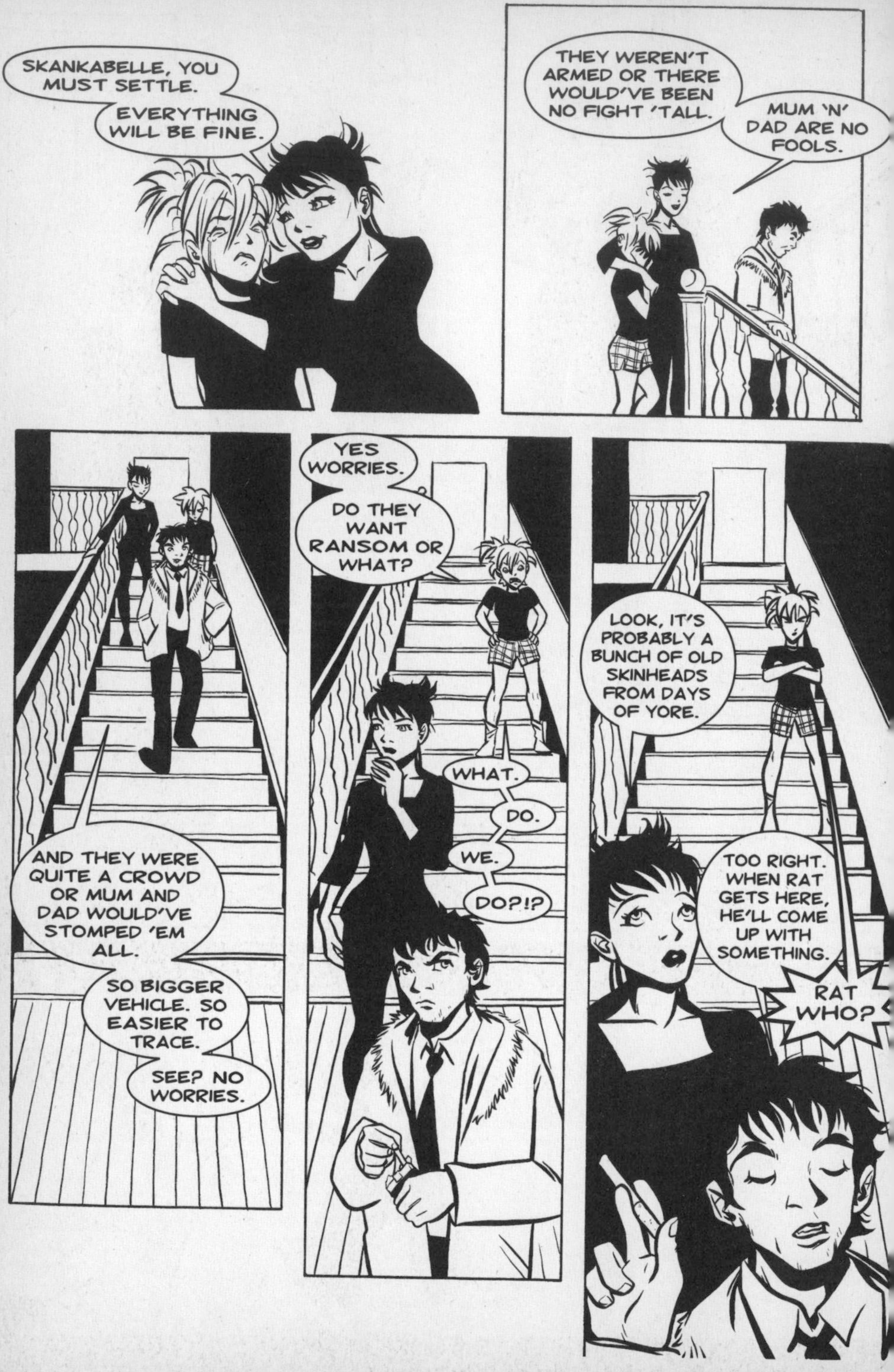
SKANKABELLE, YOU MUST SETTLE.
EVERYTHING WILL BE FINE.
THEY WEREN'T ARMED OR THERE WOULD'VE BEEN NO FIGHT 'TALL.
MUM 'N' DAD ARE NO FOOLS.
AND THEY WERE QUITE A CROWD OR MUM AND DAD WOULD'VE STOMPED 'EM ALL.
SO BIGGER VEHICLE. SO EASIER TO TRACE.
SEE? NO WORRIES.
YES WORRIES.
DO THEY WANT RANSOM OR WHAT?
WHAT.
DO.
WE.
DO?!?
LOOK, IT'S PROBABLY A BUNCH OF OLD SKINHEADS FROM DAYS OF YORE.
TOO RIGHT. WHEN RAT GETS HERE, HE'LL COME UP WITH SOMETHING.
RAT WHO?

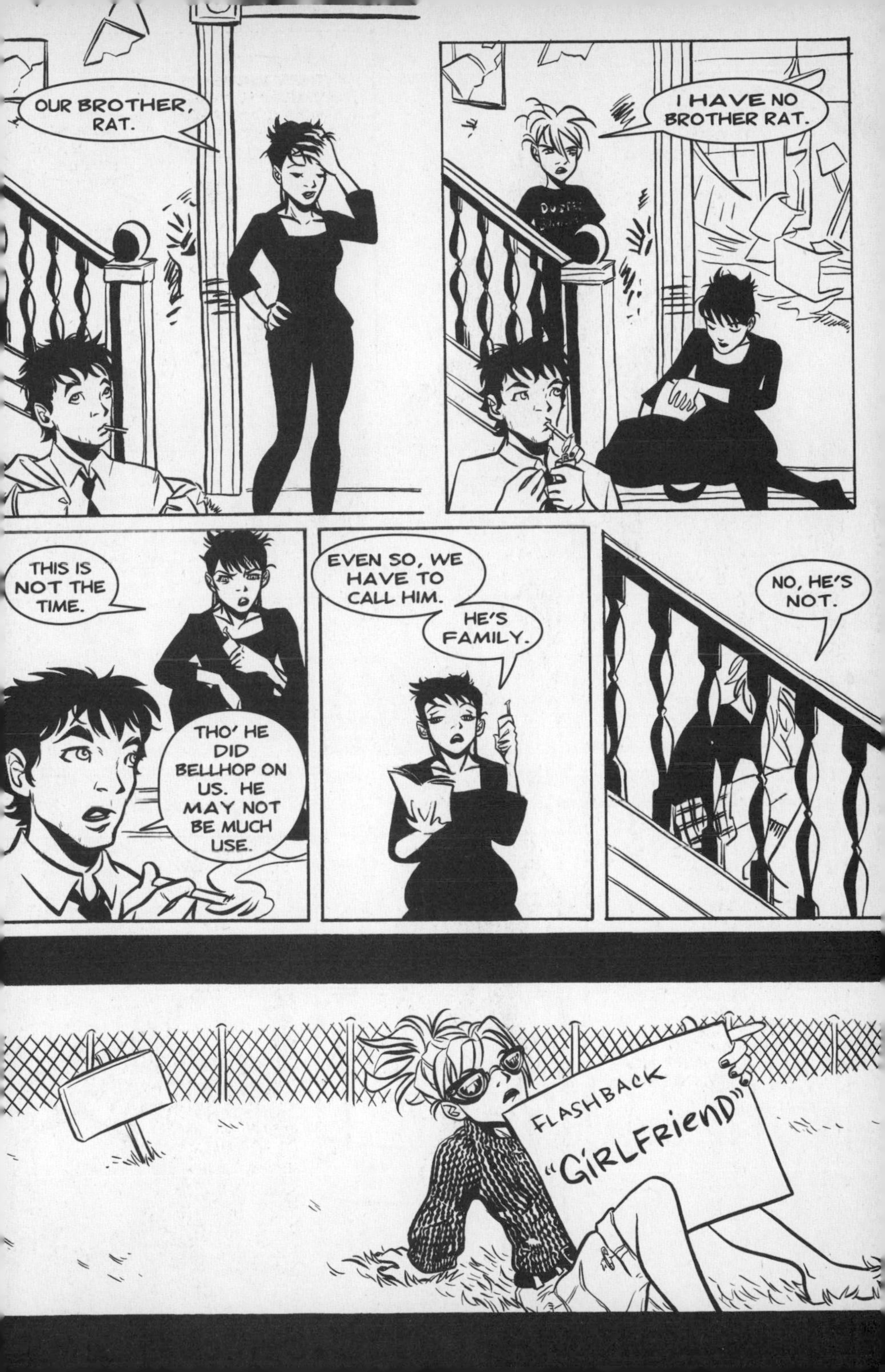
OUR BROTHER, RAT.
I HAVE NO BROTHER RAT.
THIS IS NOT THE TIME.
THO' HE DID BELLHOP ON US. HE MAY NOT BE MUCH USE.
EVEN SO, WE HAVE TO CALL HIM.
HE'S FAMILY.
NO, HE'S NOT.
FLASHBACK
"GIRLFRIEND"

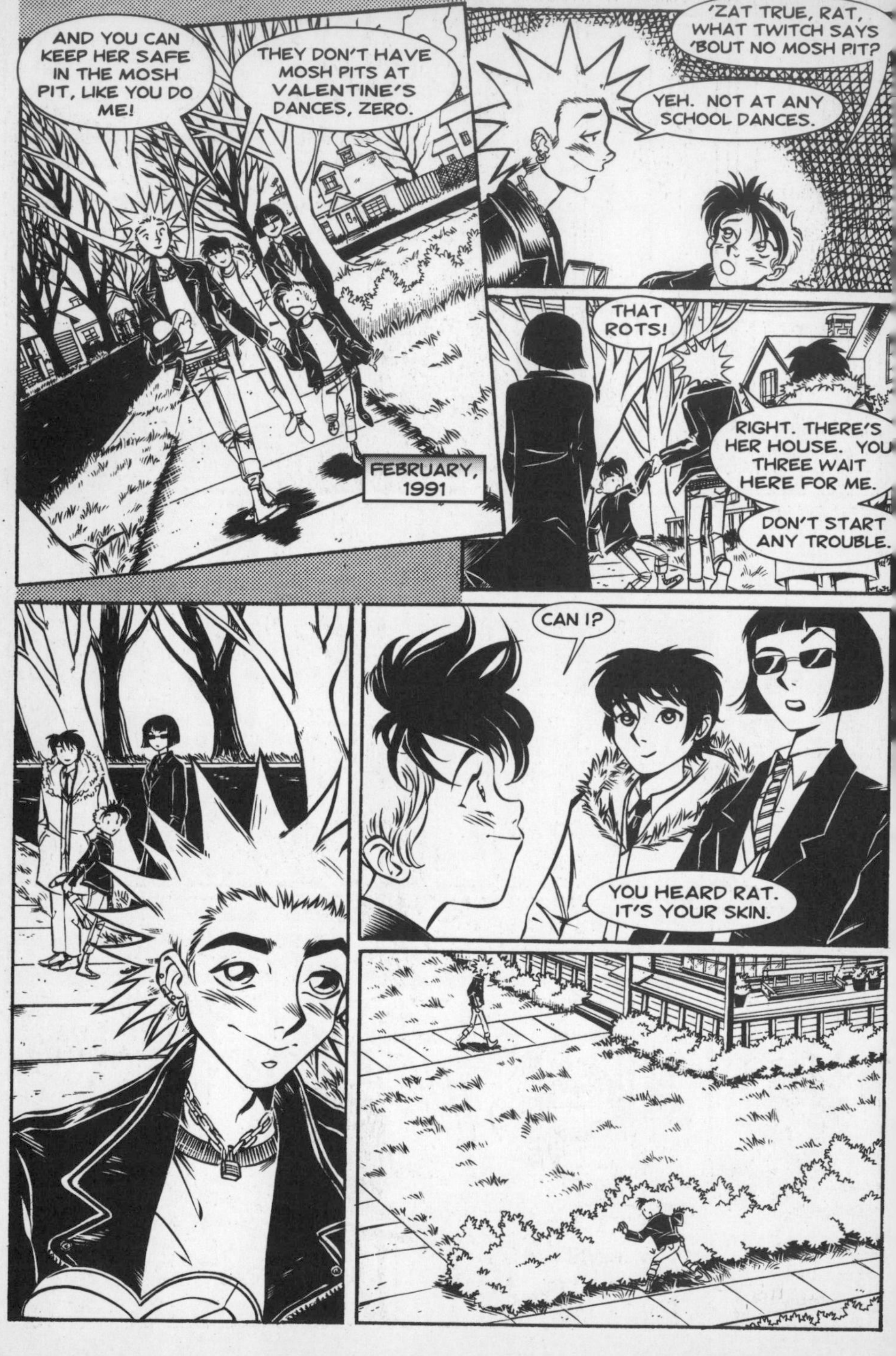

AND YOU CAN KEEP HER SAFE IN THE MOSH PIT, LIKE YOU DO ME!
THEY DON'T HAVE MOSH PITS AT VALENTINE'S DANCES, ZERO.
FEBRUARY, 1991
'ZAT TRUE, RAT, WHAT TWITCH SAYS 'BOUT NO MOSH PIT?
YEH. NOT AT ANY SCHOOL DANCES.
THAT ROTS!
RIGHT. THERE'S HER HOUSE. YOU THREE WAIT HERE FOR ME.
DON'T START ANY TROUBLE.
CAN I?
YOU HEARD RAT. IT'S YOUR SKIN.

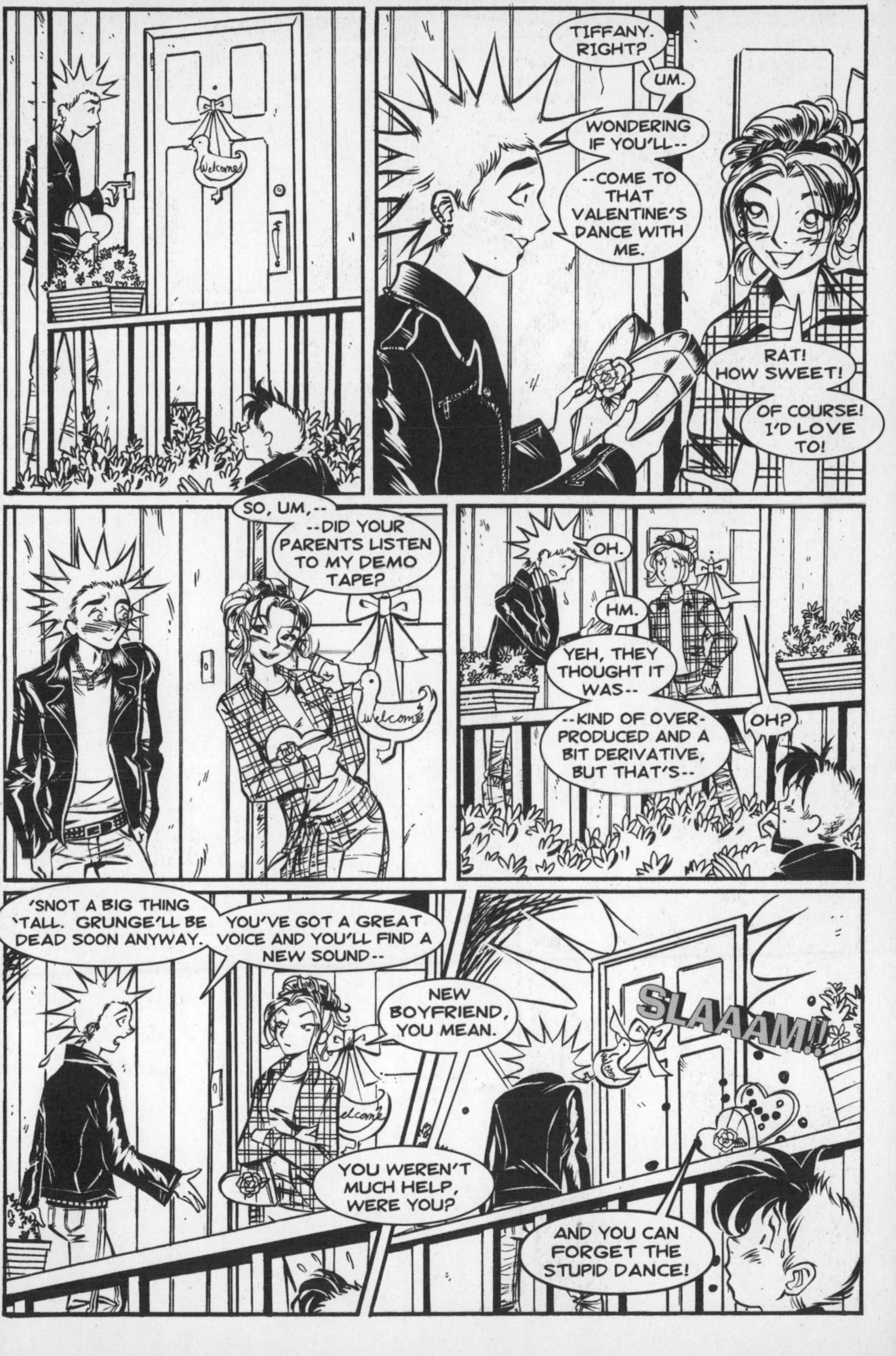
TIFFANY. RIGHT?
UM.
WONDERING IF YOU'LL--
--COME TO THAT VALENTINE'S DANCE WITH ME.
RAT! HOW SWEET!
OF COURSE! I'D LOVE TO!
SO, UM,--
--DID YOUR PARENTS LISTEN TO MY DEMO TAPE?
OH.
HM.
YEH, THEY THOUGHT IT WAS--
--KIND OF OVER-PRODUCED AND A BIT DERIVATIVE, BUT THAT'S--
OH?
'SNOT A BIG THING 'TALL. GRUNGE'LL BE DEAD SOON ANYWAY.
YOU'VE GOT A GREAT VOICE AND YOU'LL FIND A NEW SOUND--
NEW BOYFRIEND, YOU MEAN.
SLAAAM!!
YOU WEREN'T MUCH HELP, WERE YOU?
AND YOU CAN FORGET THE STUPID DANCE!

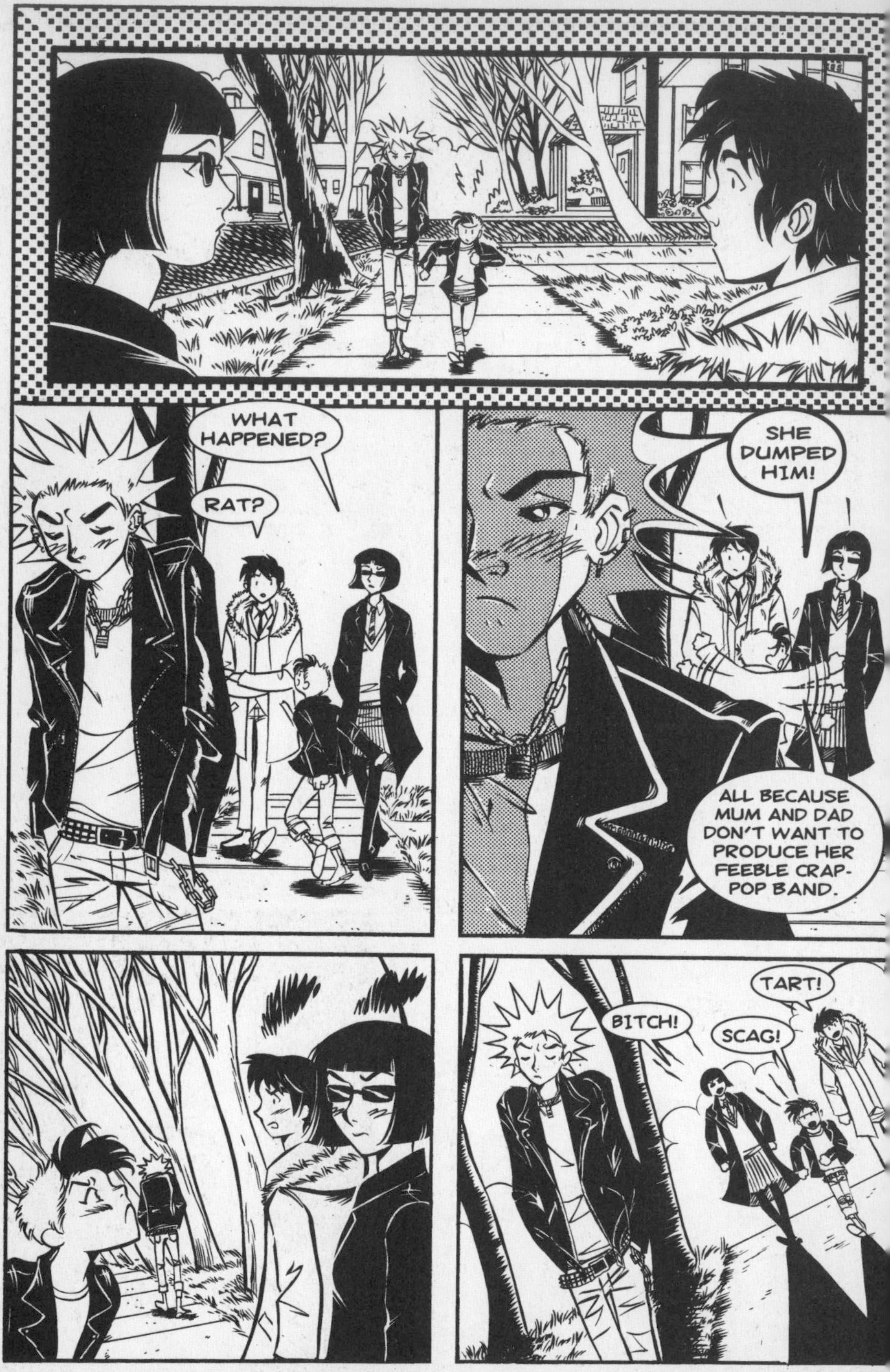
WHAT HAPPENED?
RAT?
SHE DUMPED HIM!
ALL BECAUSE MUM AND DAD DON'T WANT TO PRODUCE HER FEEBLE CRAP-POP BAND.
BITCH!
TART!
SCAG!

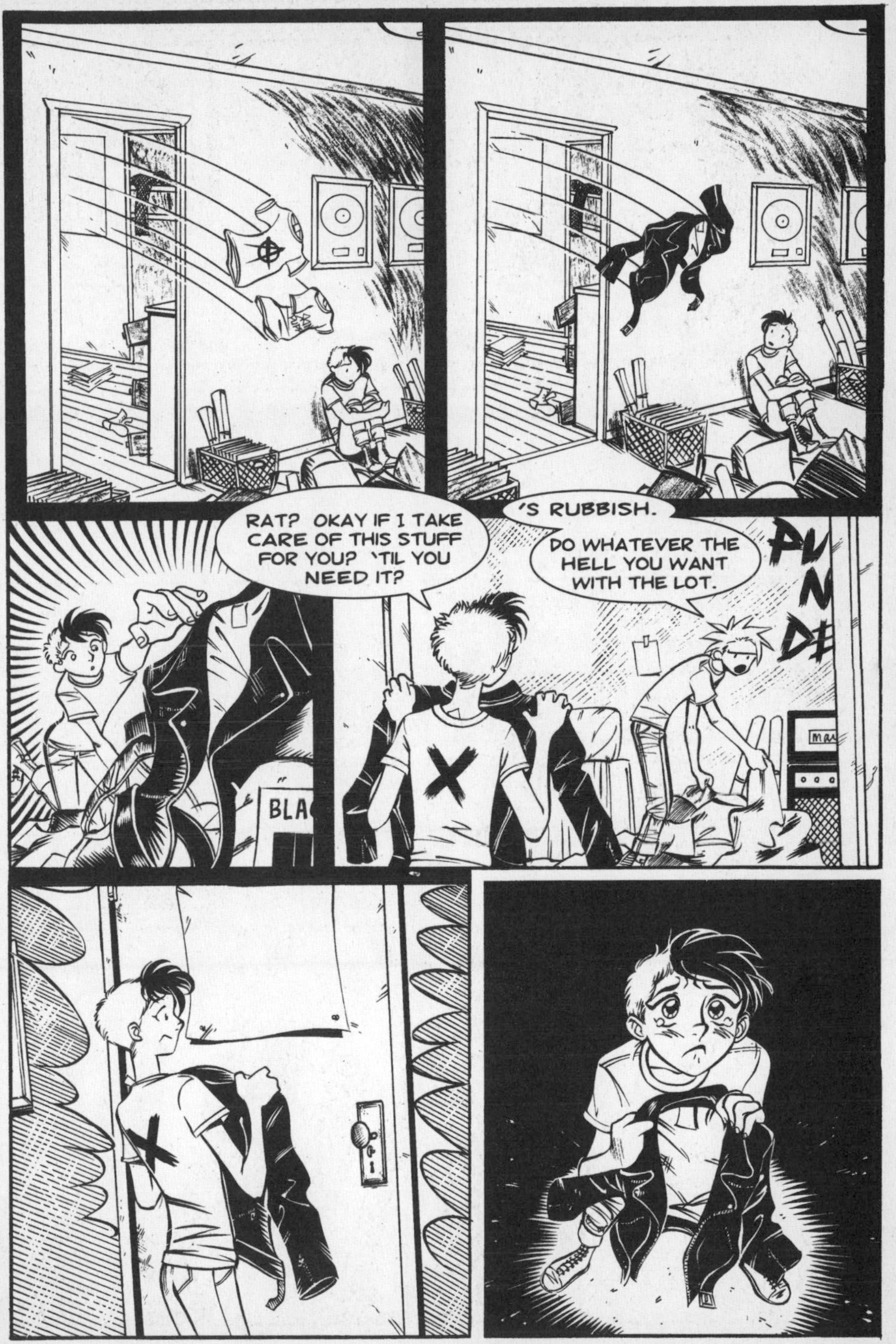
RAT? OKAY IF I TAKE CARE OF THIS STUFF FOR YOU? 'TIL YOU NEED IT?
'S RUBBISH.
DO WHATEVER THE HELL YOU WANT WITH THE LOT.
BLAC

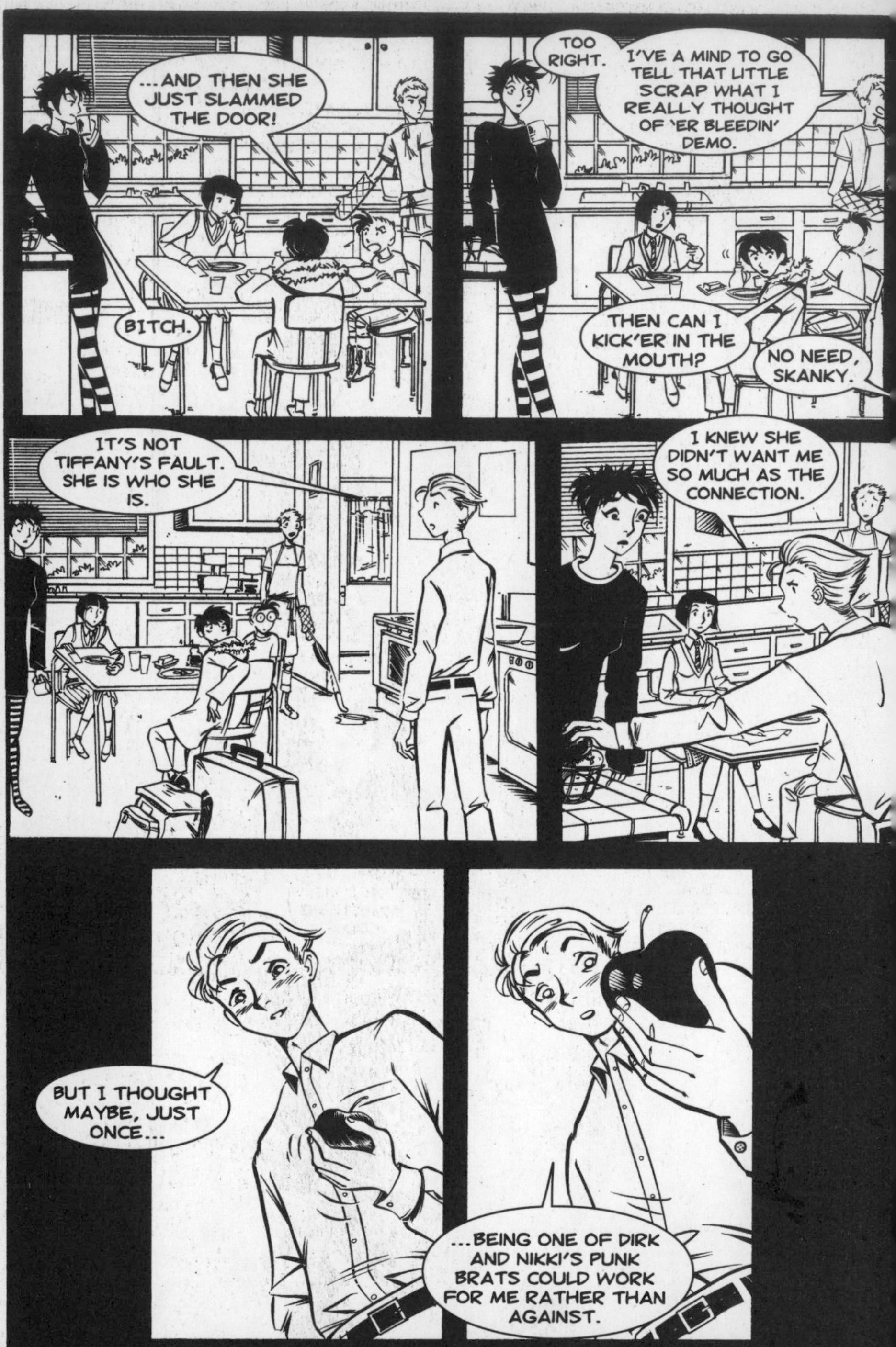
...AND THEN SHE JUST SLAMMED THE DOOR!
BITCH.
TOO RIGHT.
I'VE A MIND TO GO TELL THAT LITTLE SCRAP WHAT I REALLY THOUGHT OF 'ER BLEEDIN' DEMO.
THEN CAN I KICK'ER IN THE MOUTH?
NO NEED, SKANKY.
IT'S NOT TIFFANY'S FAULT. SHE IS WHO SHE IS.
I KNEW SHE DIDN'T WANT ME SO MUCH AS THE CONNECTION.
BUT I THOUGHT MAYBE, JUST ONCE...
...BEING ONE OF DIRK AND NIKKI'S PUNK BRATS COULD WORK FOR ME RATHER THAN AGAINST.

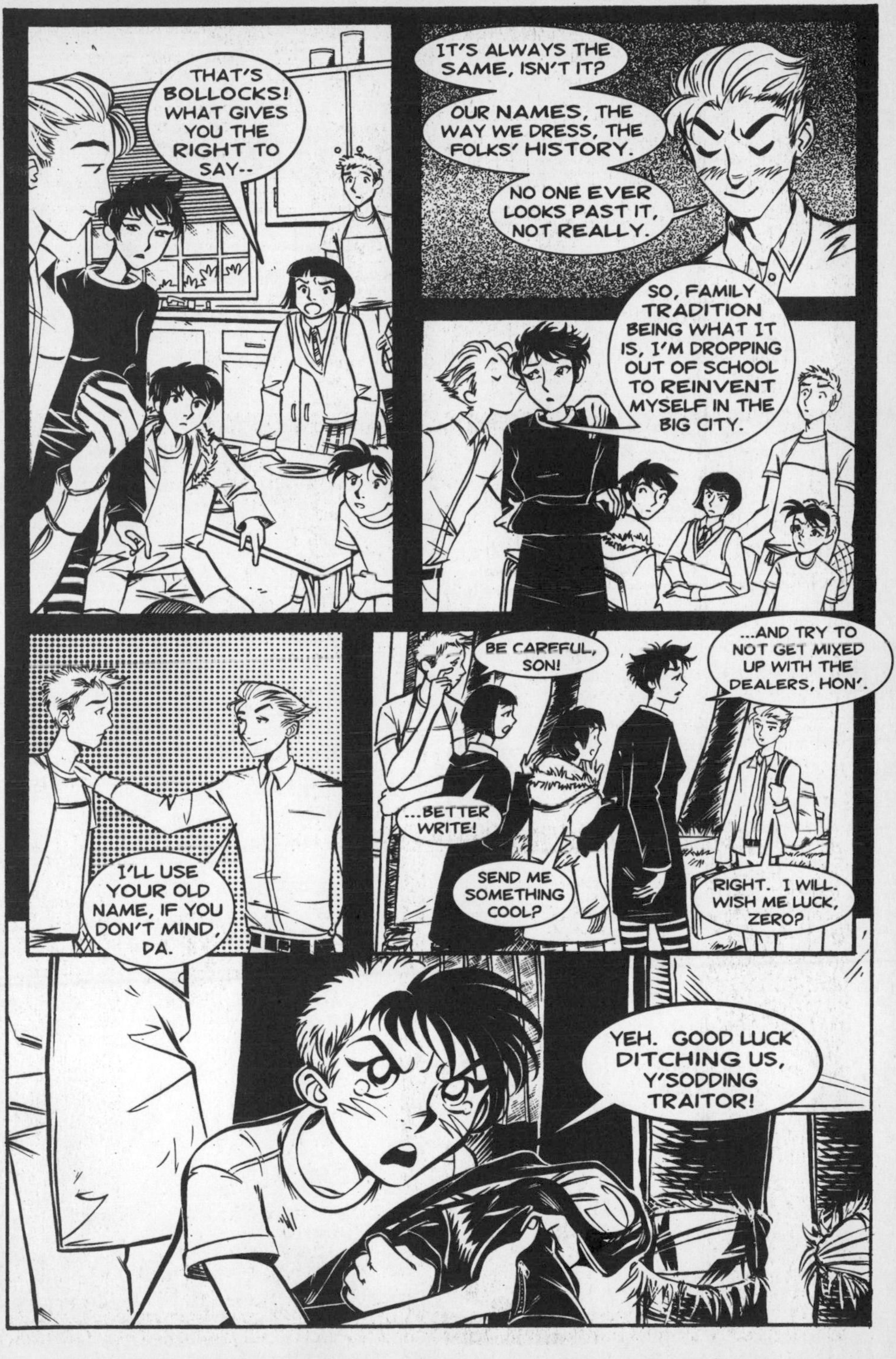
THAT'S BOLLOCKS! WHAT GIVES YOU THE RIGHT TO SAY--
IT'S ALWAYS THE SAME, ISN'T IT?
OUR NAMES, THE WAY WE DRESS, THE FOLKS' HISTORY.
NO ONE EVER LOOKS PAST IT, NOT REALLY.
SO, FAMILY TRADITION BEING WHAT IT IS, I'M DROPPING OUT OF SCHOOL TO REINVENT MYSELF IN THE BIG CITY.
I'LL USE YOUR OLD NAME, IF YOU DON'T MIND, DA.
BE CAREFUL, SON!
...AND TRY TO NOT GET MIXED UP WITH THE DEALERS, HON'.
...BETTER WRITE!
SEND ME SOMETHING COOL?
RIGHT. I WILL. WISH ME LUCK, ZERO?
YEH. GOOD LUCK DITCHING US, Y'SODDING TRAITOR!

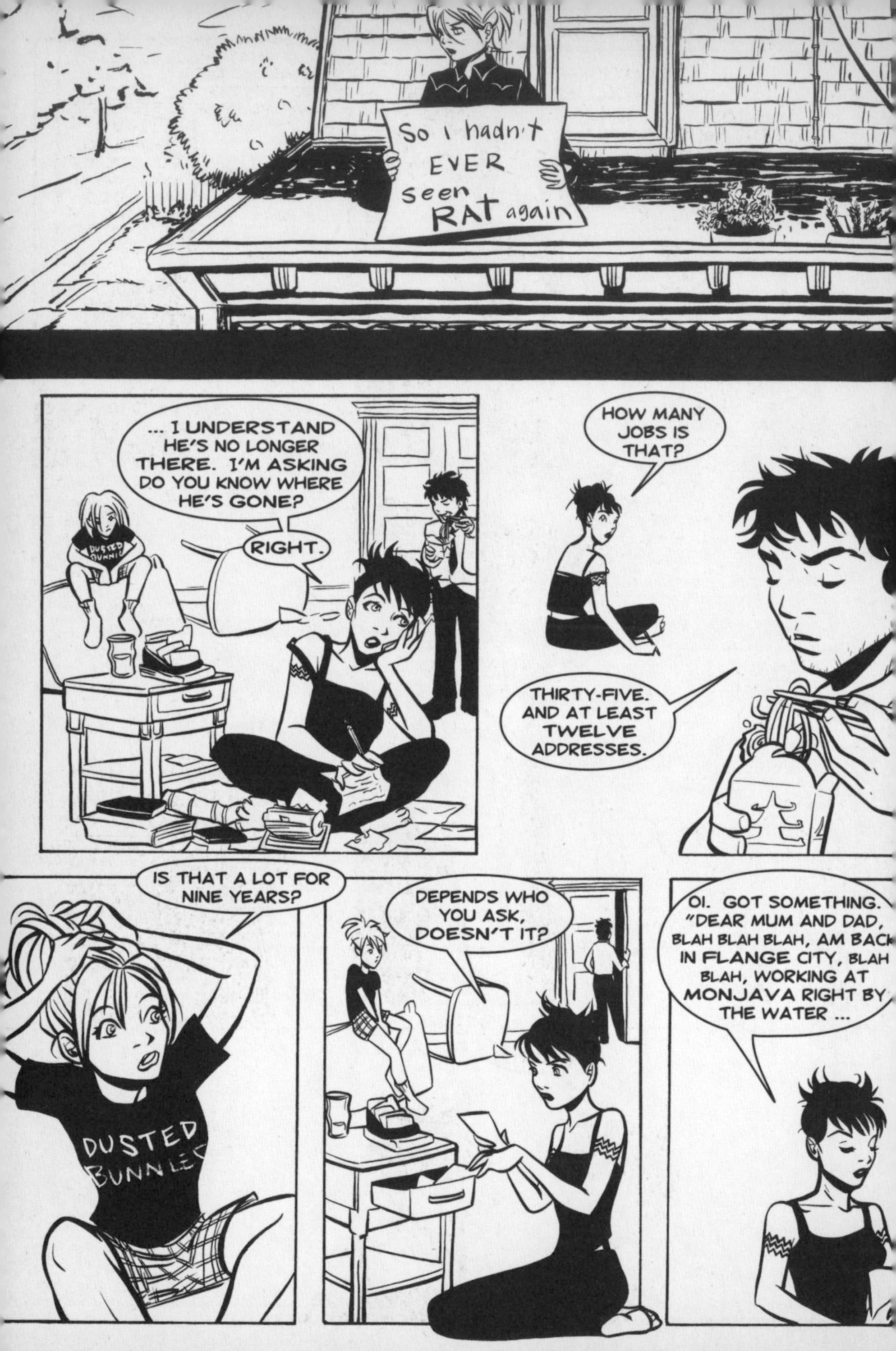
So I hadn't EVER seen RAT again
... I UNDERSTAND HE'S NO LONGER THERE. I'M ASKING DO YOU KNOW WHERE HE'S GONE?
RIGHT.
DUSTED BUNNIC
HOW MANY JOBS IS THAT?
THIRTY-FIVE. AND AT LEAST TWELVE ADDRESSES.
IS THAT A LOT FOR NINE YEARS?
DUSTED BUNNIES
DEPENDS WHO YOU ASK, DOESN'T IT?
OI. GOT SOMETHING. "DEAR MUM AND DAD, BLAH BLAH BLAH, AM BACK IN FLANGE CITY, BLAH BLAH, WORKING AT MONJAVA RIGHT BY THE WATER ...

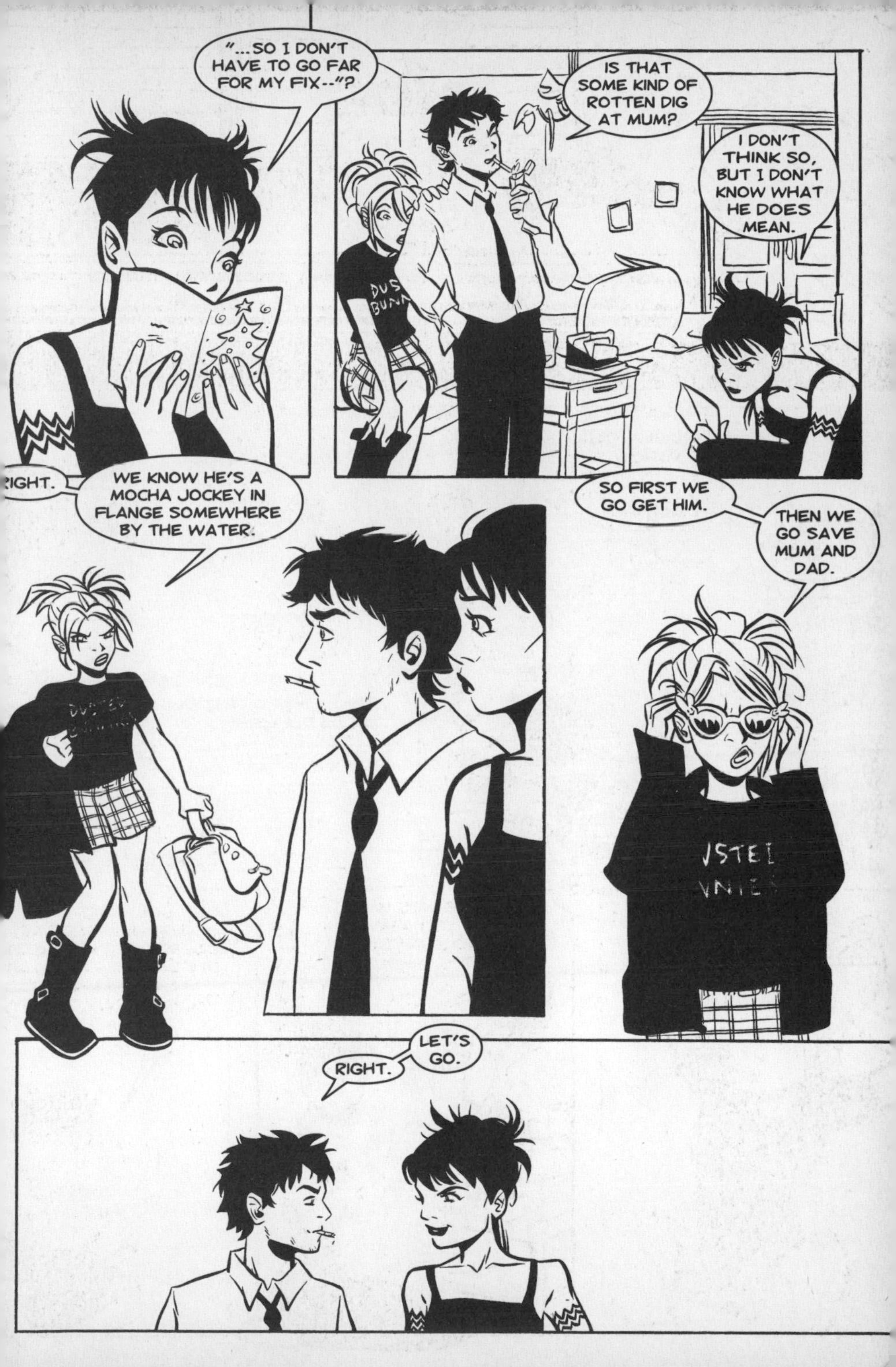
"...SO I DON'T HAVE TO GO FAR FOR MY FIX--"?
IS THAT SOME KIND OF ROTTEN DIG AT MUM?
I DON'T THINK SO, BUT I DON'T KNOW WHAT HE DOES MEAN.
DUS BUNN
RIGHT.
WE KNOW HE'S A MOCHA JOCKEY IN FLANGE SOMEWHERE BY THE WATER.
SO FIRST WE GO GET HIM.
THEN WE GO SAVE MUM AND DAD.
RIGHT.
LET'S GO.

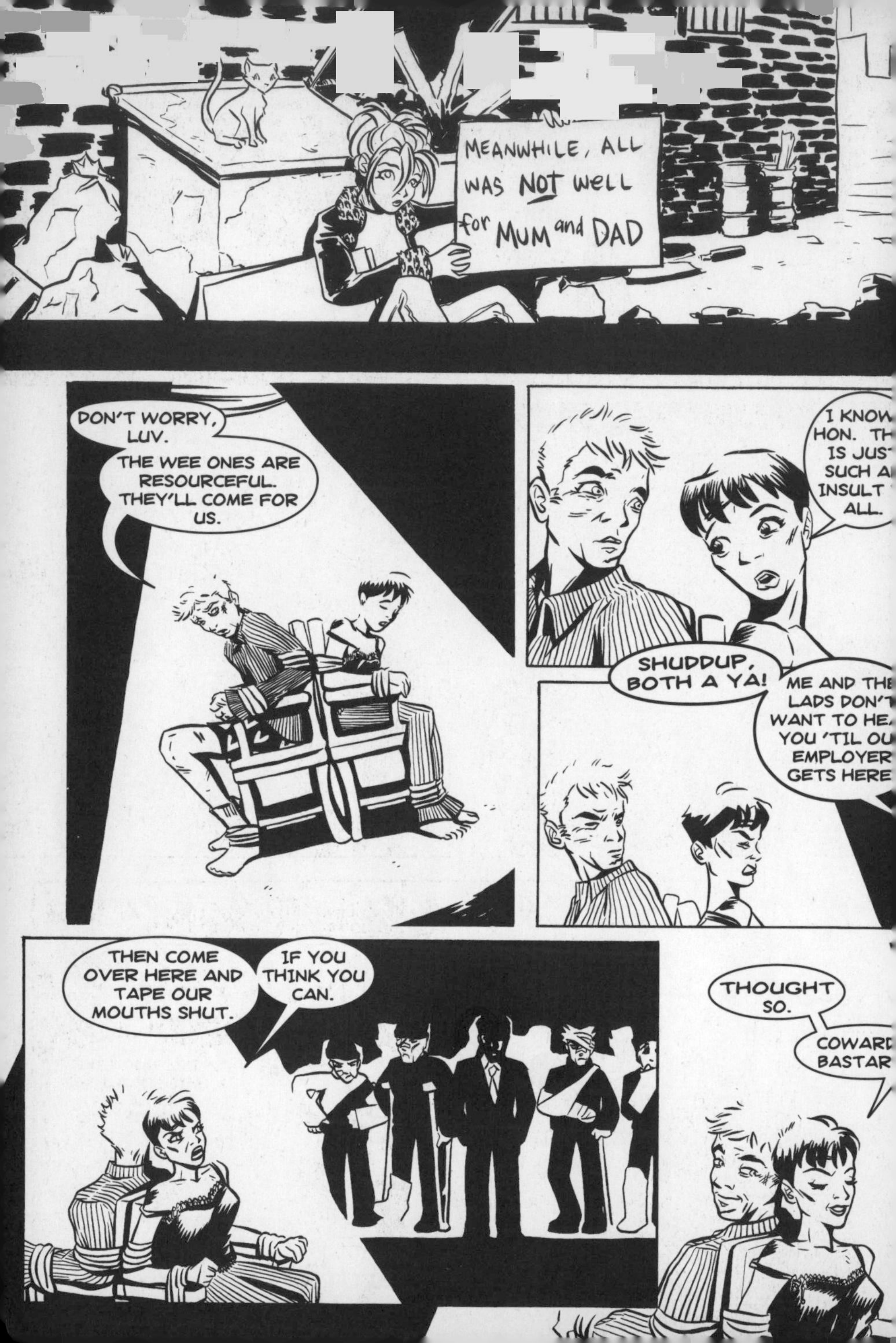
MEANWHILE, ALL WAS NOT WELL for MUM and DAD
DON'T WORRY, LUV.
THE WEE ONES ARE RESOURCEFUL. THEY'LL COME FOR US.
I KNOW HON. TH IS JUST SUCH A INSULT ALL.
SHUDDUP, BOTH A YA!
ME AND THE LADS DON'T WANT TO HE YOU 'TIL OU EMPLOYER GETS HERE
THEN COME OVER HERE AND TAPE OUR MOUTHS SHUT.
IF YOU THINK YOU CAN.
THOUGHT SO.
COWARD BASTAR

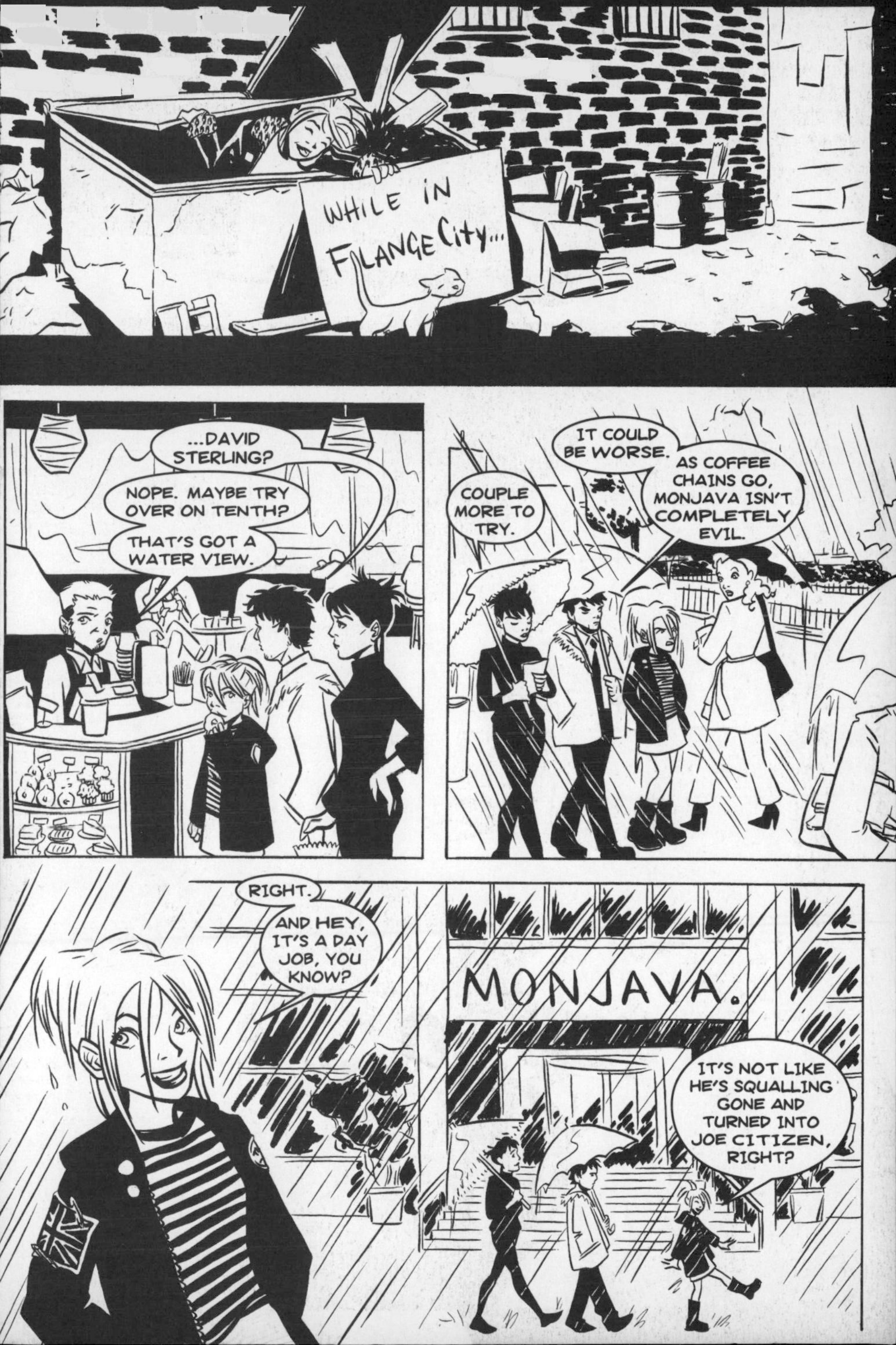
WHILE IN FLANGE City...
...DAVID STERLING?
NOPE. MAYBE TRY OVER ON TENTH?
THAT'S GOT A WATER VIEW.
COUPLE MORE TO TRY.
IT COULD BE WORSE.
AS COFFEE CHAINS GO, MONJAVA ISN'T COMPLETELY EVIL.
RIGHT.
AND HEY, IT'S A DAY JOB, YOU KNOW?
MONJAVA.
IT'S NOT LIKE HE'S SQUALLING GONE AND TURNED INTO JOE CITIZEN, RIGHT?

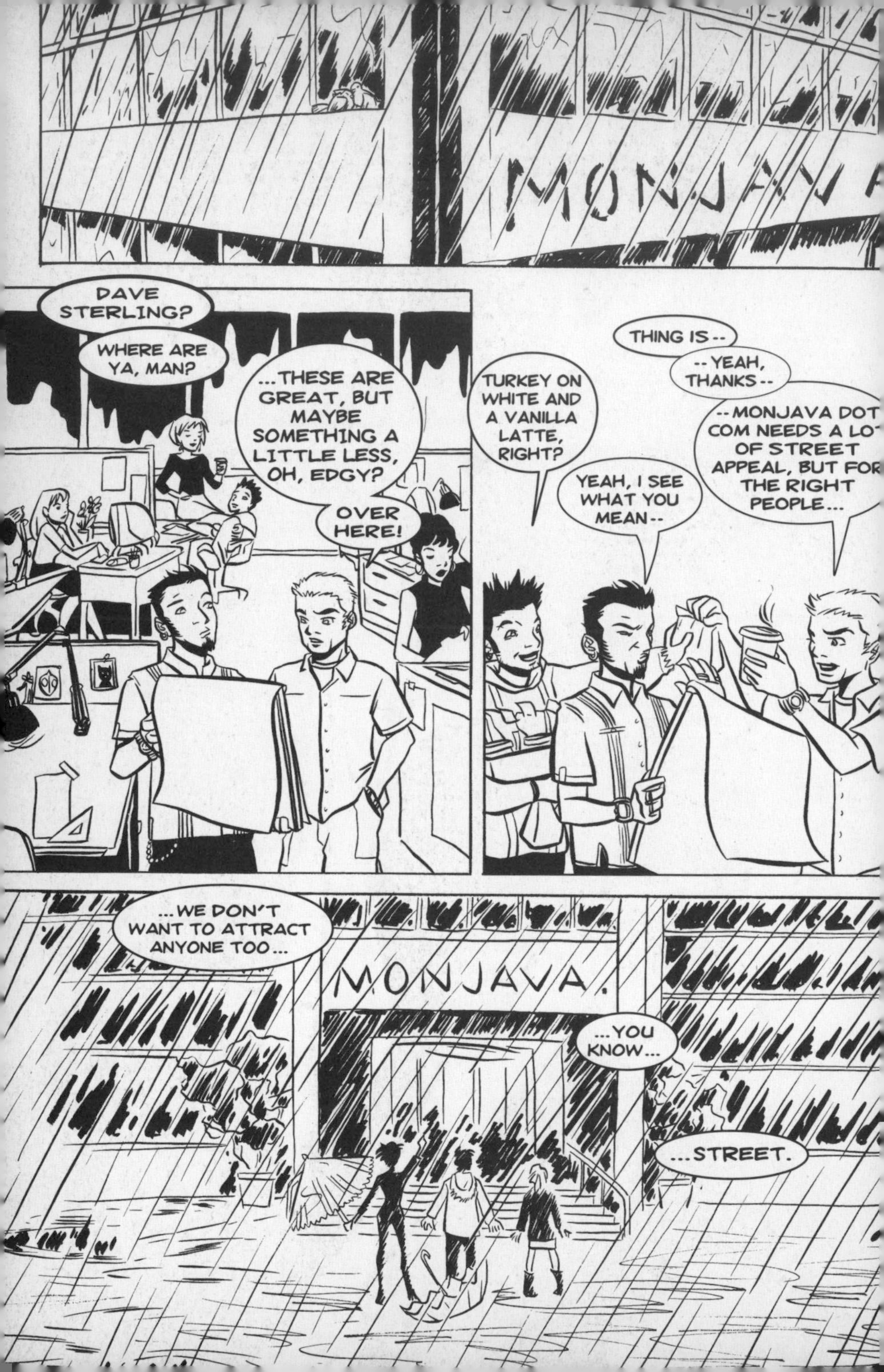
MONJAVA
DAVE STERLING?
WHERE ARE YA, MAN?
...THESE ARE GREAT, BUT MAYBE SOMETHING A LITTLE LESS, OH, EDGY?
OVER HERE!
TURKEY ON WHITE AND A VANILLA LATTE, RIGHT?
THING IS --
-- YEAH, THANKS --
YEAH, I SEE WHAT YOU MEAN --
-- MONJAVA DOT COM NEEDS A LOT OF STREET APPEAL, BUT FOR THE RIGHT PEOPLE...
...WE DON'T WANT TO ATTRACT ANYONE TOO...
MONJAVA.
...YOU KNOW...
...STREET.

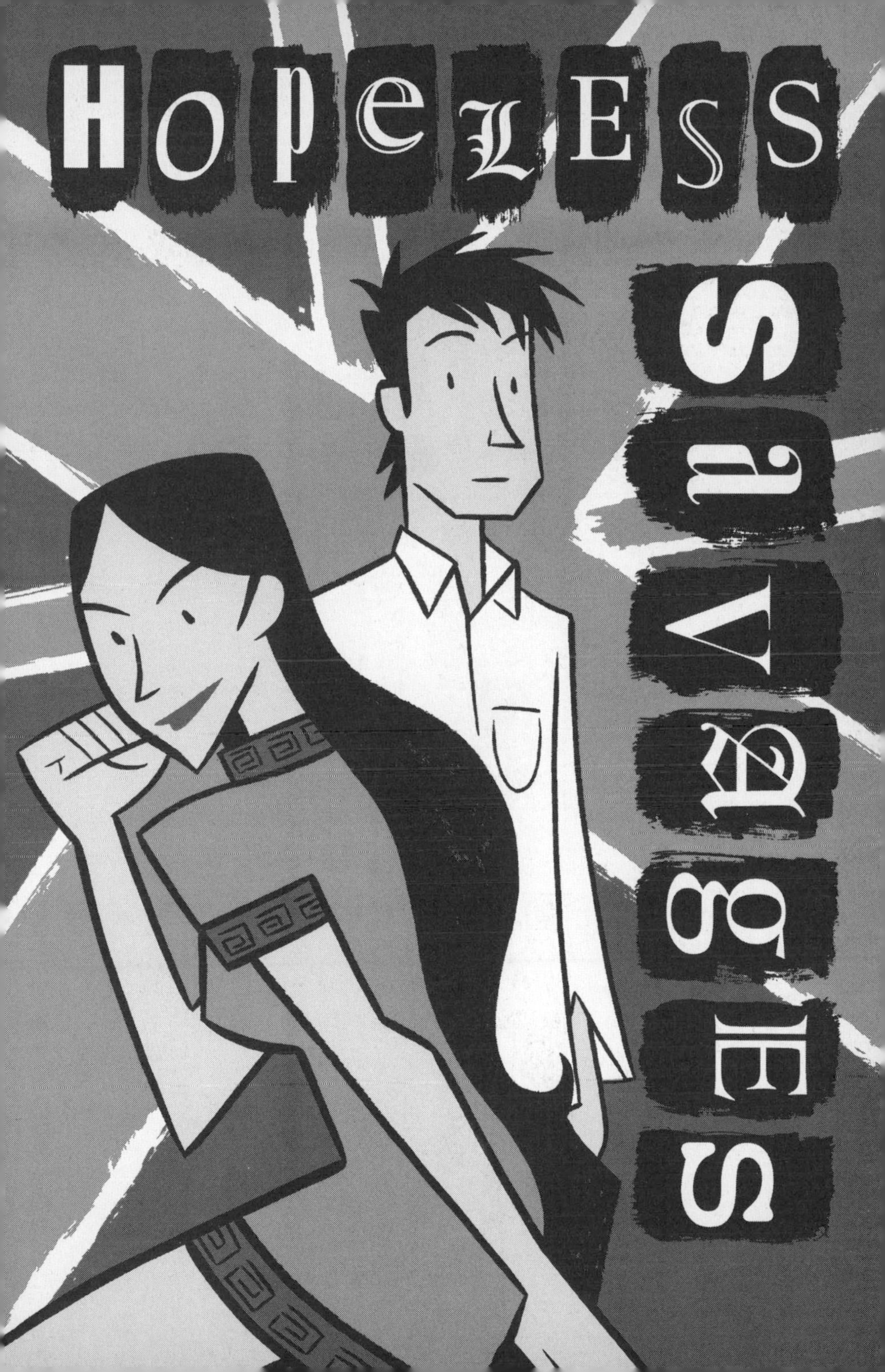
Hopeless
Savages

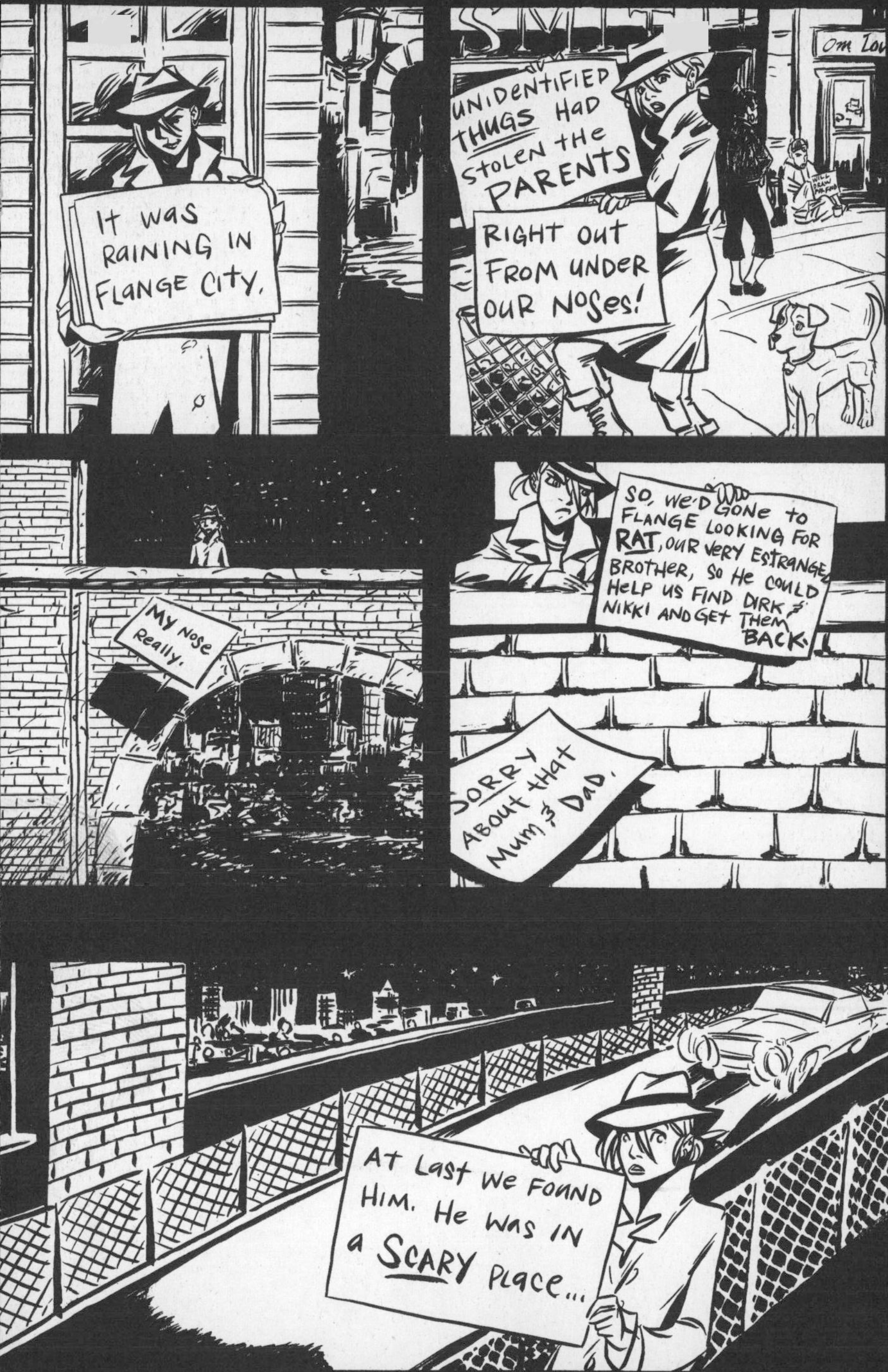
It was raining in Flange City.
Unidentified THUGS had stolen the PARENTS
Right out from under our noses!
My nose really.
So, we'd gone to Flange looking for RAT, our very estranged brother, so he could help us find Dirk & Nikki and get them BACK.
SORRY about that Mum & Dad.
At last we found him. He was in a SCARY place...

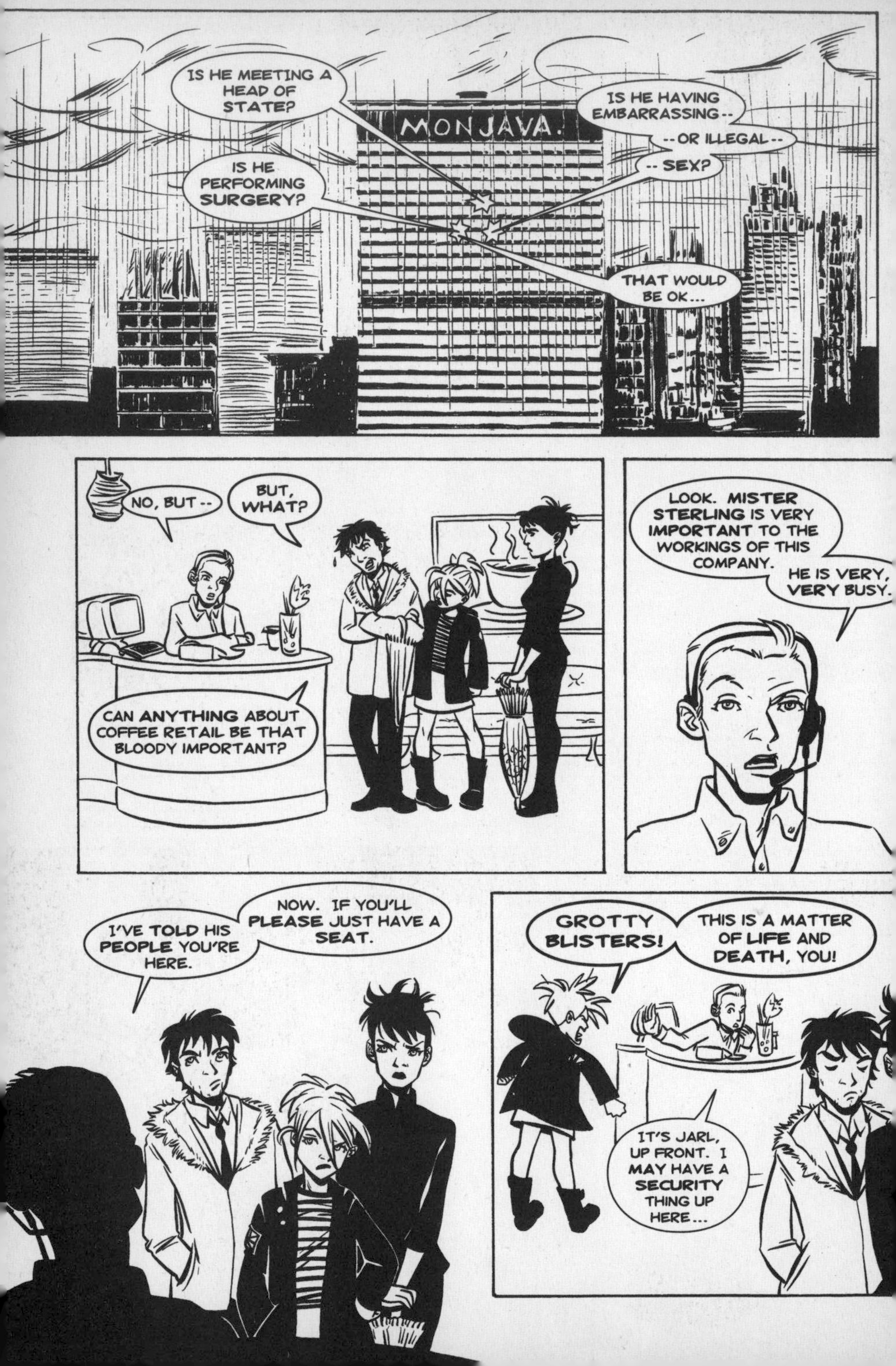
IS HE MEETING A HEAD OF STATE?
IS HE HAVING EMBARRASSING --
-- OR ILLEGAL --
-- SEX?
IS HE PERFORMING SURGERY?
THAT WOULD BE OK...
MONJAVA.
NO, BUT --
BUT, WHAT?
CAN ANYTHING ABOUT COFFEE RETAIL BE THAT BLOODY IMPORTANT?
LOOK. MISTER STERLING IS VERY IMPORTANT TO THE WORKINGS OF THIS COMPANY.
HE IS VERY, VERY BUSY.
I'VE TOLD HIS PEOPLE YOU'RE HERE.
NOW. IF YOU'LL PLEASE JUST HAVE A SEAT.
GROTTY BLISTERS!
THIS IS A MATTER OF LIFE AND DEATH, YOU!
IT'S JARL, UP FRONT. I MAY HAVE A SECURITY THING UP HERE...

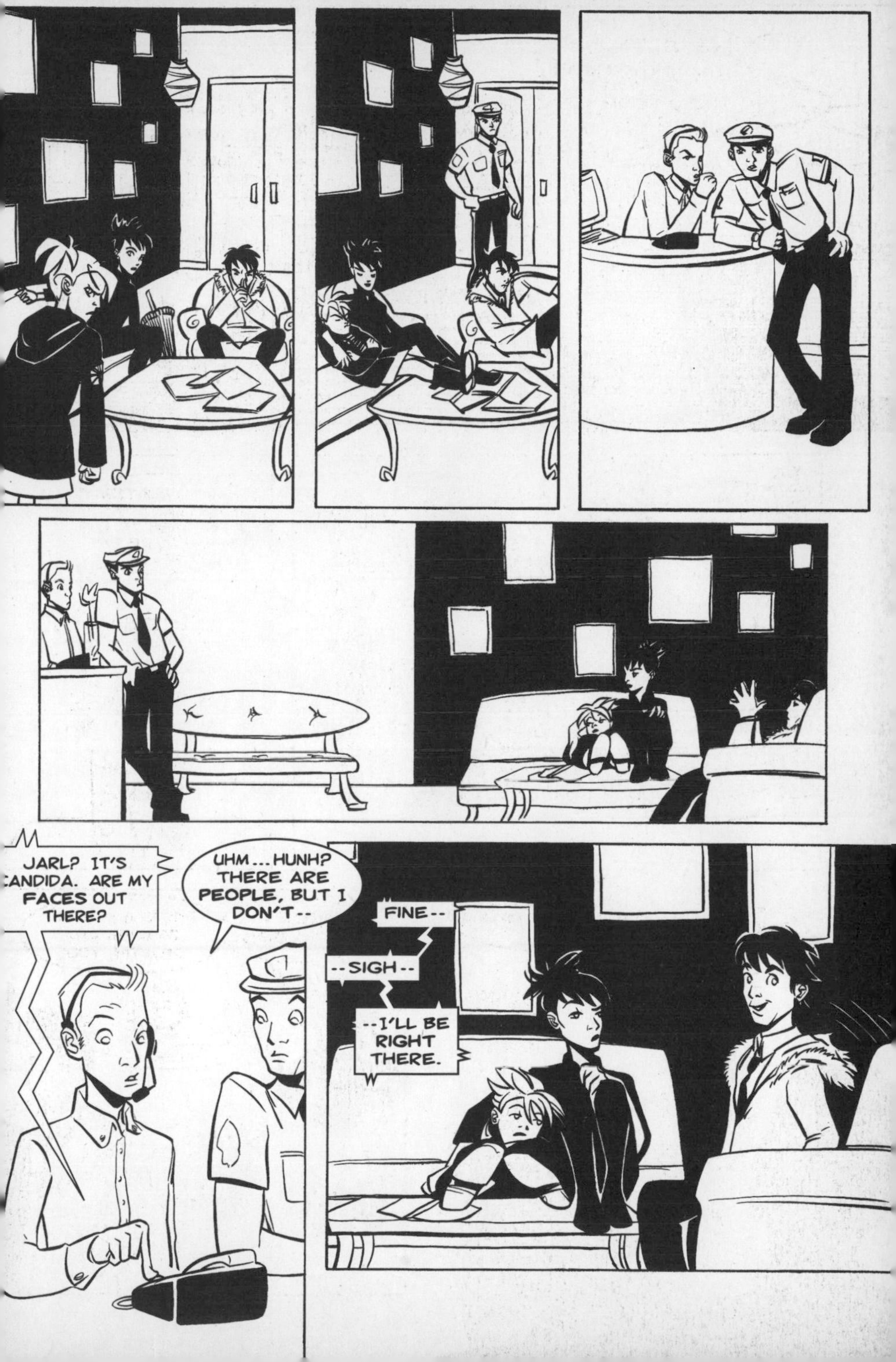
JARL? IT'S CANDIDA. ARE MY FACES OUT THERE?
UHM... HUNH? THERE ARE PEOPLE, BUT I DON'T--
FINE--
--SIGH--
--I'LL BE RIGHT THERE.

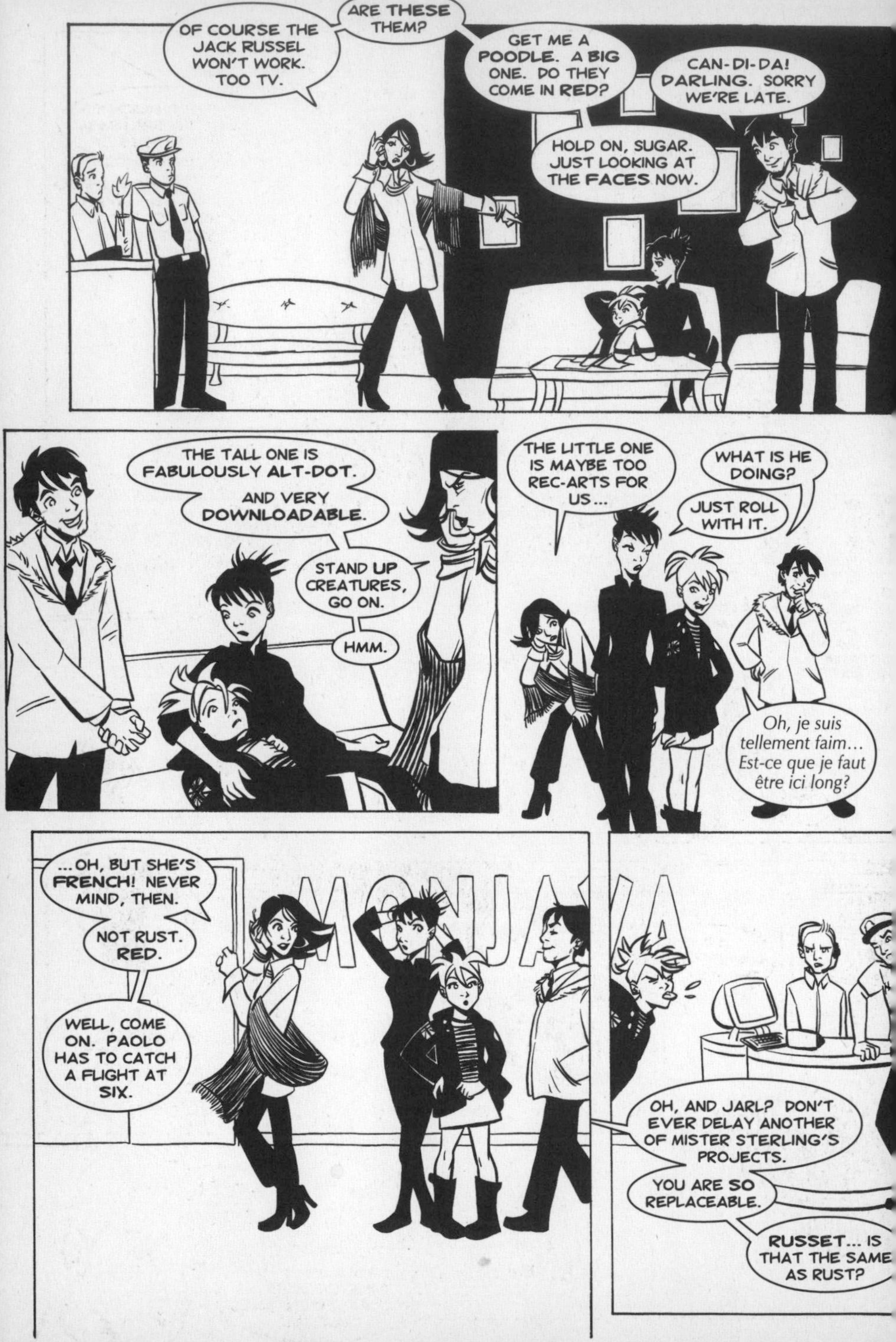
OF COURSE THE JACK RUSSEL WON'T WORK. TOO TV.
ARE THESE THEM?
GET ME A POODLE. A BIG ONE. DO THEY COME IN RED?
CAN-DI-DA! DARLING. SORRY WE'RE LATE.
HOLD ON, SUGAR. JUST LOOKING AT THE FACES NOW.
THE TALL ONE IS FABULOUSLY ALT-DOT.
AND VERY DOWNLOADABLE.
STAND UP CREATURES, GO ON.
HMM.
THE LITTLE ONE IS MAYBE TOO REC-ARTS FOR US...
WHAT IS HE DOING?
JUST ROLL WITH IT.
Oh, je suis tellement faim... Est-ce que je faut être ici long?
...OH, BUT SHE'S FRENCH! NEVER MIND, THEN.
NOT RUST. RED.
WELL, COME ON. PAOLO HAS TO CATCH A FLIGHT AT SIX.
OH, AND JARL? DON'T EVER DELAY ANOTHER OF MISTER STERLING'S PROJECTS.
YOU ARE SO REPLACEABLE.
RUSSET... IS THAT THE SAME AS RUST?

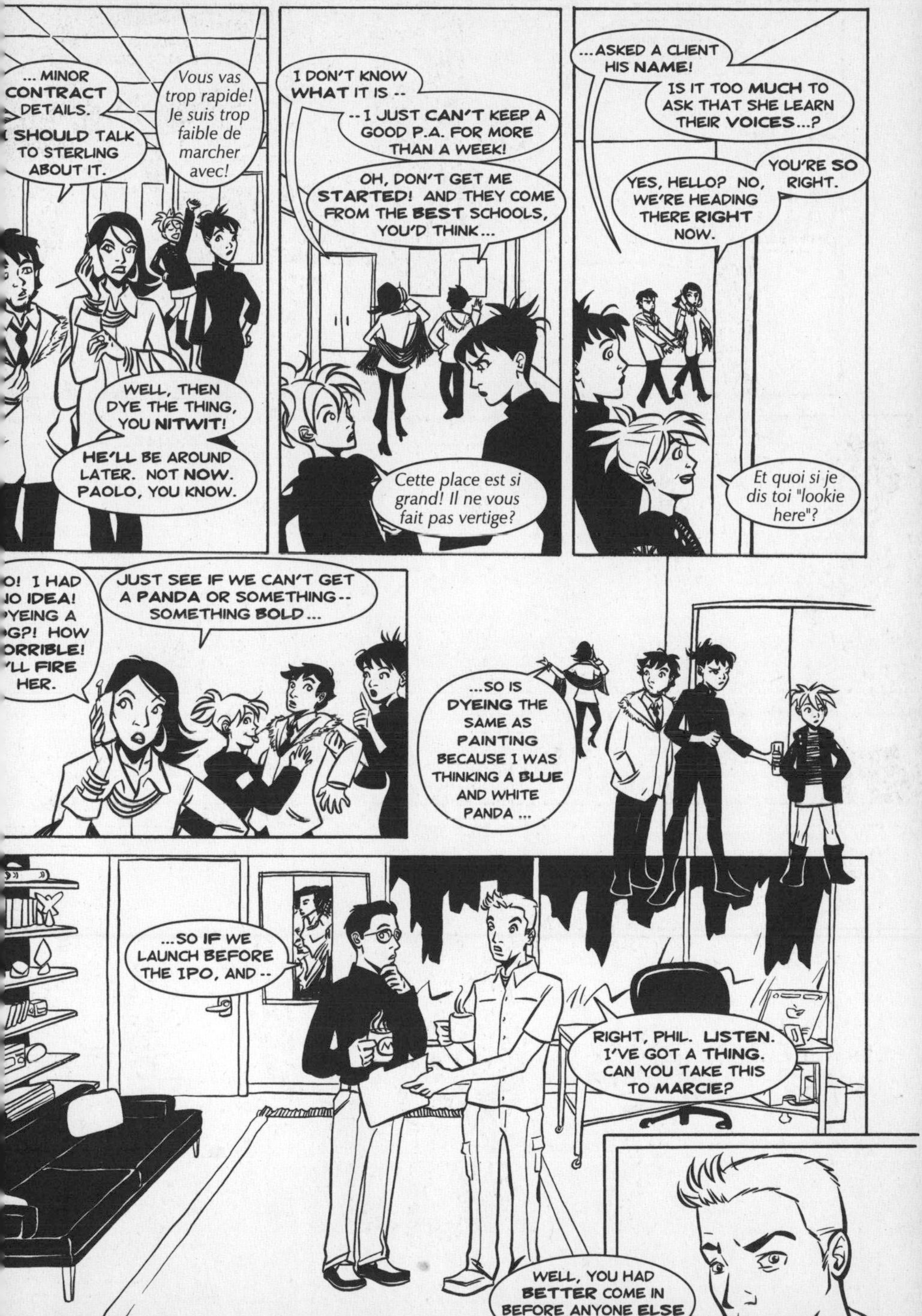
... MINOR CONTRACT DETAILS.
I SHOULD TALK TO STERLING ABOUT IT.
Vous vas trop rapide! Je suis trop faible de marcher avec!
WELL, THEN DYE THE THING, YOU NITWIT!
HE'LL BE AROUND LATER. NOT NOW. PAOLO, YOU KNOW.
I DON'T KNOW WHAT IT IS --
-- I JUST CAN'T KEEP A GOOD P.A. FOR MORE THAN A WEEK!
OH, DON'T GET ME STARTED! AND THEY COME FROM THE BEST SCHOOLS, YOU'D THINK...
Cette place est si grand! Il ne vous fait pas vertige?
...ASKED A CLIENT HIS NAME!
IS IT TOO MUCH TO ASK THAT SHE LEARN THEIR VOICES...?
YES, HELLO? NO, WE'RE HEADING THERE RIGHT NOW.
YOU'RE SO RIGHT.
Et quoi si je dis toi "lookie here"?
O! I HAD IO IDEA! YEING A G?! HOW ORRIBLE! 'LL FIRE HER.
JUST SEE IF WE CAN'T GET A PANDA OR SOMETHING -- SOMETHING BOLD...
...SO IS DYEING THE SAME AS PAINTING BECAUSE I WAS THINKING A BLUE AND WHITE PANDA ...
...SO IF WE LAUNCH BEFORE THE IPO, AND --
RIGHT, PHIL. LISTEN. I'VE GOT A THING. CAN YOU TAKE THIS TO MARCIE?
WELL, YOU HAD BETTER COME IN BEFORE ANYONE ELSE SEES YOU.

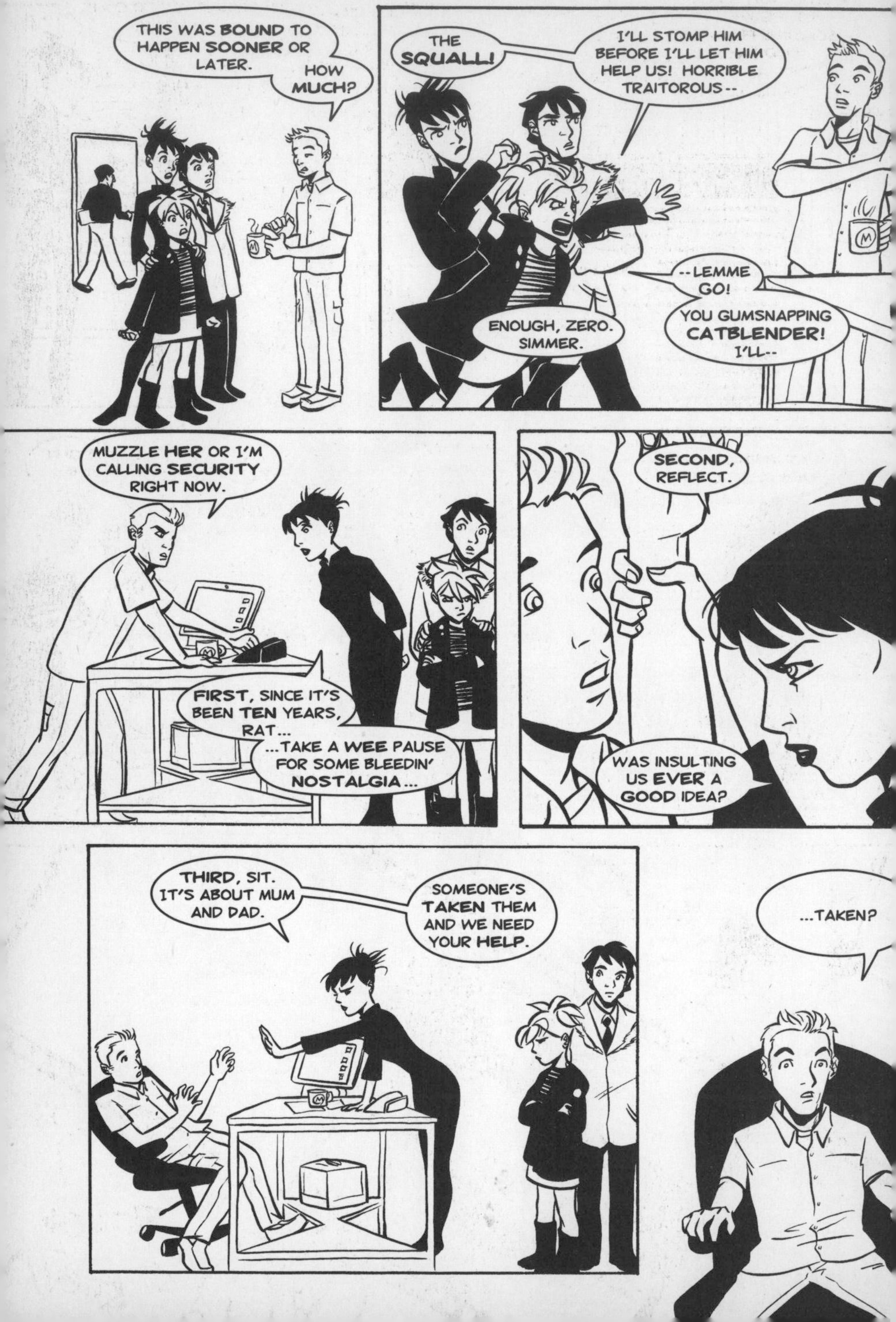
THIS WAS BOUND TO HAPPEN SOONER OR LATER.
HOW MUCH?
THE SQUALL!
I'LL STOMP HIM BEFORE I'LL LET HIM HELP US! HORRIBLE TRAITOROUS--
--LEMME GO!
YOU GUMSNAPPING CATBLENDER! I'LL--
ENOUGH, ZERO. SIMMER.
MUZZLE HER OR I'M CALLING SECURITY RIGHT NOW.
FIRST, SINCE IT'S BEEN TEN YEARS, RAT...
...TAKE A WEE PAUSE FOR SOME BLEEDIN' NOSTALGIA...
SECOND, REFLECT.
WAS INSULTING US EVER A GOOD IDEA?
THIRD, SIT. IT'S ABOUT MUM AND DAD.
SOMEONE'S TAKEN THEM AND WE NEED YOUR HELP.
...TAKEN?

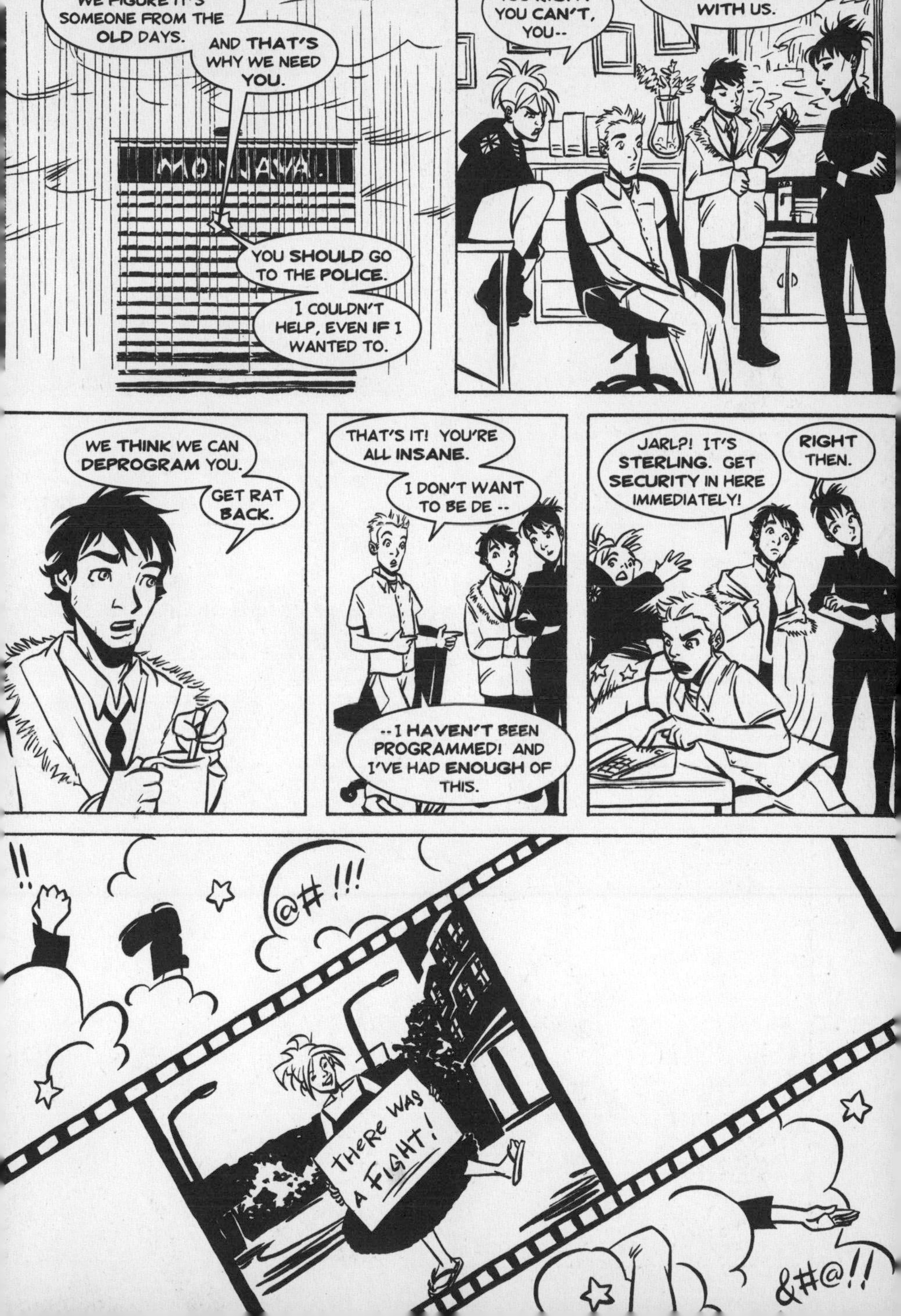
...SO THAT'S WHY WE FIGURE IT'S SOMEONE FROM THE OLD DAYS.
AND THAT'S WHY WE NEED YOU.
MONJAVA.
YOU SHOULD GO TO THE POLICE.
I COULDN'T HELP, EVEN IF I WANTED TO.
TOO RIGHT YOU CAN'T, YOU--
BUT RAT CAN. WE NEED YOU TO COME WITH US.
WE THINK WE CAN DEPROGRAM YOU.
GET RAT BACK.
THAT'S IT! YOU'RE ALL INSANE.
I DON'T WANT TO BE DE --
--I HAVEN'T BEEN PROGRAMMED! AND I'VE HAD ENOUGH OF THIS.
JARL?! IT'S STERLING. GET SECURITY IN HERE IMMEDIATELY!
RIGHT THEN.
!!
@# !!!
there was a FIGHT!
&#@!!

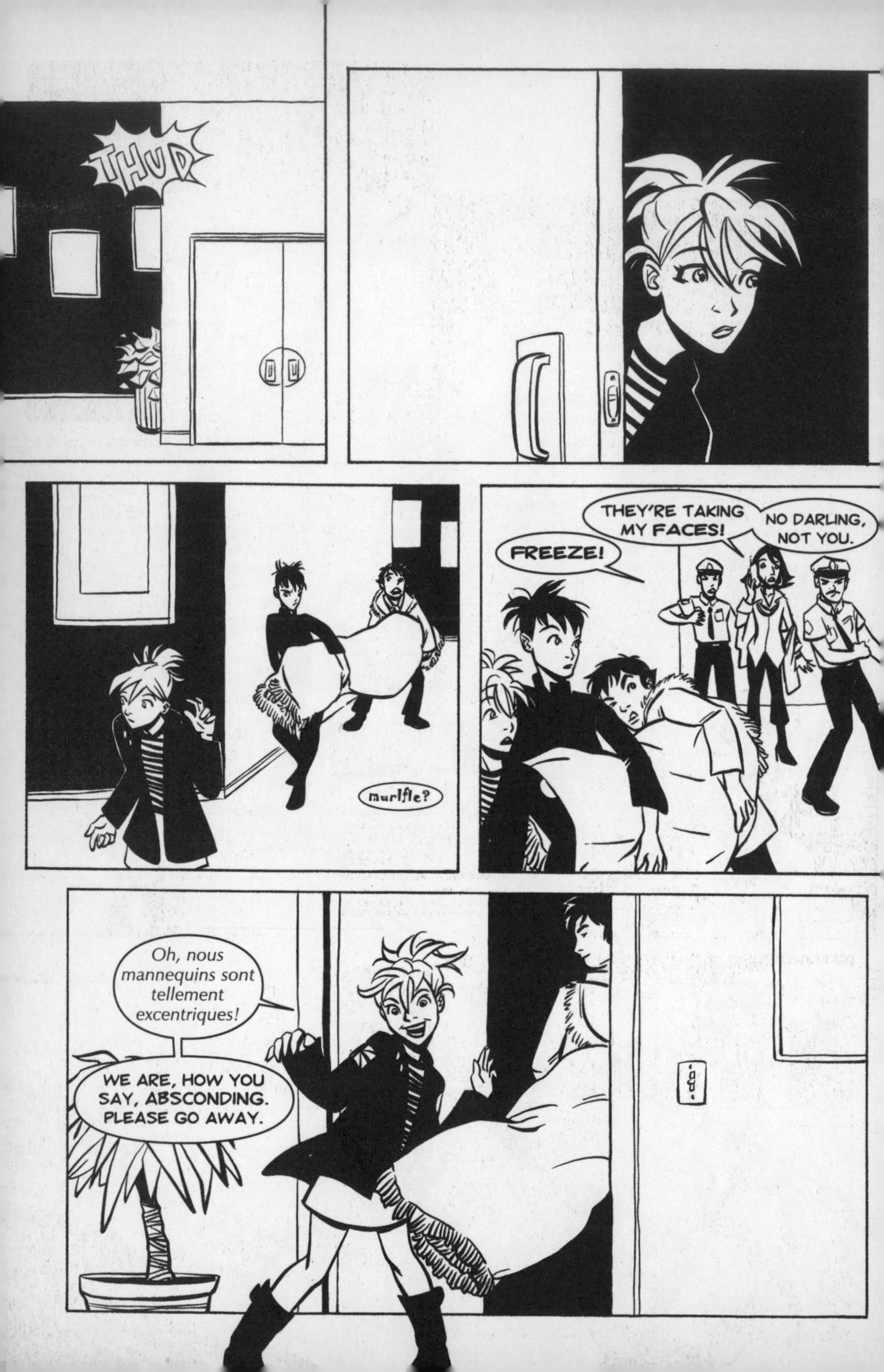
THUD
murlfle?
FREEZE!
THEY'RE TAKING MY FACES!
NO DARLING, NOT YOU.
Oh, nous mannequins sont tellement excentriques!
WE ARE, HOW YOU SAY, ABSCONDING. PLEASE GO AWAY.

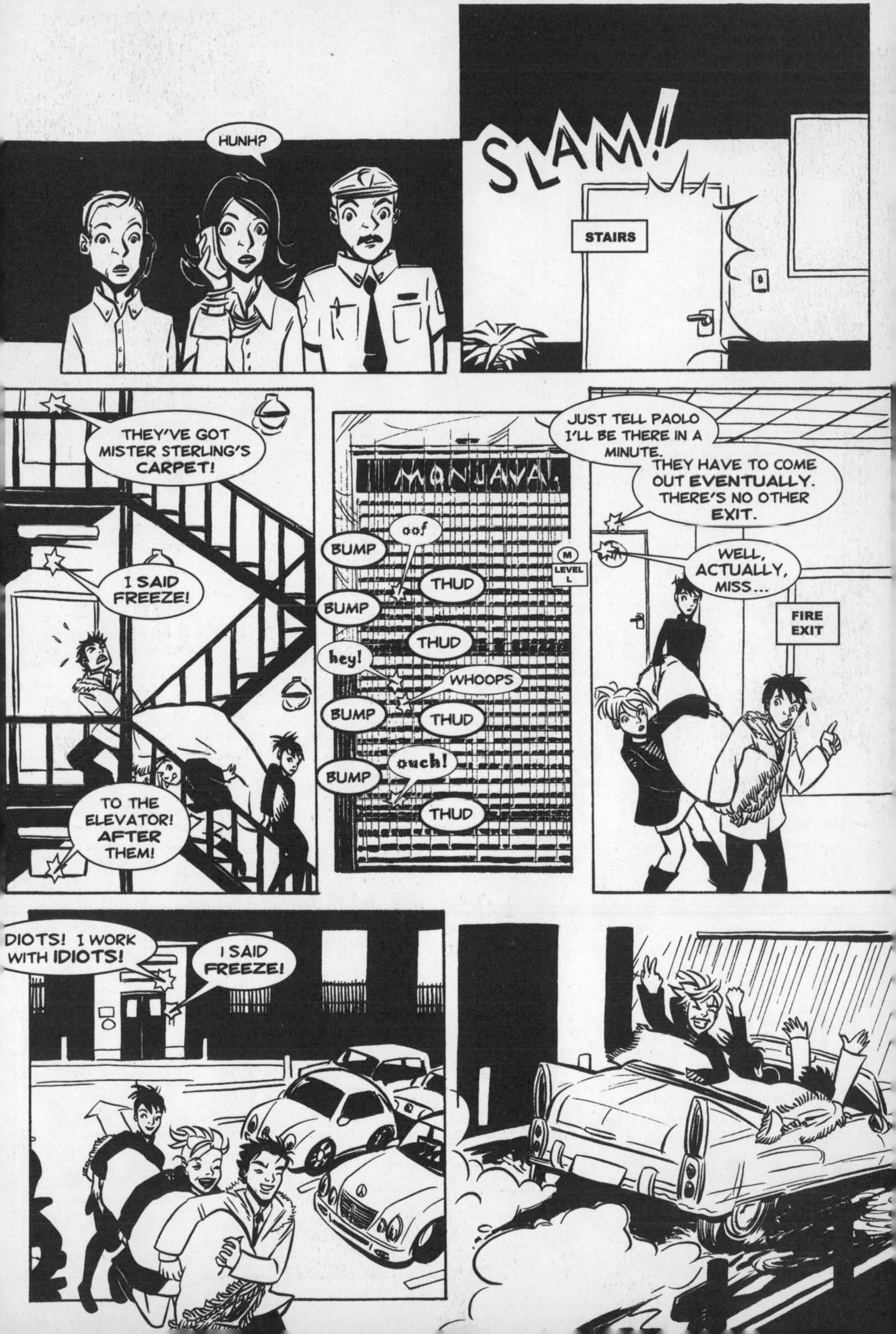
HUNH?
SLAM!
STAIRS
THEY'VE GOT MISTER STERLING'S CARPET!
I SAID FREEZE!
TO THE ELEVATOR! AFTER THEM!
MONJAVA
BUMP
oof
THUD
BUMP
THUD
hey!
WHOOPS
BUMP
THUD
BUMP
ouch!
THUD
JUST TELL PAOLO I'LL BE THERE IN A MINUTE.
THEY HAVE TO COME OUT EVENTUALLY. THERE'S NO OTHER EXIT.
M
LEVEL L
WELL, ACTUALLY, MISS...
FIRE EXIT
DIOTS! I WORK WITH IDIOTS!
I SAID FREEZE!

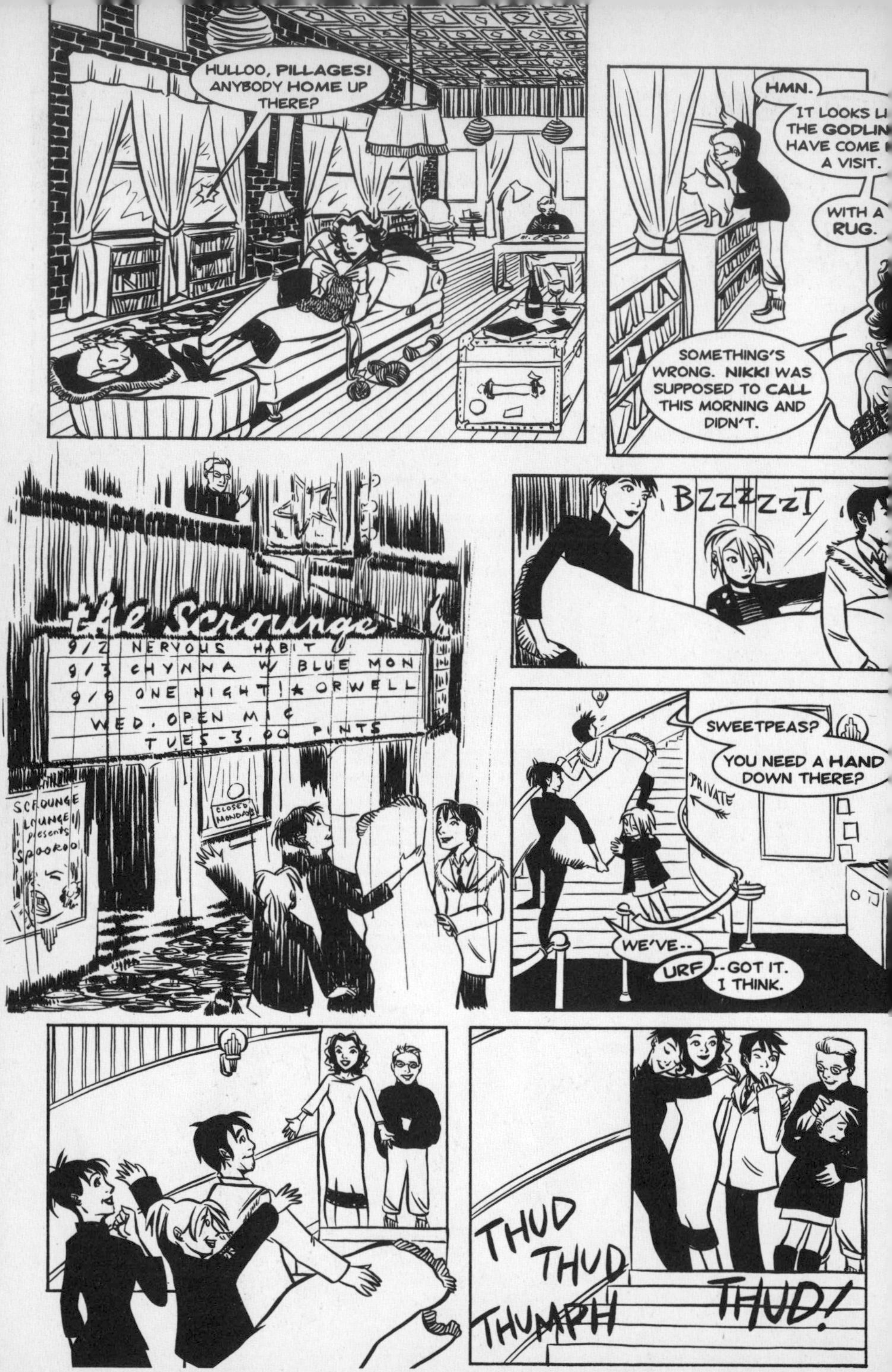

HULLOO, PILLAGES! ANYBODY HOME UP THERE?
HMN.
IT LOOKS LI THE GODLIN HAVE COME A VISIT.
WITH A RUG.
SOMETHING'S WRONG. NIKKI WAS SUPPOSED TO CALL THIS MORNING AND DIDN'T.
the Scrounge
9/2 NERVOUS HABIT
9/3 CHYNNA W BLUE MON
9/9 ONE NIGHT! ★ ORWELL
WED. OPEN MIC
TUES - 3.00 PINTS
SCROUNGE LOUNGE presents
CLOSED MONDAYS
BZZZZZT
SWEETPEAS?
YOU NEED A HAND DOWN THERE?
PRIVATE
WE'VE..
URF
--GOT IT. I THINK.
THUD
THUD
THUMPH
THUD!

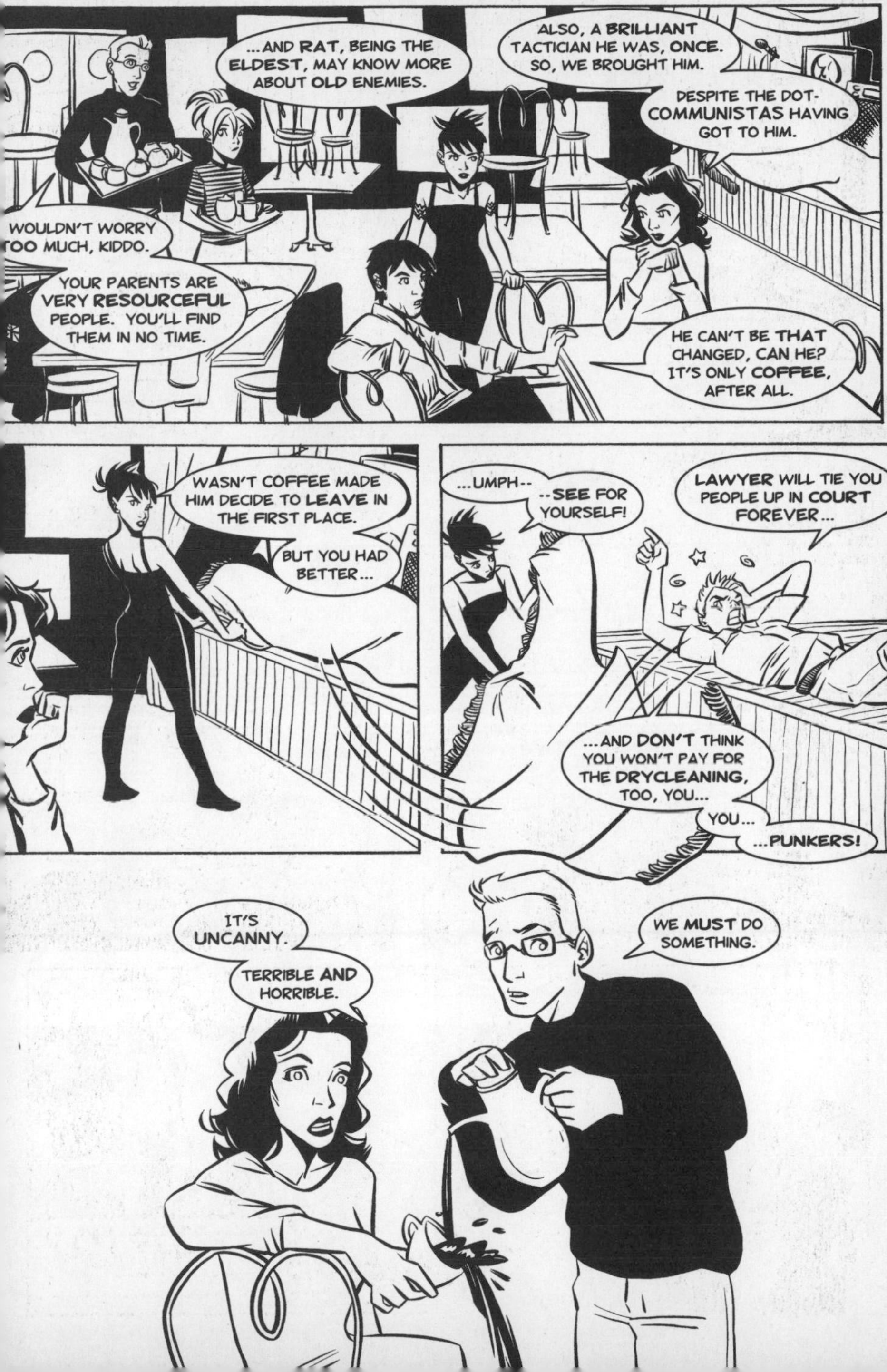
...AND RAT, BEING THE ELDEST, MAY KNOW MORE ABOUT OLD ENEMIES.
ALSO, A BRILLIANT TACTICIAN HE WAS, ONCE. SO, WE BROUGHT HIM.
DESPITE THE DOT-COMMUNISTAS HAVING GOT TO HIM.
WOULDN'T WORRY TOO MUCH, KIDDO.
YOUR PARENTS ARE VERY RESOURCEFUL PEOPLE. YOU'LL FIND THEM IN NO TIME.
HE CAN'T BE THAT CHANGED, CAN HE? IT'S ONLY COFFEE, AFTER ALL.
WASN'T COFFEE MADE HIM DECIDE TO LEAVE IN THE FIRST PLACE.
BUT YOU HAD BETTER...
...UMPH--
--SEE FOR YOURSELF!
LAWYER WILL TIE YOU PEOPLE UP IN COURT FOREVER...
...AND DON'T THINK YOU WON'T PAY FOR THE DRYCLEANING, TOO, YOU...
YOU...
...PUNKERS!
IT'S UNCANNY.
TERRIBLE AND HORRIBLE.
WE MUST DO SOMETHING.

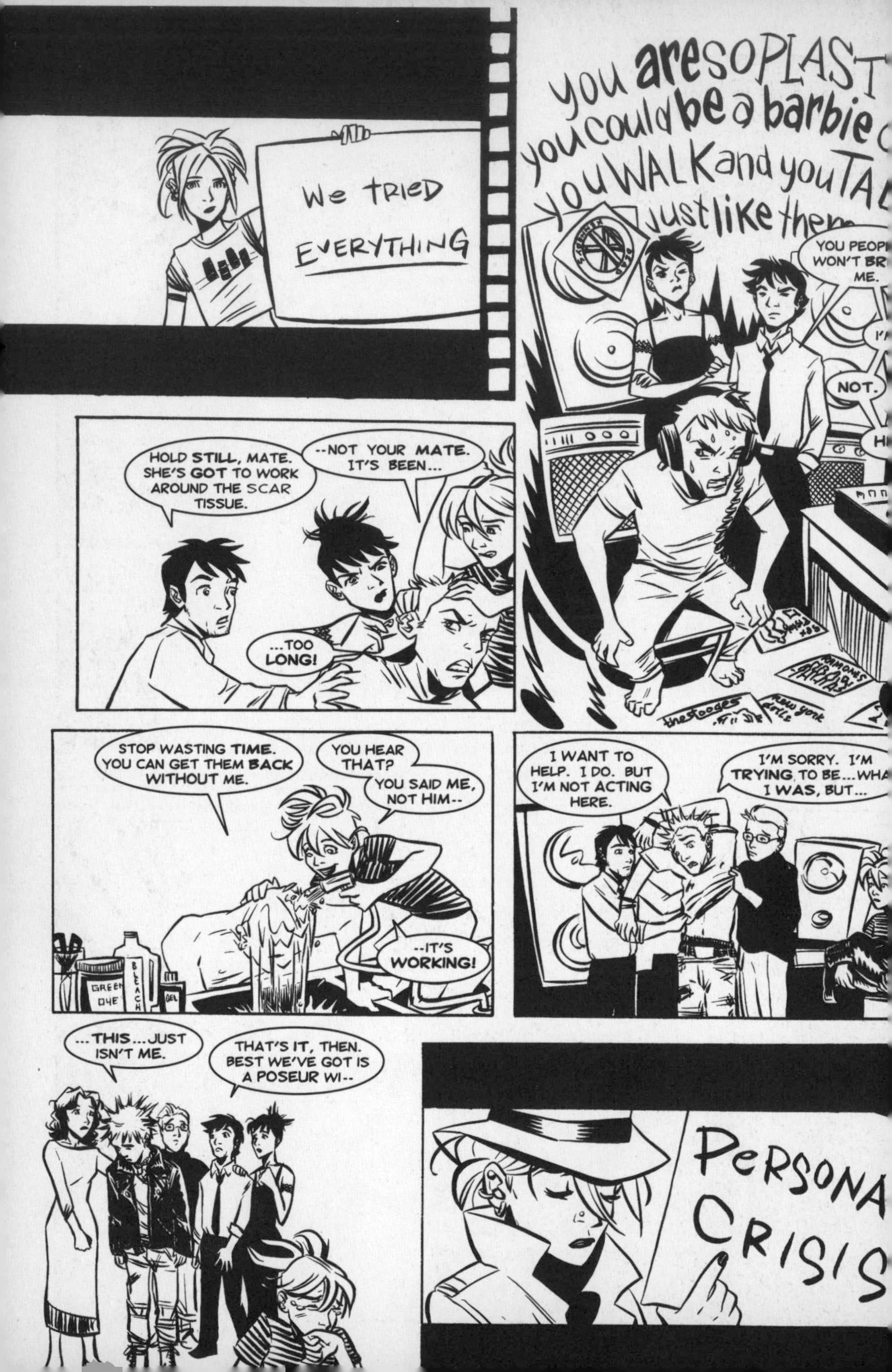
We TRIED EVERYTHING
HOLD STILL, MATE. SHE'S GOT TO WORK AROUND THE SCAR TISSUE.
--NOT YOUR MATE. IT'S BEEN...
...TOO LONG!
STOP WASTING TIME. YOU CAN GET THEM BACK WITHOUT ME.
YOU HEAR THAT?
YOU SAID ME, NOT HIM--
--IT'S WORKING!
GREEN DYE
BLEACH
GEL
...THIS...JUST ISN'T ME.
THAT'S IT, THEN. BEST WE'VE GOT IS A POSEUR WI--
you are so PLAST
you could be a barbie
you WALK and you TAL
just like the
YOU PEOP
WON'T BR
ME.
NOT.
the stooges
new york dolls
RAMONES
I WANT TO HELP. I DO. BUT I'M NOT ACTING HERE.
I'M SORRY. I'M TRYING TO BE...WHA I WAS, BUT...
PERSONA CRISIS

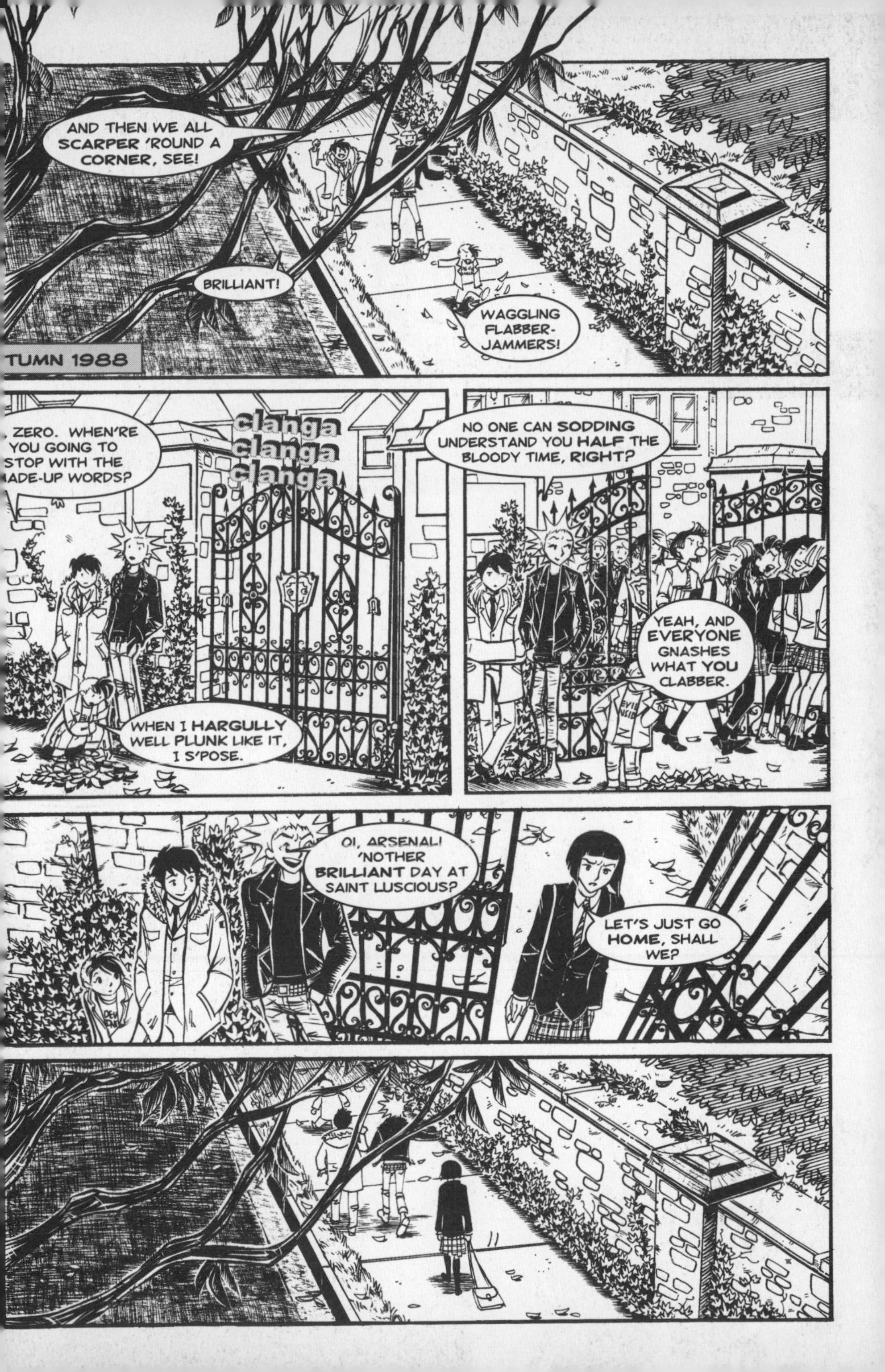
AND THEN WE ALL SCARPER 'ROUND A CORNER, SEE!
BRILLIANT!
WAGGLING FLABBER-JAMMERS!
TUMN 1988
ZERO. WHEN'RE YOU GOING TO STOP WITH THE ADE-UP WORDS?
clanga clanga clanga
WHEN I HARGULLY WELL PLUNK LIKE IT, I S'POSE.
NO ONE CAN SODDING UNDERSTAND YOU HALF THE BLOODY TIME, RIGHT?
YEAH, AND EVERYONE GNASHES WHAT YOU CLABBER.
OI, ARSENAL! 'NOTHER BRILLIANT DAY AT SAINT LUSCIOUS?
LET'S JUST GO HOME, SHALL WE?

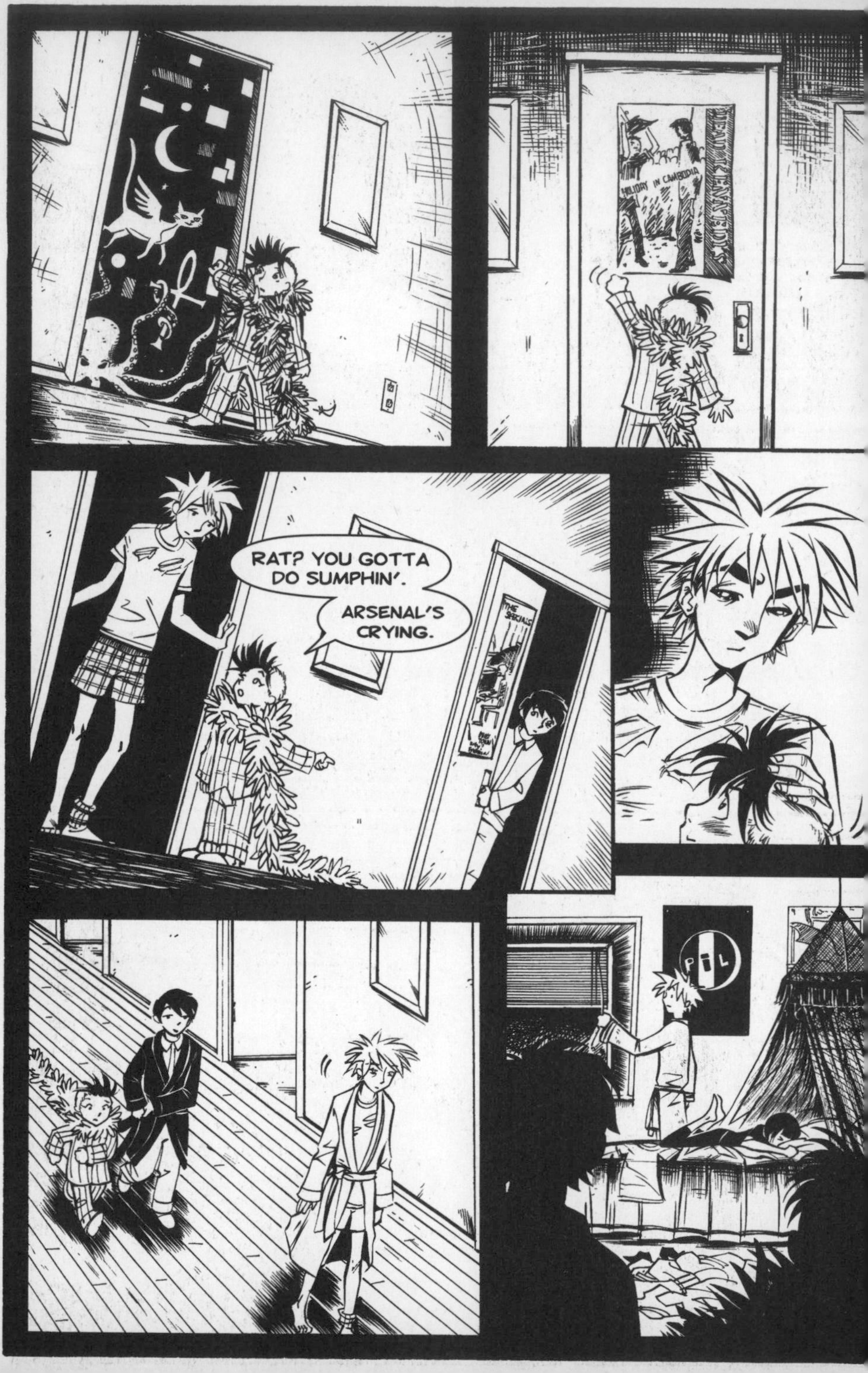
HOLIDAY IN CAMBODIA
RAT? YOU GOTTA DO SUMPHIN'.
ARSENAL'S CRYING.
THE SPECIALS
PiL

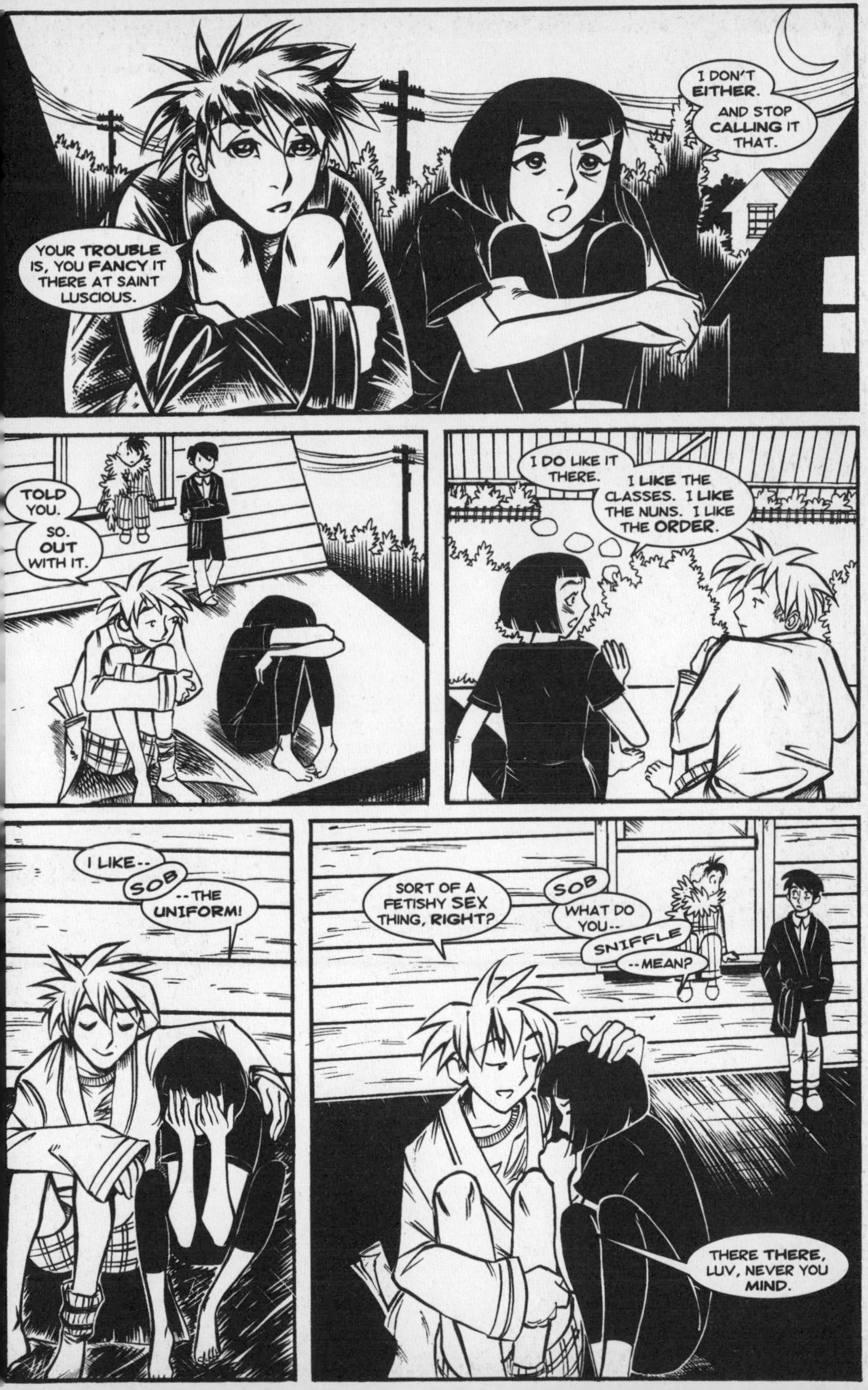
I DON'T EITHER.
AND STOP CALLING IT THAT.
YOUR TROUBLE IS, YOU FANCY IT THERE AT SAINT LUSCIOUS.
TOLD YOU.
SO. OUT WITH IT.
I DO LIKE IT THERE.
I LIKE THE CLASSES. I LIKE THE NUNS. I LIKE THE ORDER.
I LIKE--
SOB
--THE UNIFORM!
SORT OF A FETISHY SEX THING, RIGHT?
SOB
WHAT DO YOU--
SNIFFLE
--MEAN?
THERE THERE, LUV, NEVER YOU MIND.

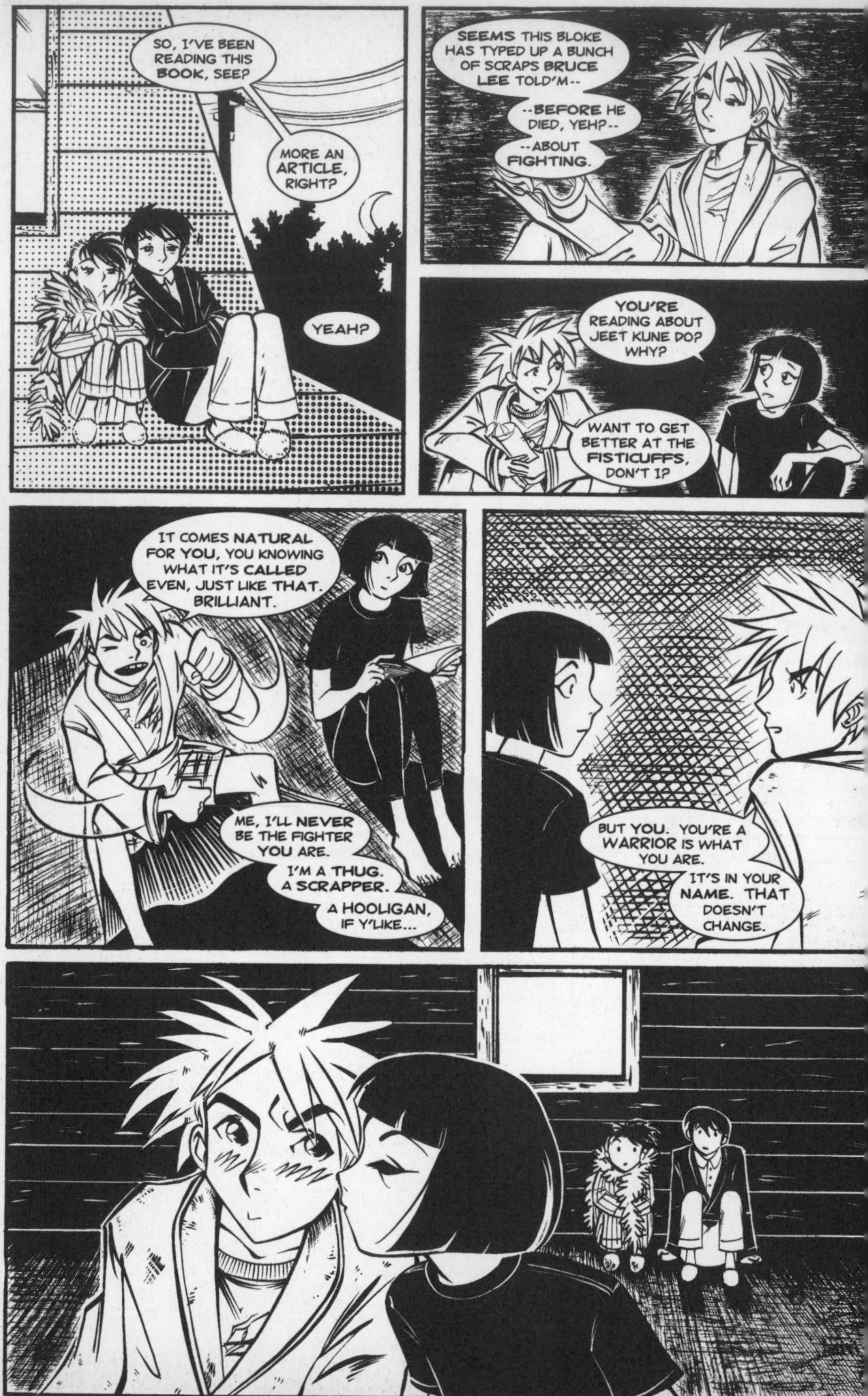
SO, I'VE BEEN READING THIS BOOK, SEE?
MORE AN ARTICLE, RIGHT?
YEAH?
SEEMS THIS BLOKE HAS TYPED UP A BUNCH OF SCRAPS BRUCE LEE TOLD'M--
--BEFORE HE DIED, YEH?--
--ABOUT FIGHTING.
YOU'RE READING ABOUT JEET KUNE DO? WHY?
WANT TO GET BETTER AT THE FISTICUFFS, DON'T I?
IT COMES NATURAL FOR YOU, YOU KNOWING WHAT IT'S CALLED EVEN, JUST LIKE THAT. BRILLIANT.
ME, I'LL NEVER BE THE FIGHTER YOU ARE.
I'M A THUG. A SCRAPPER.
A HOOLIGAN, IF Y'LIKE...
BUT YOU. YOU'RE A WARRIOR IS WHAT YOU ARE.
IT'S IN YOUR NAME. THAT DOESN'T CHANGE.

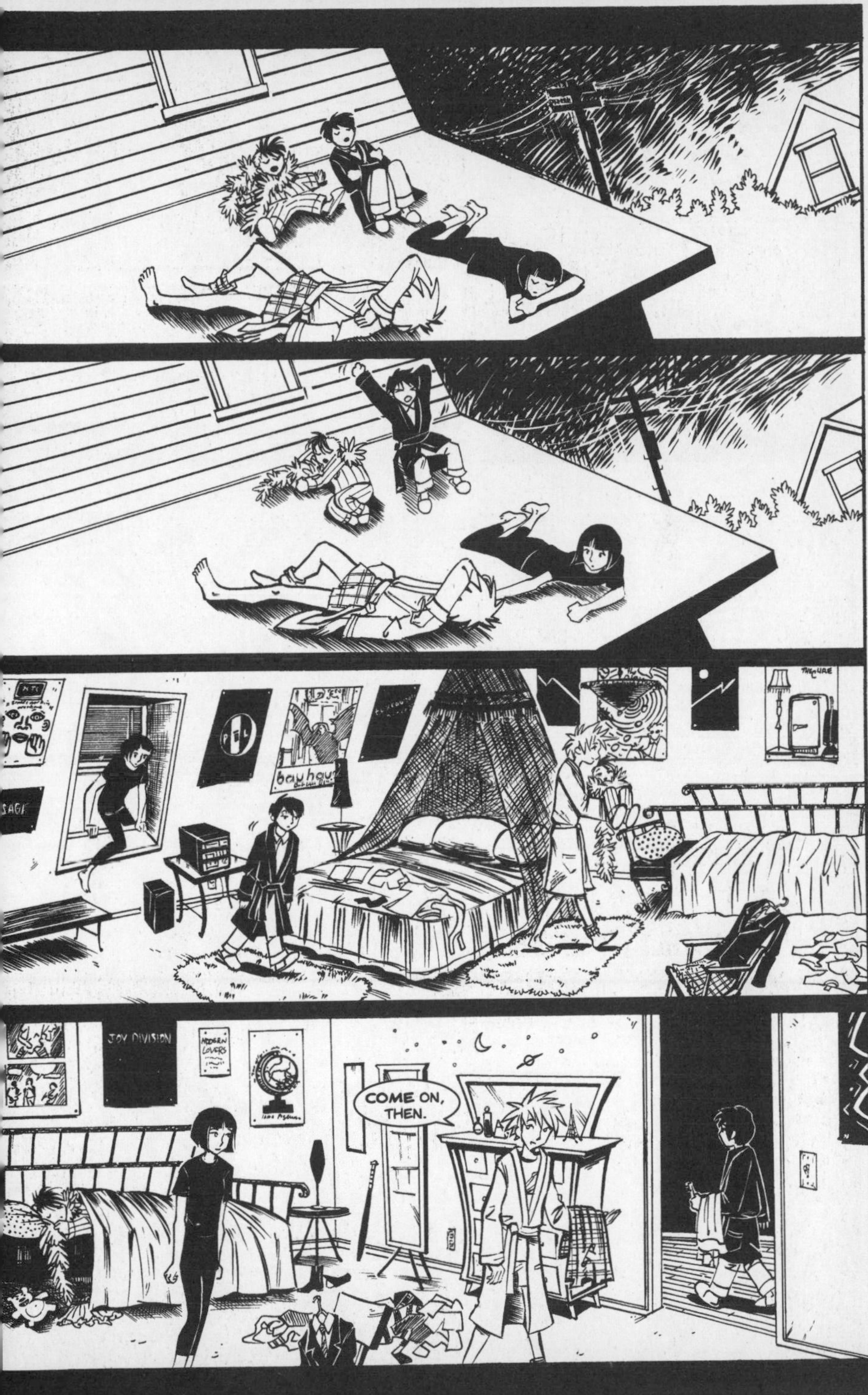
JOY DIVISION
MODERN LOVERS
COME ON, THEN.

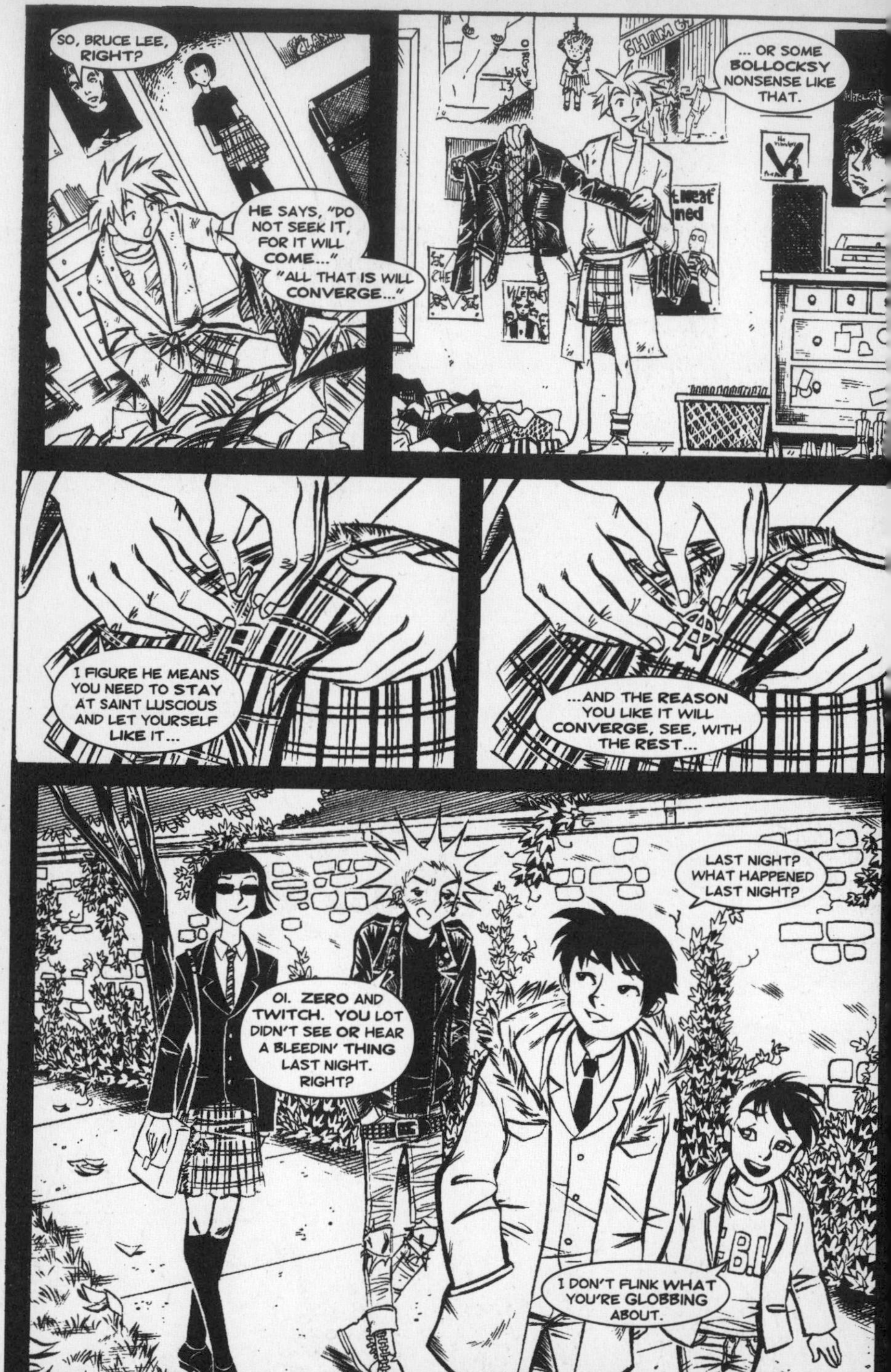
SO, BRUCE LEE, RIGHT?
HE SAYS, "DO NOT SEEK IT, FOR IT WILL COME..."
"ALL THAT IS WILL CONVERGE..."
... OR SOME BOLLOCKSY NONSENSE LIKE THAT.
I FIGURE HE MEANS YOU NEED TO STAY AT SAINT LUSCIOUS AND LET YOURSELF LIKE IT...
...AND THE REASON YOU LIKE IT WILL CONVERGE, SEE, WITH THE REST...
OI. ZERO AND TWITCH. YOU LOT DIDN'T SEE OR HEAR A BLEEDIN' THING LAST NIGHT. RIGHT?
LAST NIGHT? WHAT HAPPENED LAST NIGHT?
I DON'T FLINK WHAT YOU'RE GLOBBING ABOUT.

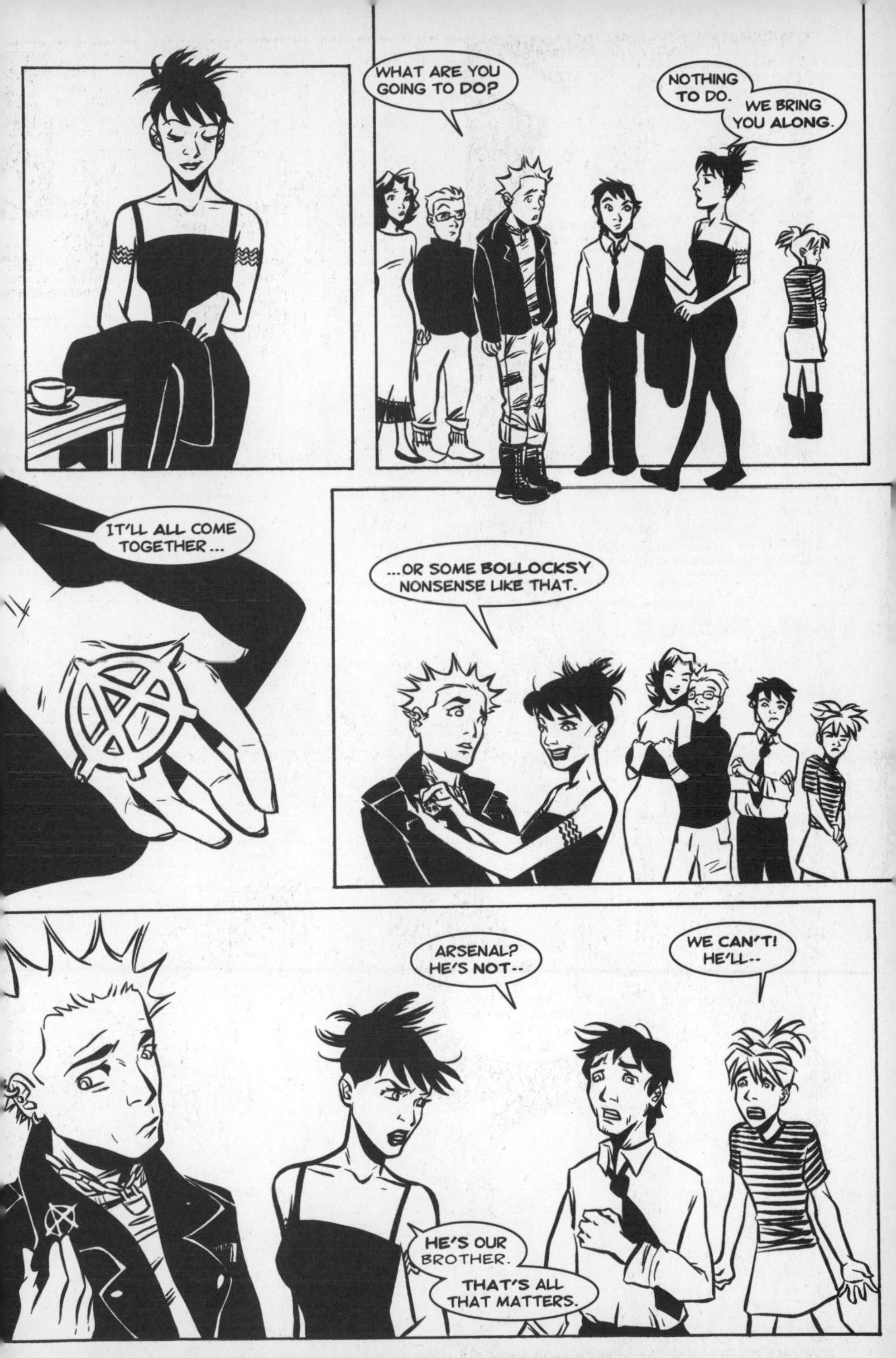
WHAT ARE YOU GOING TO DO?
NOTHING TO DO.
WE BRING YOU ALONG.
IT'LL ALL COME TOGETHER...
...OR SOME BOLLOCKSY NONSENSE LIKE THAT.
ARSENAL? HE'S NOT--
WE CAN'T! HE'LL--
HE'S OUR BROTHER.
THAT'S ALL THAT MATTERS.

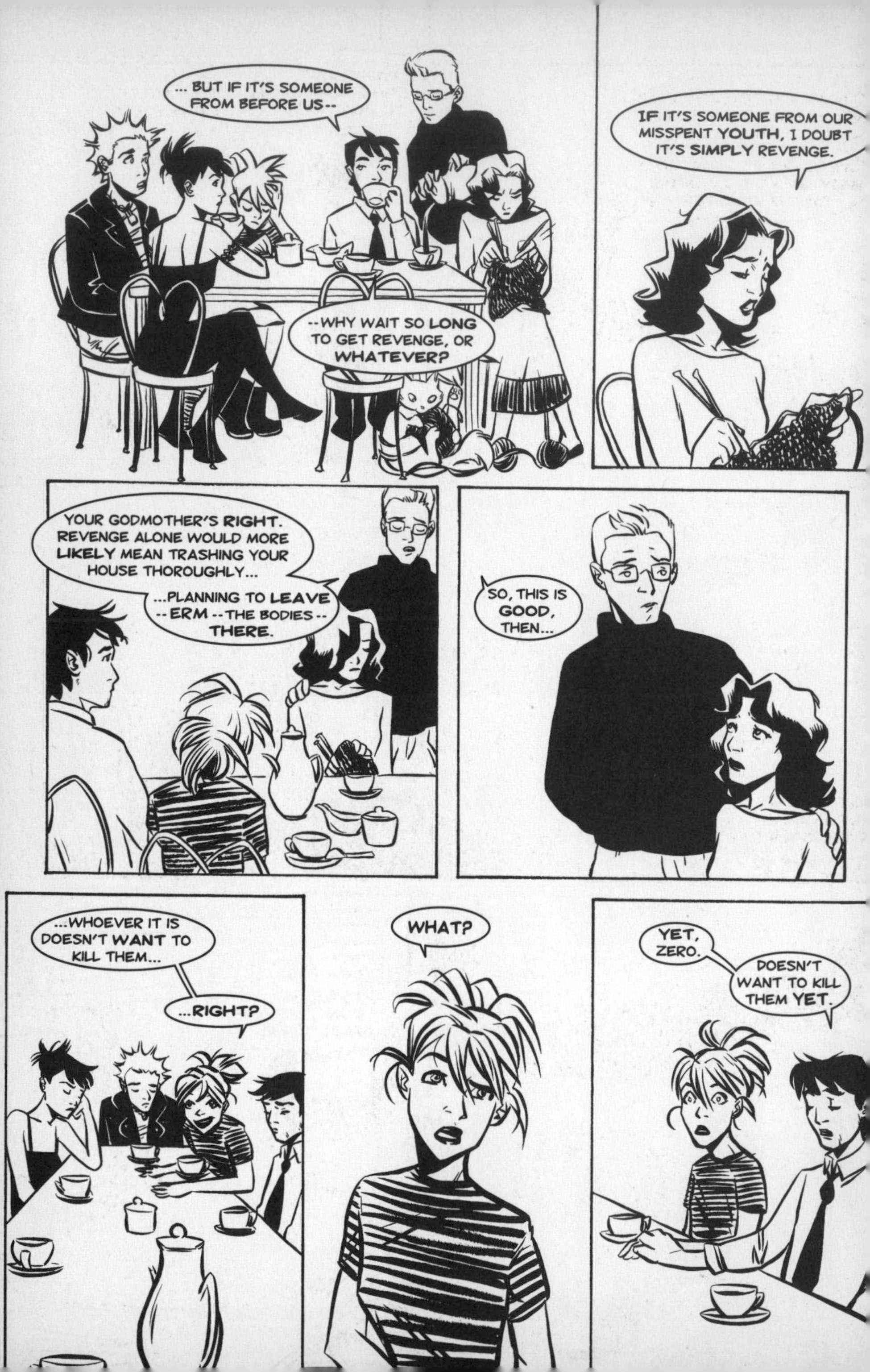
... BUT IF IT'S SOMEONE FROM BEFORE US--
--WHY WAIT SO LONG TO GET REVENGE, OR WHATEVER?
IF IT'S SOMEONE FROM OUR MISSPENT YOUTH, I DOUBT IT'S SIMPLY REVENGE.
YOUR GODMOTHER'S RIGHT. REVENGE ALONE WOULD MORE LIKELY MEAN TRASHING YOUR HOUSE THOROUGHLY...
...PLANNING TO LEAVE --ERM --THE BODIES-- THERE.
SO, THIS IS GOOD, THEN...
...WHOEVER IT IS DOESN'T WANT TO KILL THEM...
...RIGHT?
WHAT?
YET, ZERO.
DOESN'T WANT TO KILL THEM YET.

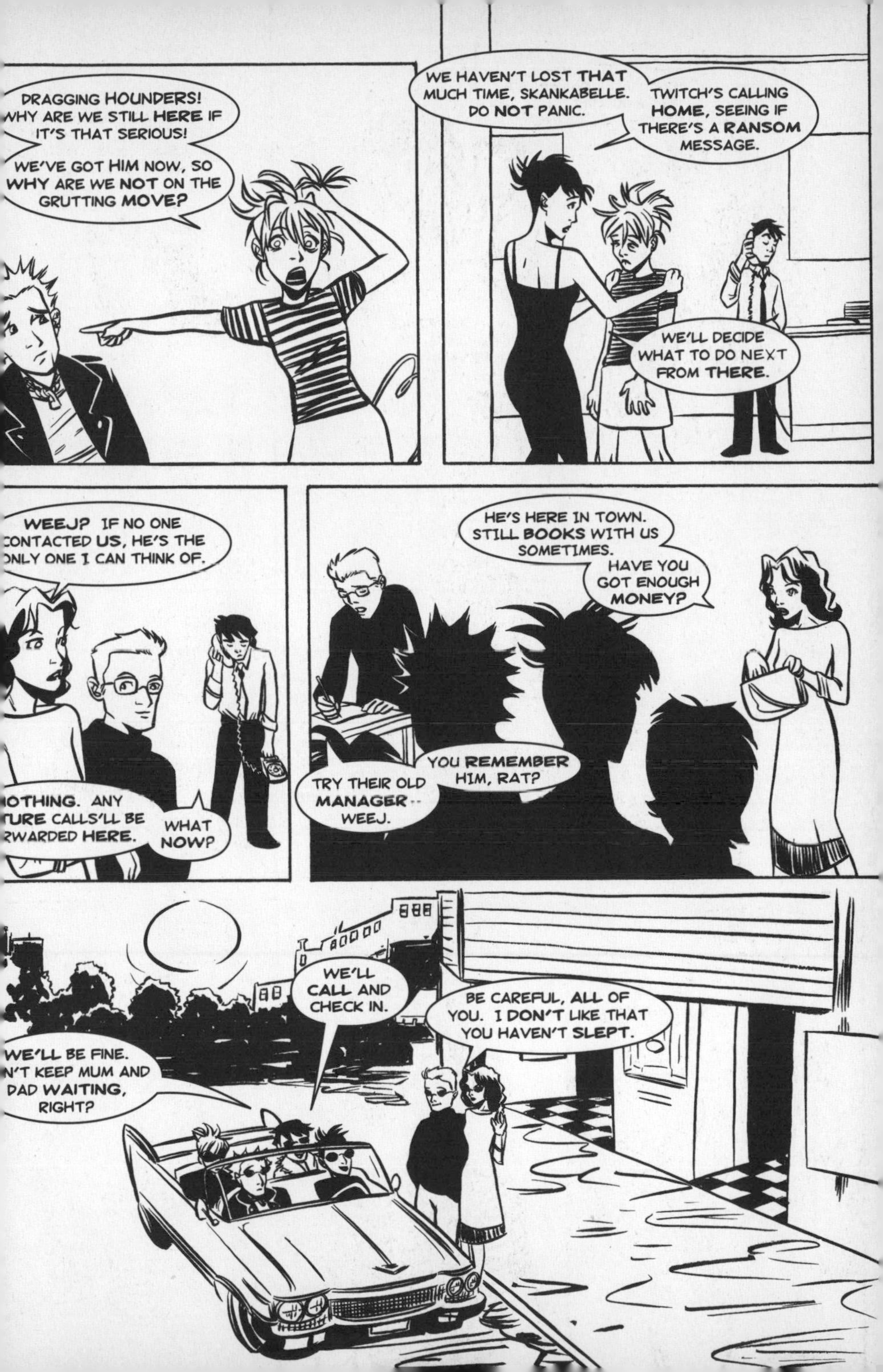
DRAGGING HOUNDERS! WHY ARE WE STILL HERE IF IT'S THAT SERIOUS!
WE'VE GOT HIM NOW, SO WHY ARE WE NOT ON THE GRUTTING MOVE?
WE HAVEN'T LOST THAT MUCH TIME, SKANKABELLE. DO NOT PANIC.
TWITCH'S CALLING HOME, SEEING IF THERE'S A RANSOM MESSAGE.
WE'LL DECIDE WHAT TO DO NEXT FROM THERE.
WEEJ? IF NO ONE CONTACTED US, HE'S THE ONLY ONE I CAN THINK OF.
OTHING. ANY TURE CALLS'LL BE RWARDED HERE.
WHAT NOW?
TRY THEIR OLD MANAGER -- WEEJ.
YOU REMEMBER HIM, RAT?
HE'S HERE IN TOWN. STILL BOOKS WITH US SOMETIMES.
HAVE YOU GOT ENOUGH MONEY?
WE'LL BE FINE. N'T KEEP MUM AND DAD WAITING, RIGHT?
WE'LL CALL AND CHECK IN.
BE CAREFUL, ALL OF YOU. I DON'T LIKE THAT YOU HAVEN'T SLEPT.

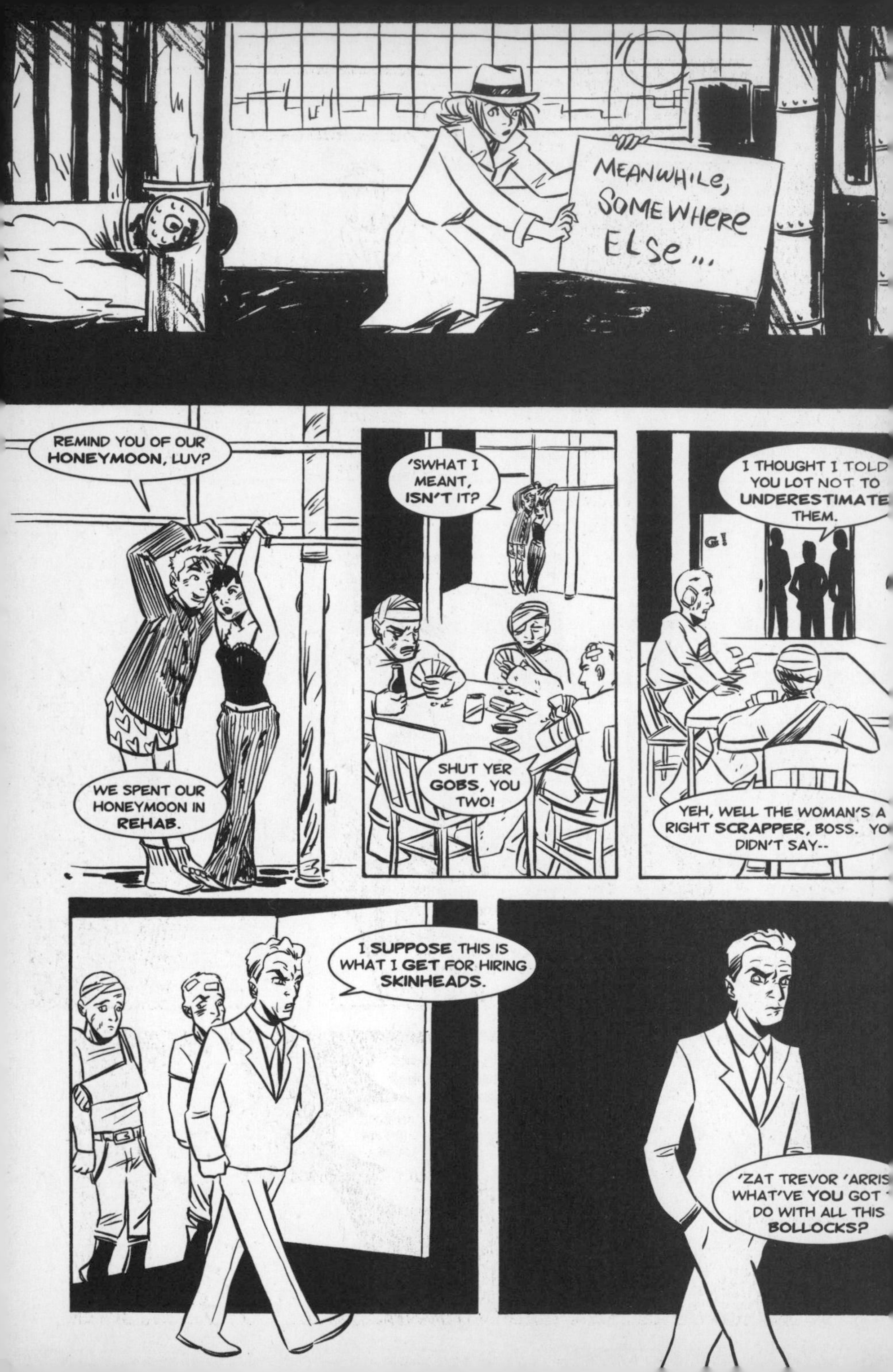
MEANWHILE, SOMEWHERE ELSE...
REMIND YOU OF OUR HONEYMOON, LUV?
WE SPENT OUR HONEYMOON IN REHAB.
'SWHAT I MEANT, ISN'T IT?
SHUT YER GOBS, YOU TWO!
I THOUGHT I TOLD YOU LOT NOT TO UNDERESTIMATE THEM.
G!
YEH, WELL THE WOMAN'S A RIGHT SCRAPPER, BOSS. YO
DIDN'T SAY--
I SUPPOSE THIS IS WHAT I GET FOR HIRING SKINHEADS.
'ZAT TREVOR 'ARRIS
WHAT'VE YOU GOT
DO WITH ALL THIS BOLLOCKS?

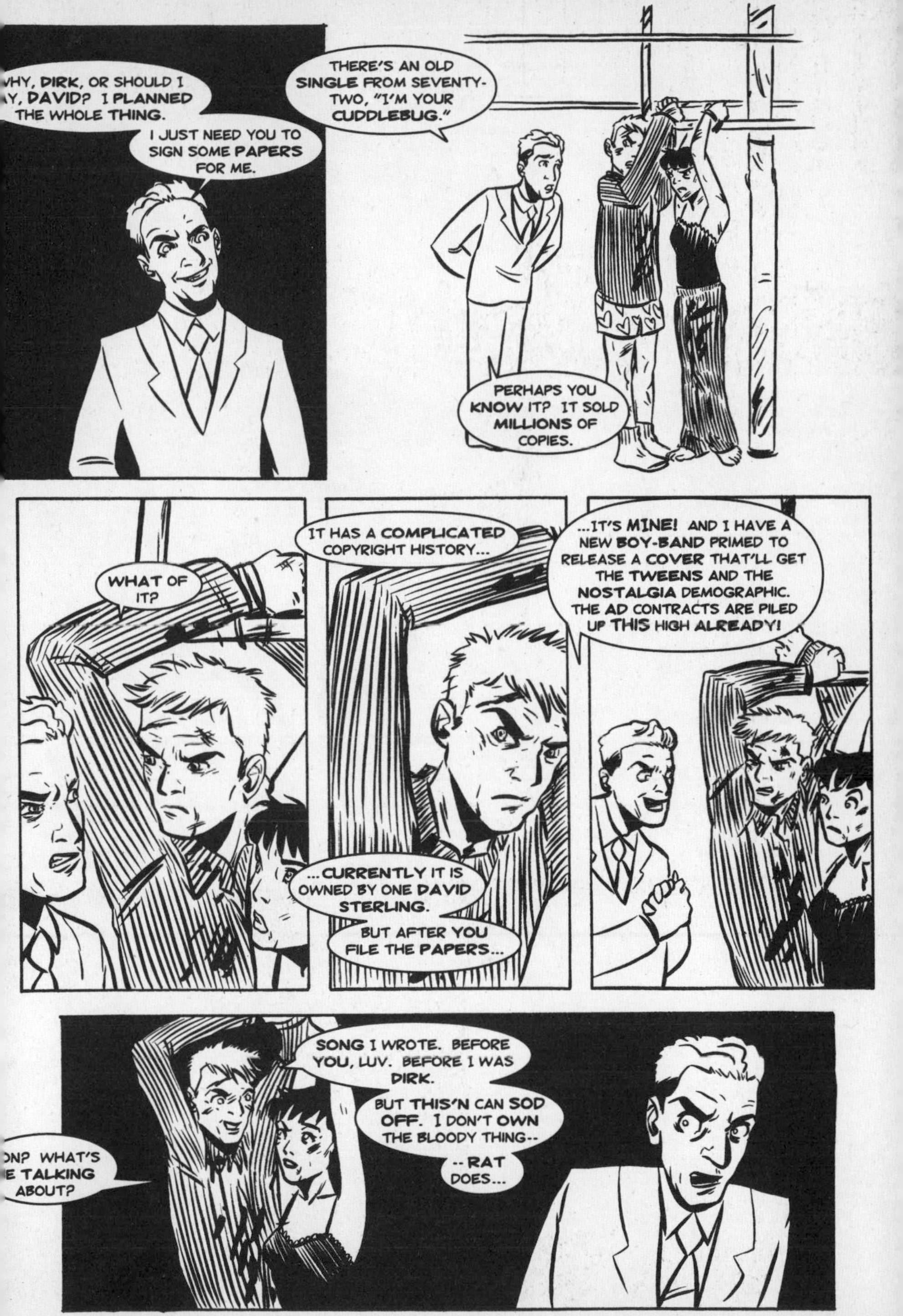

VHY, DIRK, OR SHOULD I
Y, DAVID? I PLANNED THE WHOLE THING.
I JUST NEED YOU TO SIGN SOME PAPERS FOR ME.
THERE'S AN OLD SINGLE FROM SEVENTY-TWO, "I'M YOUR CUDDLEBUG."
PERHAPS YOU KNOW IT? IT SOLD MILLIONS OF COPIES.
WHAT OF IT?
IT HAS A COMPLICATED COPYRIGHT HISTORY...
...CURRENTLY IT IS OWNED BY ONE DAVID STERLING.
BUT AFTER YOU FILE THE PAPERS...
...IT'S MINE! AND I HAVE A NEW BOY-BAND PRIMED TO RELEASE A COVER THAT'LL GET THE TWEENS AND THE NOSTALGIA DEMOGRAPHIC. THE AD CONTRACTS ARE PILED UP THIS HIGH ALREADY!
ON? WHAT'S
E TALKING ABOUT?
SONG I WROTE. BEFORE YOU, LUV. BEFORE I WAS DIRK.
BUT THIS'N CAN SOD OFF. I DON'T OWN THE BLOODY THING--
--RAT DOES...

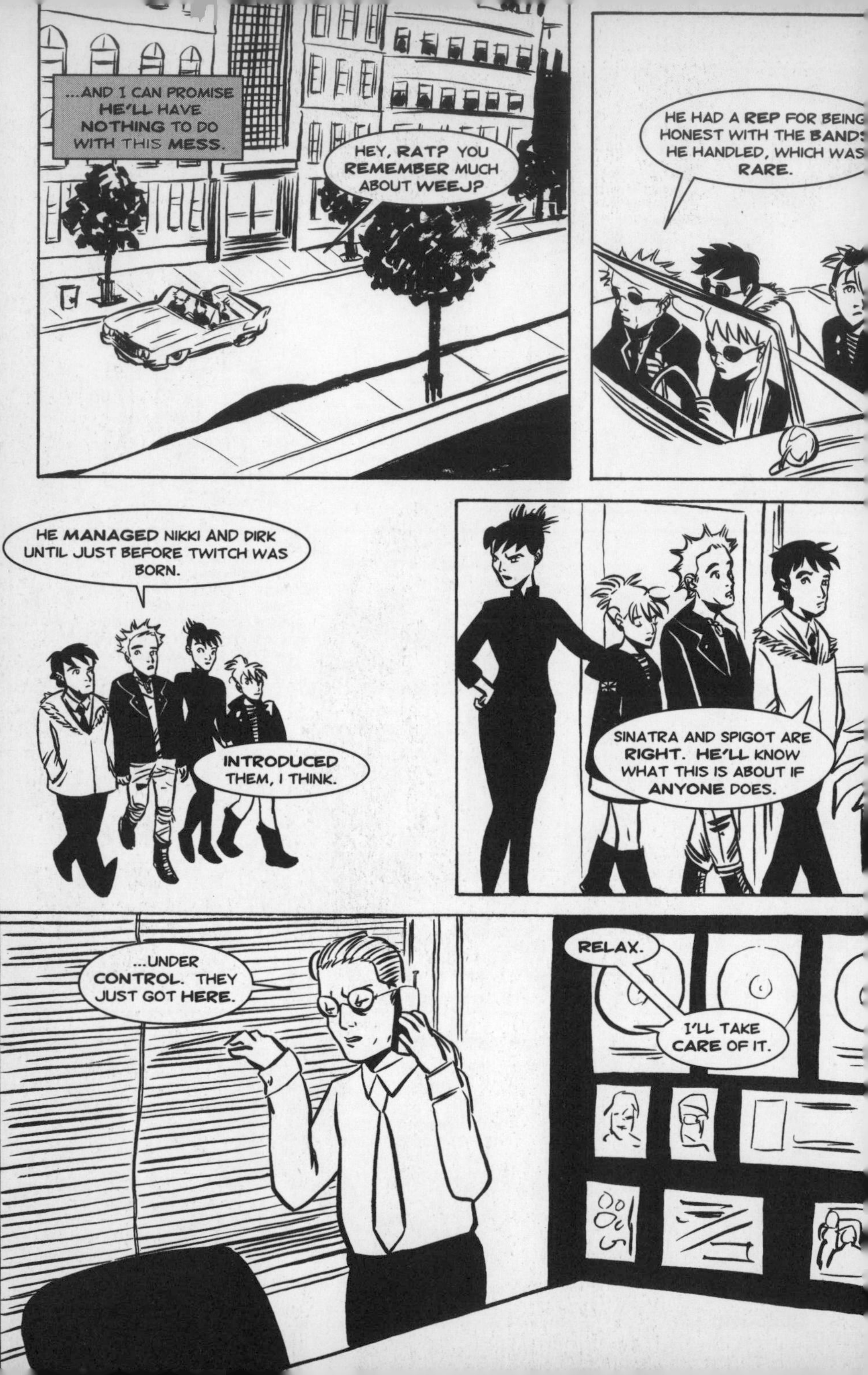
...AND I CAN PROMISE HE'LL HAVE NOTHING TO DO WITH THIS MESS.
HEY, RAT? YOU REMEMBER MUCH ABOUT WEEJ?
HE HAD A REP FOR BEING HONEST WITH THE BANDS HE HANDLED, WHICH WAS RARE.
HE MANAGED NIKKI AND DIRK UNTIL JUST BEFORE TWITCH WAS BORN.
INTRODUCED THEM, I THINK.
SINATRA AND SPIGOT ARE RIGHT. HE'LL KNOW WHAT THIS IS ABOUT IF ANYONE DOES.
...UNDER CONTROL. THEY JUST GOT HERE.
RELAX.
I'LL TAKE CARE OF IT.

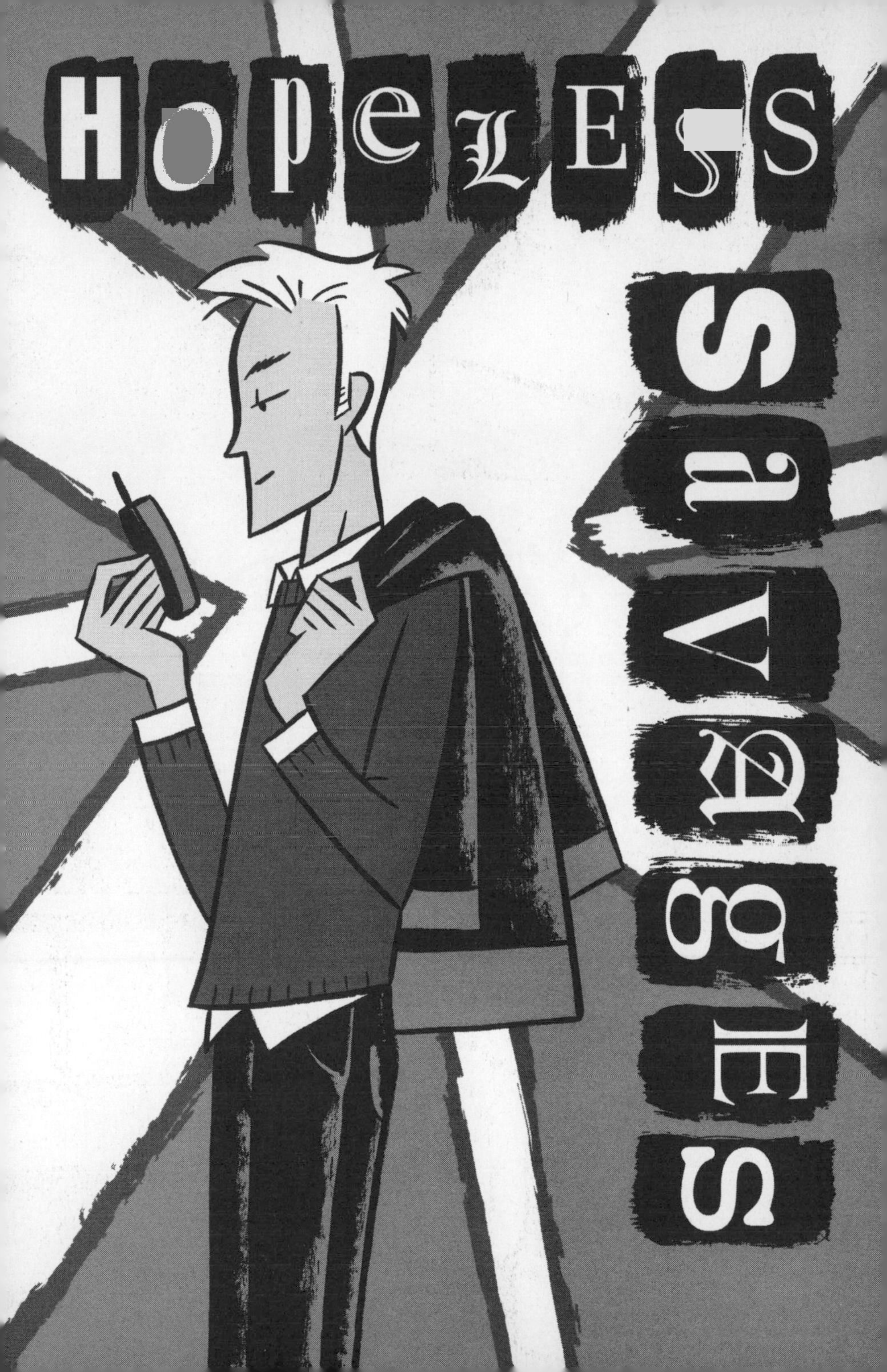

HopeLEsS
SaVAgES

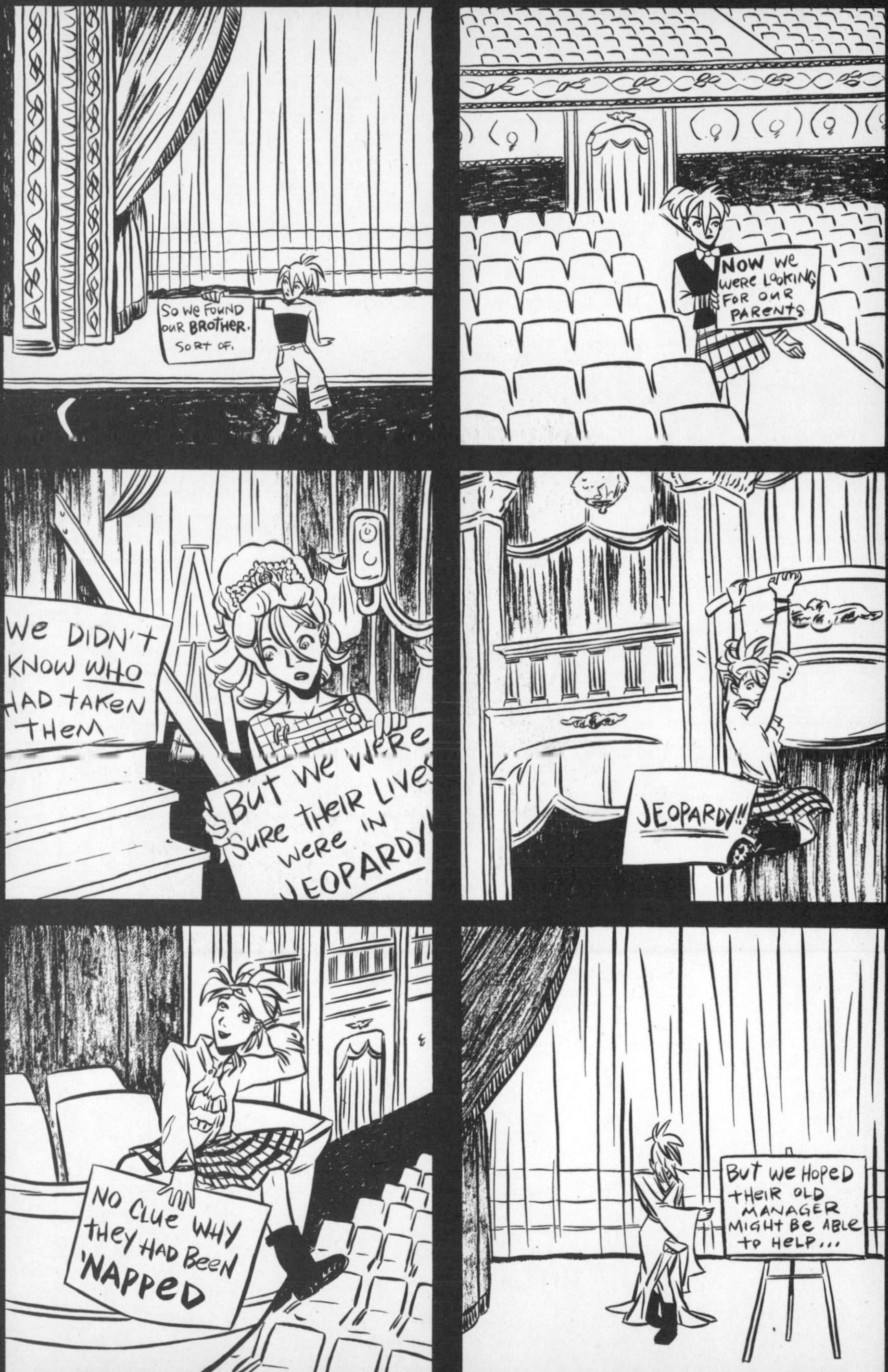
So we FOUND our BROTHER.
SORT OF.
NOW we were LOOKING FOR OUR PARENTS
We DIDN'T KNOW WHO HAD TAKEN THEM
But we were Sure THEIR LIVES were in JEOPARDY!
JEOPARDY!!
NO CLUE WHY THEY HAD BEEN 'NAPPED
But we HOPED THEIR OLD MANAGER MIGHT BE ABLE to HELP...

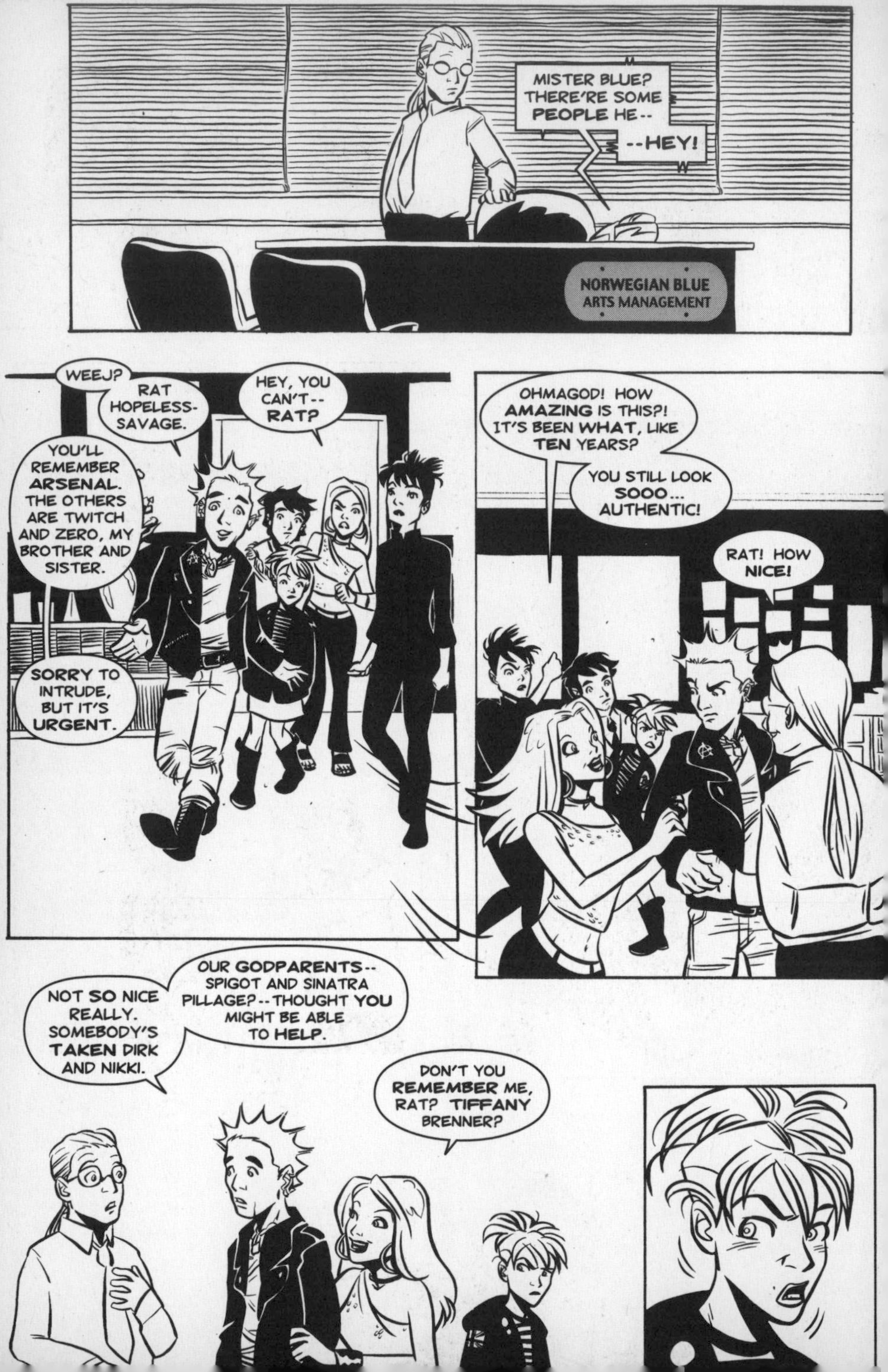
MISTER BLUE? THERE'RE SOME PEOPLE HE--
--HEY!
NORWEGIAN BLUE ARTS MANAGEMENT
WEEJ?
RAT HOPELESS-SAVAGE.
HEY, YOU CAN'T-- RAT?
YOU'LL REMEMBER ARSENAL. THE OTHERS ARE TWITCH AND ZERO, MY BROTHER AND SISTER.
SORRY TO INTRUDE, BUT IT'S URGENT.
OHMAGOD! HOW AMAZING IS THIS?! IT'S BEEN WHAT, LIKE TEN YEARS?
YOU STILL LOOK SOOO... AUTHENTIC!
RAT! HOW NICE!
NOT SO NICE REALLY. SOMEBODY'S TAKEN DIRK AND NIKKI.
OUR GODPARENTS-- SPIGOT AND SINATRA PILLAGE?--THOUGHT YOU MIGHT BE ABLE TO HELP.
DON'T YOU REMEMBER ME, RAT? TIFFANY BRENNER?

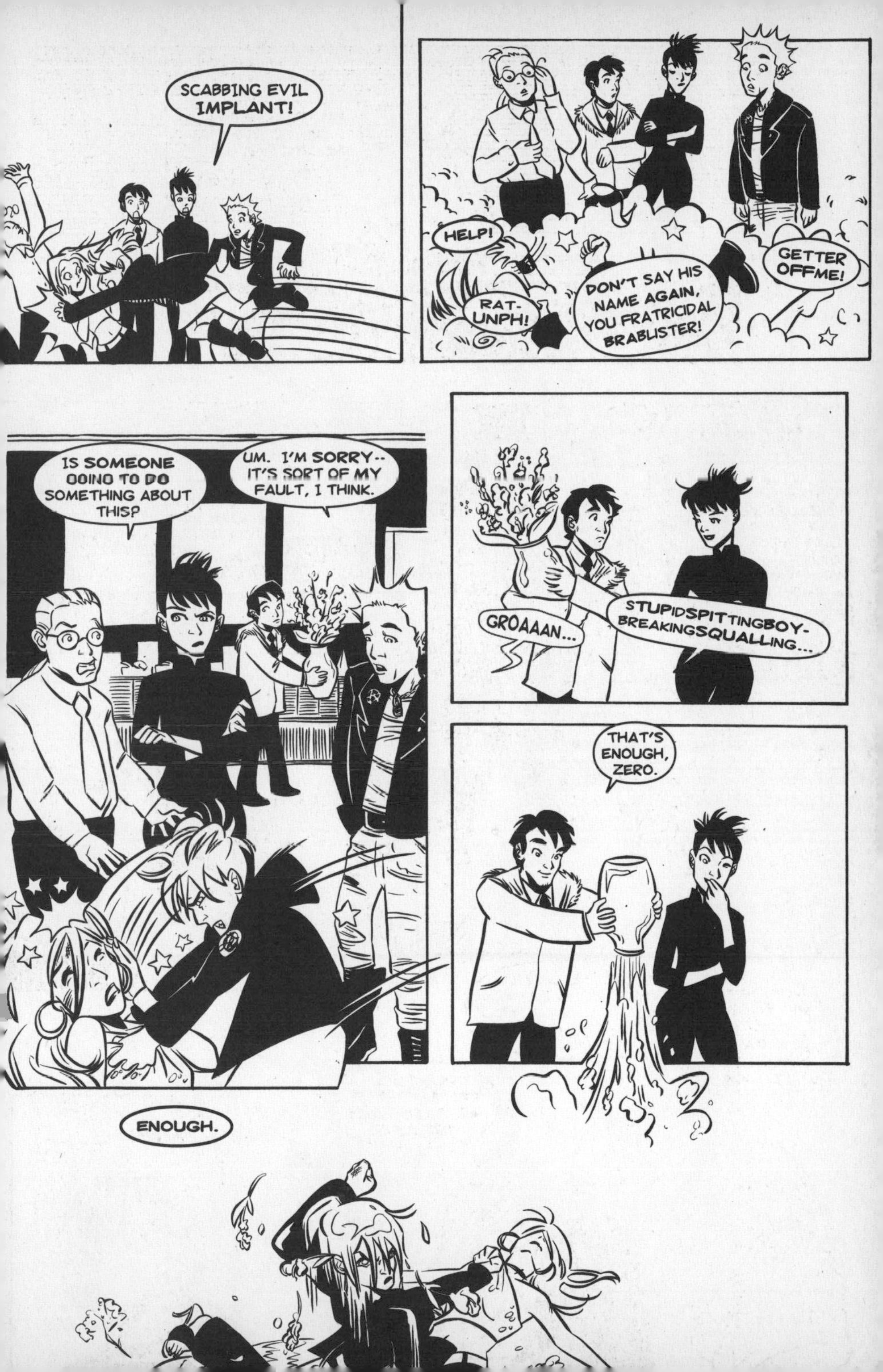
SCABBING EVIL IMPLANT!
HELP!
RAT-UNPH!
DON'T SAY HIS NAME AGAIN, YOU FRATRICIDAL BRABLISTER!
GETTER OFFME!
IS SOMEONE GOING TO DO SOMETHING ABOUT THIS?
UM. I'M SORRY-- IT'S SORT OF MY FAULT, I THINK.
GROAAAN...
STUPIDSPITTINGBOY-BREAKINGSQUALLING...
THAT'S ENOUGH, ZERO.
ENOUGH.

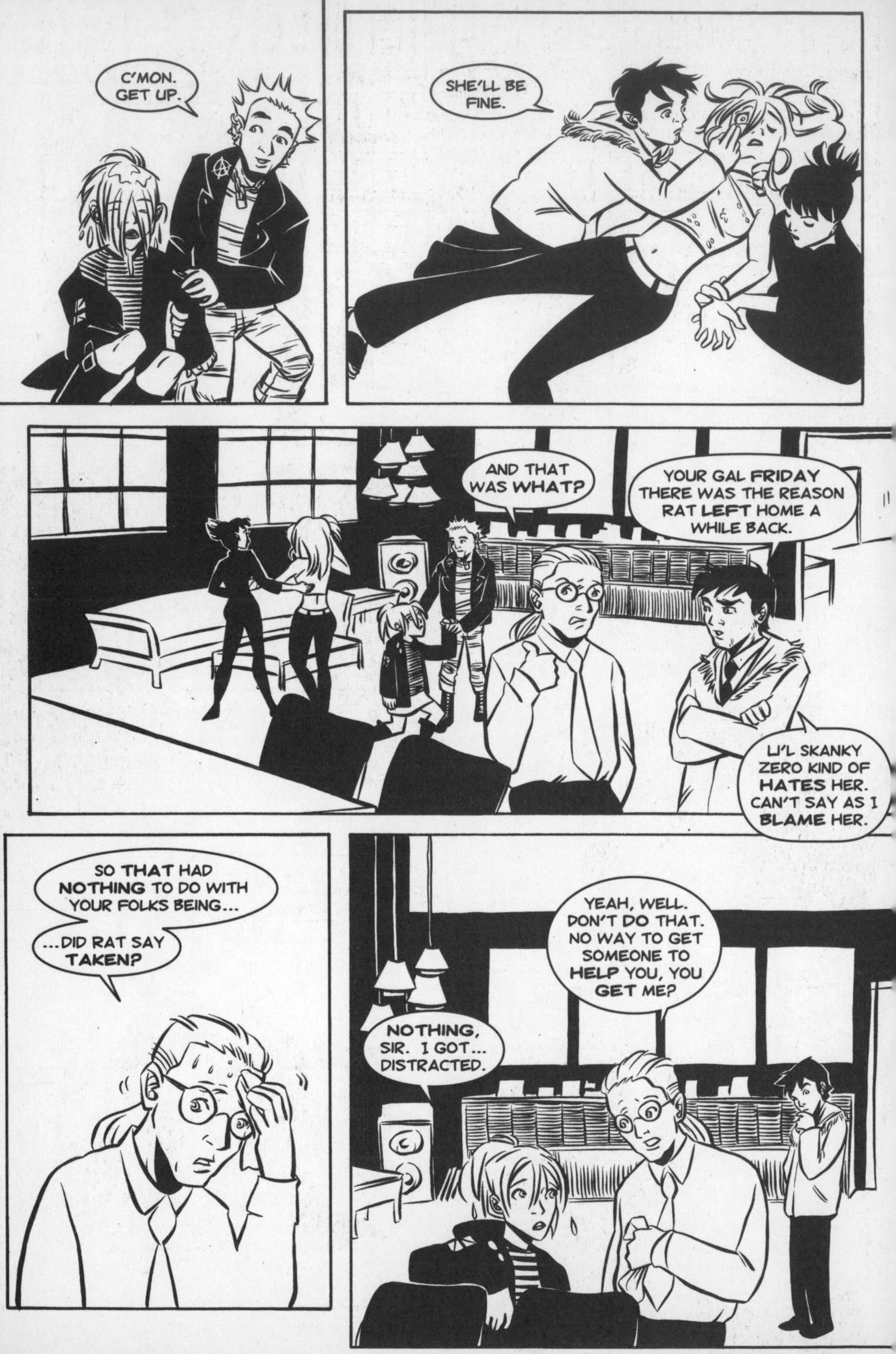
C'MON. GET UP.
SHE'LL BE FINE.
AND THAT WAS WHAT?
YOUR GAL FRIDAY THERE WAS THE REASON RAT LEFT HOME A WHILE BACK.
LI'L SKANKY ZERO KIND OF HATES HER. CAN'T SAY AS I BLAME HER.
SO THAT HAD NOTHING TO DO WITH YOUR FOLKS BEING...
...DID RAT SAY TAKEN?
YEAH, WELL. DON'T DO THAT. NO WAY TO GET SOMEONE TO HELP YOU, YOU GET ME?
NOTHING, SIR. I GOT... DISTRACTED.

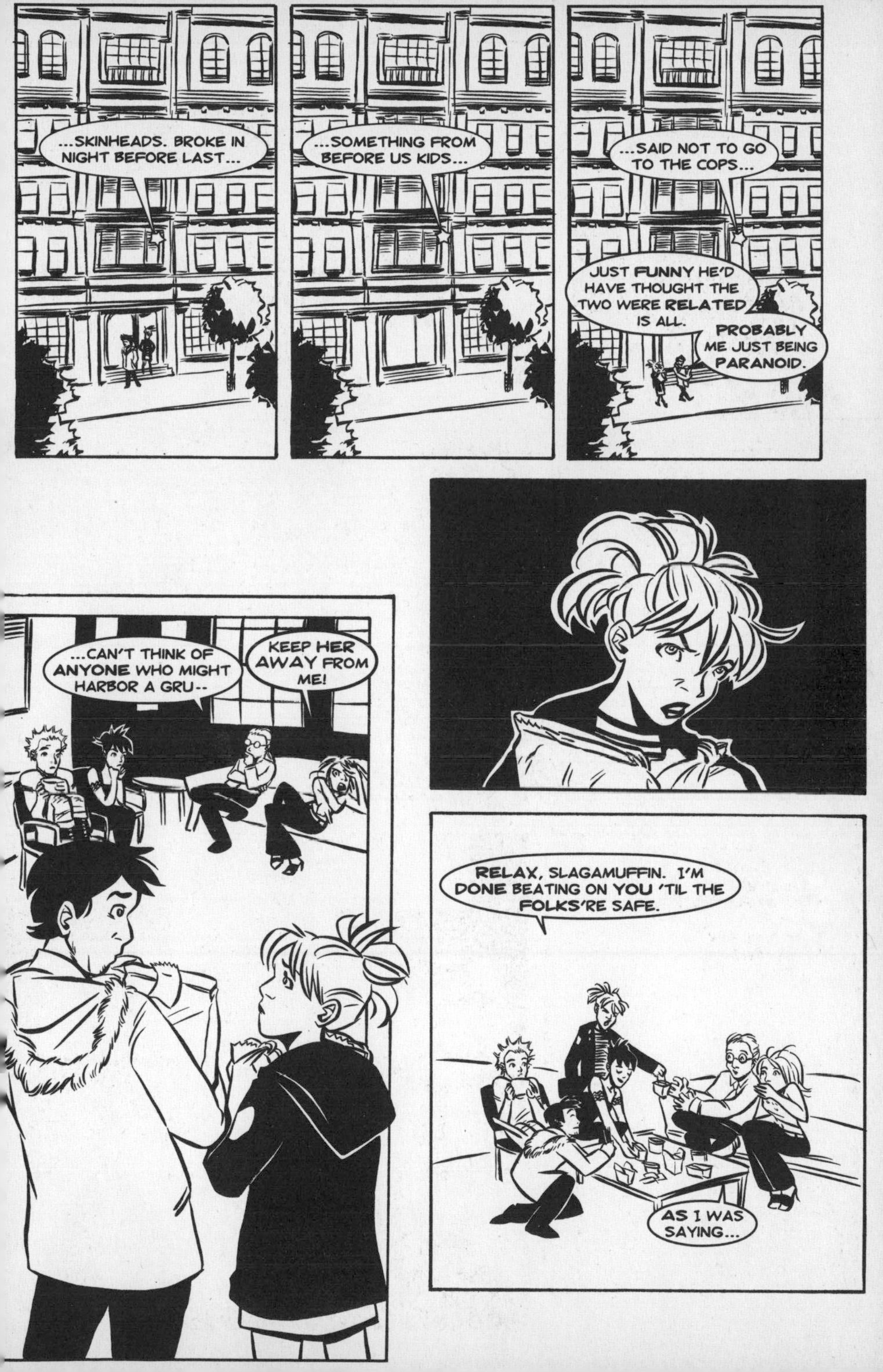
...SKINHEADS. BROKE IN NIGHT BEFORE LAST...
...SOMETHING FROM BEFORE US KIDS...
...SAID NOT TO GO TO THE COPS...
JUST FUNNY HE'D HAVE THOUGHT THE TWO WERE RELATED IS ALL.
PROBABLY ME JUST BEING PARANOID.
...CAN'T THINK OF ANYONE WHO MIGHT HARBOR A GRU--
KEEP HER AWAY FROM ME!
RELAX, SLAGAMUFFIN. I'M DONE BEATING ON YOU 'TIL THE FOLKS'RE SAFE.
AS I WAS SAYING...

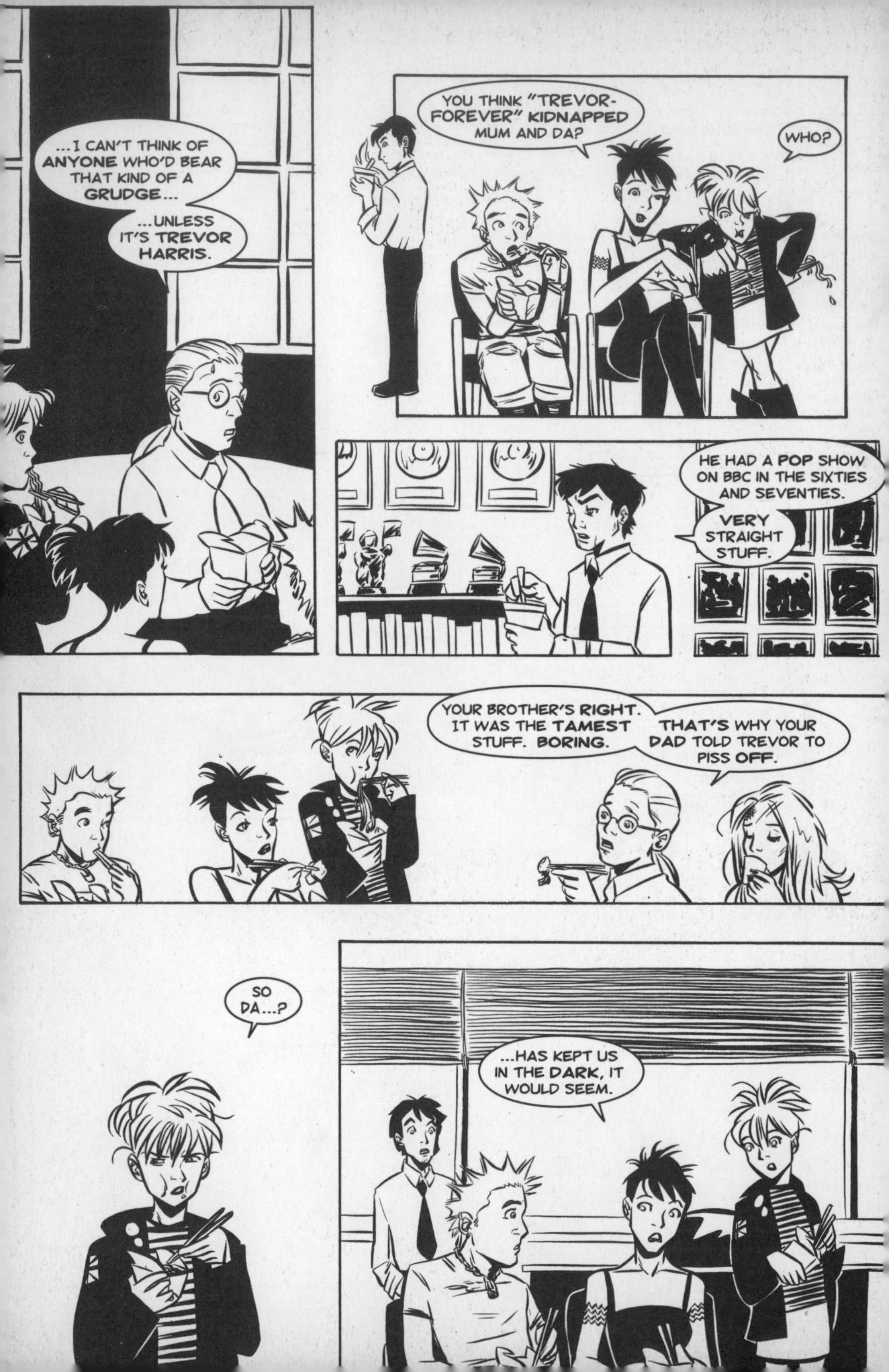

...I CAN'T THINK OF ANYONE WHO'D BEAR THAT KIND OF A GRUDGE...
...UNLESS IT'S TREVOR HARRIS.
YOU THINK "TREVOR-FOREVER" KIDNAPPED MUM AND DA?
WHO?
HE HAD A POP SHOW ON BBC IN THE SIXTIES AND SEVENTIES.
VERY STRAIGHT STUFF.
YOUR BROTHER'S RIGHT. IT WAS THE TAMEST STUFF. BORING.
THAT'S WHY YOUR DAD TOLD TREVOR TO PISS OFF.
SO DA...?
...HAS KEPT US IN THE DARK, IT WOULD SEEM.

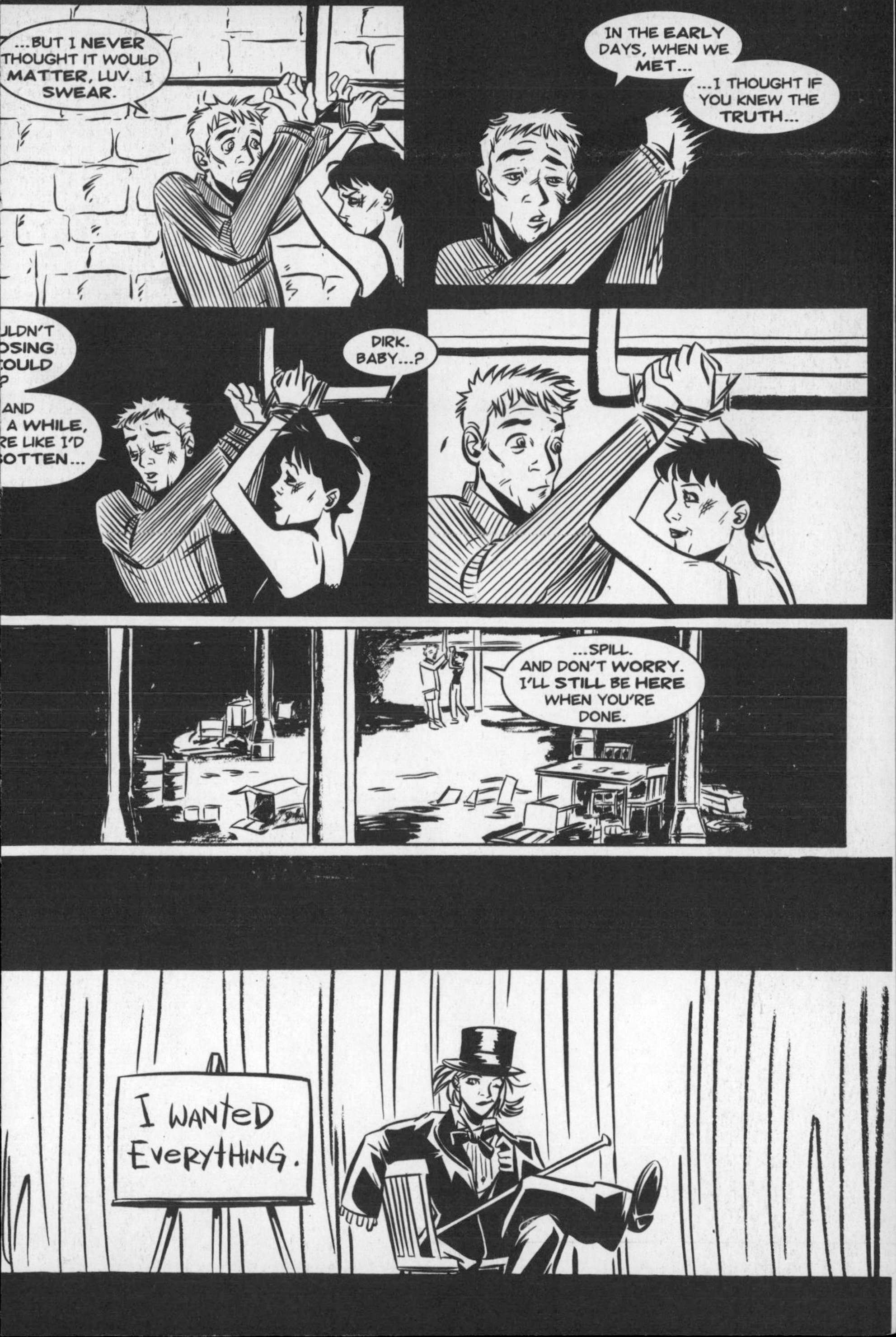
...BUT I NEVER THOUGHT IT WOULD MATTER, LUV. I SWEAR.
IN THE EARLY DAYS, WHEN WE MET...
...I THOUGHT IF YOU KNEW THE TRUTH...
AND A WHILE,
DIRK. BABY...?
...SPILL. AND DON'T WORRY. I'LL STILL BE HERE WHEN YOU'RE DONE.
I WANTED EVERYTHING.

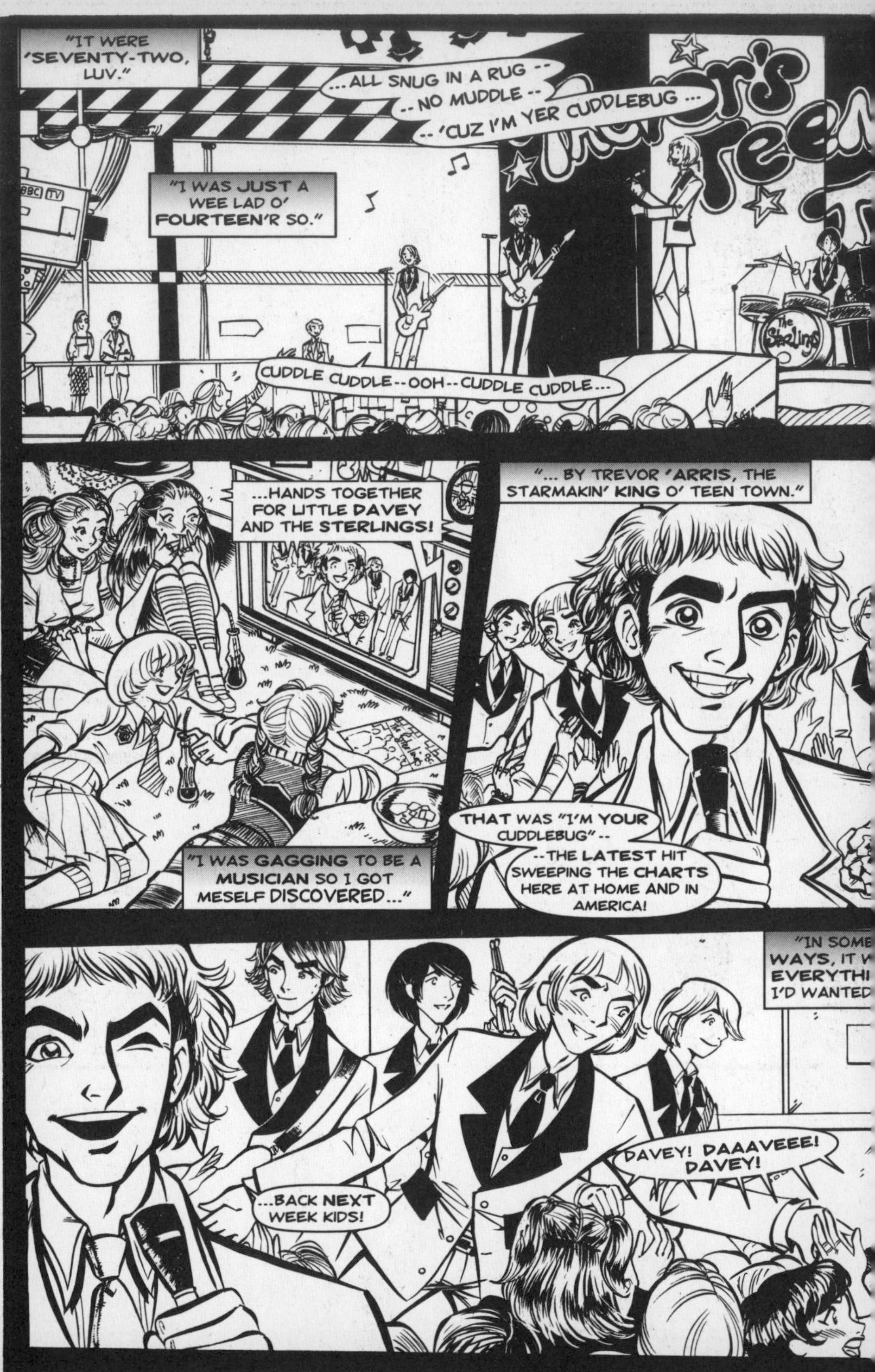
"IT WERE 'SEVENTY-TWO, LUV."
...ALL SNUG IN A RUG --
-- NO MUDDLE --
-- 'CUZ I'M YER CUDDLEBUG ...
"I WAS JUST A WEE LAD O' FOURTEEN'R SO."
CUDDLE CUDDLE--OOH--CUDDLE CUDDLE...
...HANDS TOGETHER FOR LITTLE DAVEY AND THE STERLINGS!
"I WAS GAGGING TO BE A MUSICIAN SO I GOT MESELF DISCOVERED..."
"... BY TREVOR 'ARRIS, THE STARMAKIN' KING O' TEEN TOWN."
THAT WAS "I'M YOUR CUDDLEBUG" --
--THE LATEST HIT SWEEPING THE CHARTS HERE AT HOME AND IN AMERICA!
"IN SOME WAYS, IT W EVERYTHI I'D WANTED
...BACK NEXT WEEK KIDS!
DAVEY! DAAAVEEE! DAVEY!

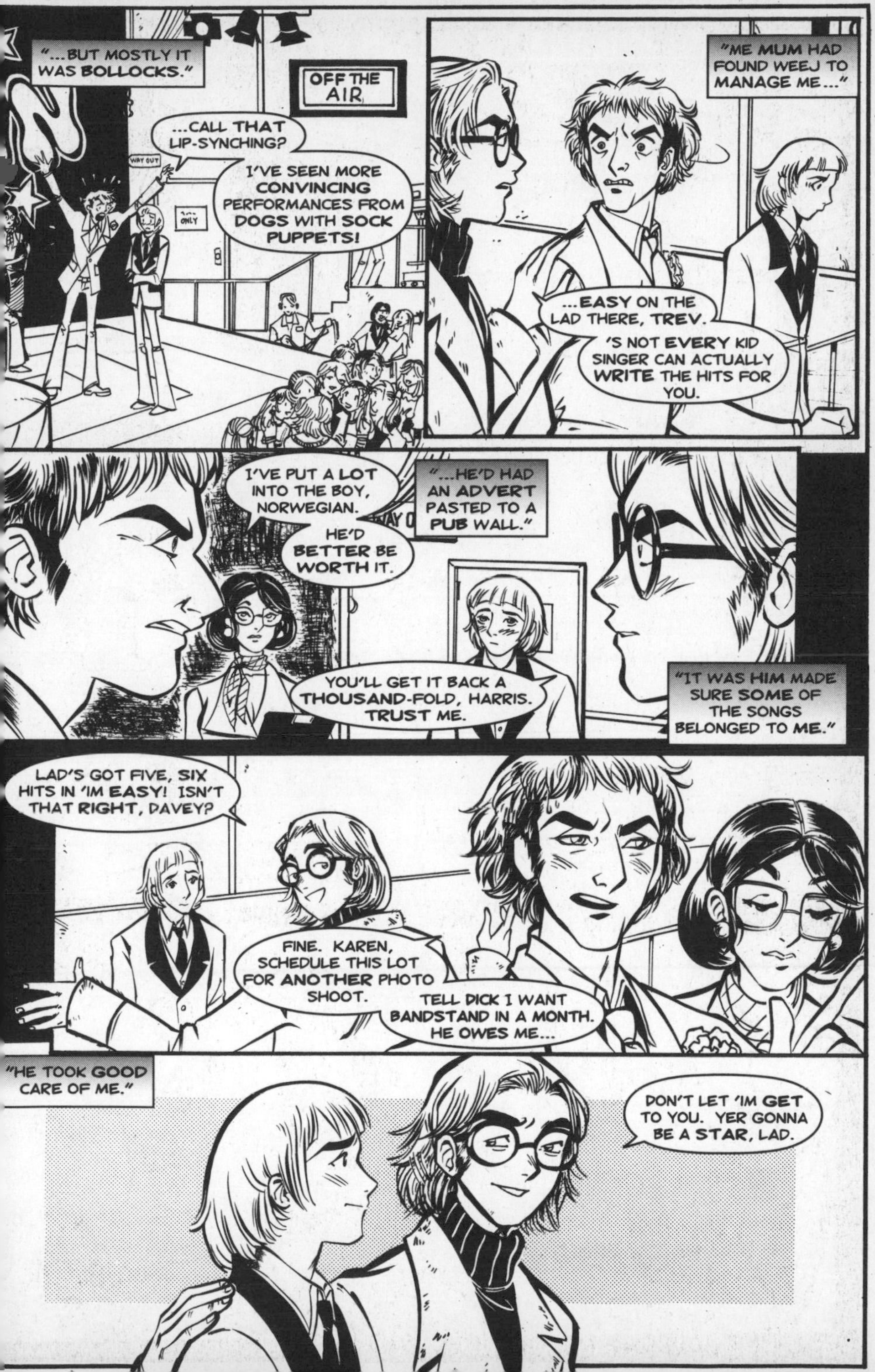
"...BUT MOSTLY IT WAS BOLLOCKS."
OFF THE AIR
WAY OUT
ONLY
...CALL THAT LIP-SYNCHING?
I'VE SEEN MORE CONVINCING PERFORMANCES FROM DOGS WITH SOCK PUPPETS!
"ME MUM HAD FOUND WEEJ TO MANAGE ME..."
...EASY ON THE LAD THERE, TREV.
'S NOT EVERY KID SINGER CAN ACTUALLY WRITE THE HITS FOR YOU.
I'VE PUT A LOT INTO THE BOY, NORWEGIAN.
HE'D BETTER BE WORTH IT.
"...HE'D HAD AN ADVERT PASTED TO A PUB WALL."
YOU'LL GET IT BACK A THOUSAND-FOLD, HARRIS. TRUST ME.
"IT WAS HIM MADE SURE SOME OF THE SONGS BELONGED TO ME."
LAD'S GOT FIVE, SIX HITS IN 'IM EASY! ISN'T THAT RIGHT, DAVEY?
FINE. KAREN, SCHEDULE THIS LOT FOR ANOTHER PHOTO SHOOT.
TELL DICK I WANT BANDSTAND IN A MONTH. HE OWES ME...
"HE TOOK GOOD CARE OF ME."
DON'T LET 'IM GET TO YOU. YER GONNA BE A STAR, LAD.

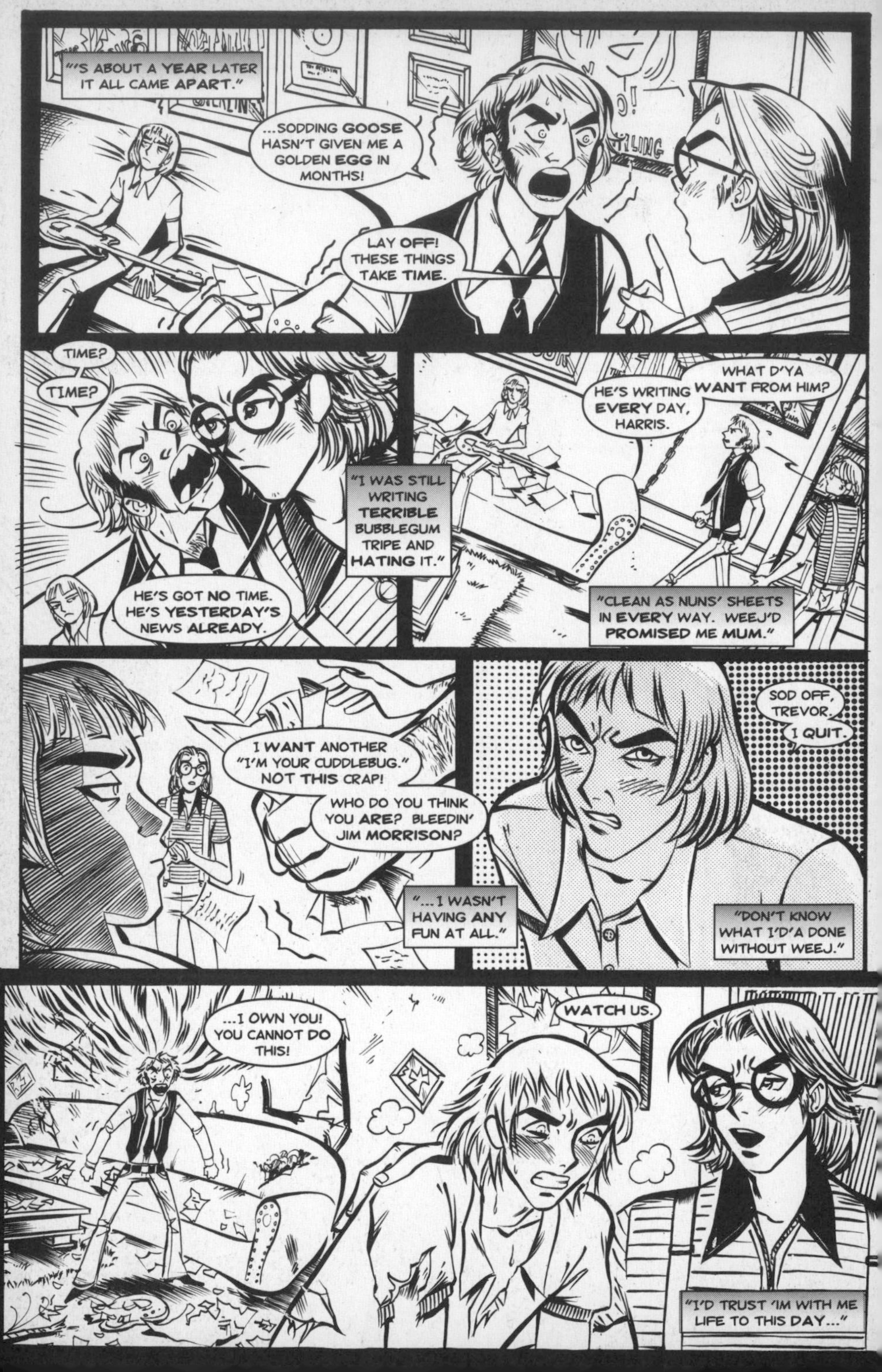

"'S ABOUT A YEAR LATER IT ALL CAME APART."
...SODDING GOOSE HASN'T GIVEN ME A GOLDEN EGG IN MONTHS!
LAY OFF! THESE THINGS TAKE TIME.
TIME?
TIME?
"I WAS STILL WRITING TERRIBLE BUBBLEGUM TRIPE AND HATING IT."
HE'S GOT NO TIME. HE'S YESTERDAY'S NEWS ALREADY.
HE'S WRITING EVERY DAY, HARRIS.
WHAT D'YA WANT FROM HIM?
"CLEAN AS NUNS' SHEETS IN EVERY WAY. WEEJ'D PROMISED ME MUM."
I WANT ANOTHER "I'M YOUR CUDDLEBUG." NOT THIS CRAP!
WHO DO YOU THINK YOU ARE? BLEEDIN' JIM MORRISON?
"...I WASN'T HAVING ANY FUN AT ALL."
SOD OFF, TREVOR.
I QUIT.
"DON'T KNOW WHAT I'D'A DONE WITHOUT WEEJ."
...I OWN YOU! YOU CANNOT DO THIS!
WATCH US.
"I'D TRUST 'IM WITH ME LIFE TO THIS DAY..."

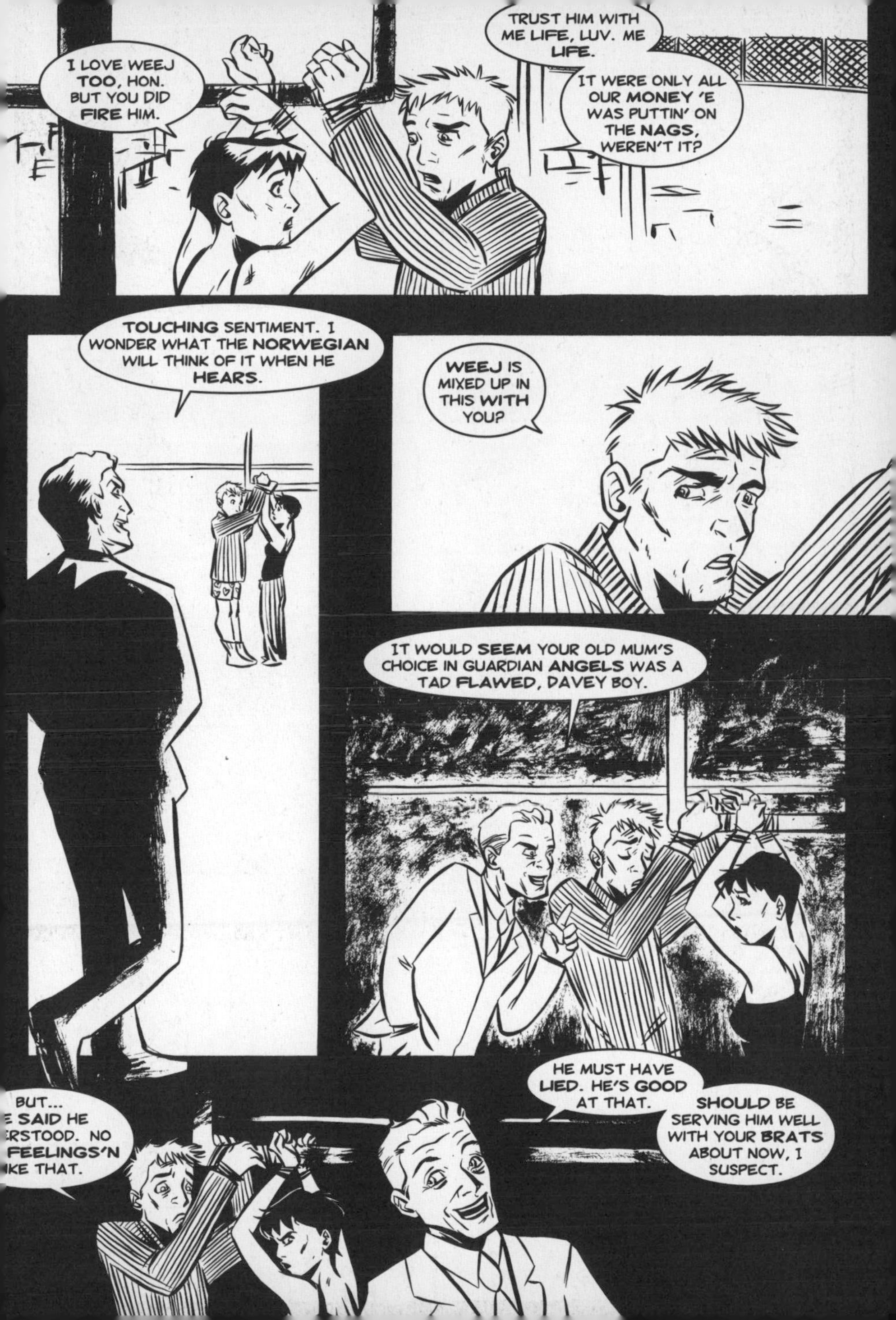
I LOVE WEEJ TOO, HON. BUT YOU DID FIRE HIM.
TRUST HIM WITH ME LIFE, LUV. ME LIFE.
IT WERE ONLY ALL OUR MONEY 'E WAS PUTTIN' ON THE NAGS, WEREN'T IT?
TOUCHING SENTIMENT. I WONDER WHAT THE NORWEGIAN WILL THINK OF IT WHEN HE HEARS.
WEEJ IS MIXED UP IN THIS WITH YOU?
IT WOULD SEEM YOUR OLD MUM'S CHOICE IN GUARDIAN ANGELS WAS A TAD FLAWED, DAVEY BOY.
BUT... E SAID HE ERSTOOD. NO FEELINGS'N KE THAT.
HE MUST HAVE LIED. HE'S GOOD AT THAT.
SHOULD BE SERVING HIM WELL WITH YOUR BRATS ABOUT NOW, I SUSPECT.

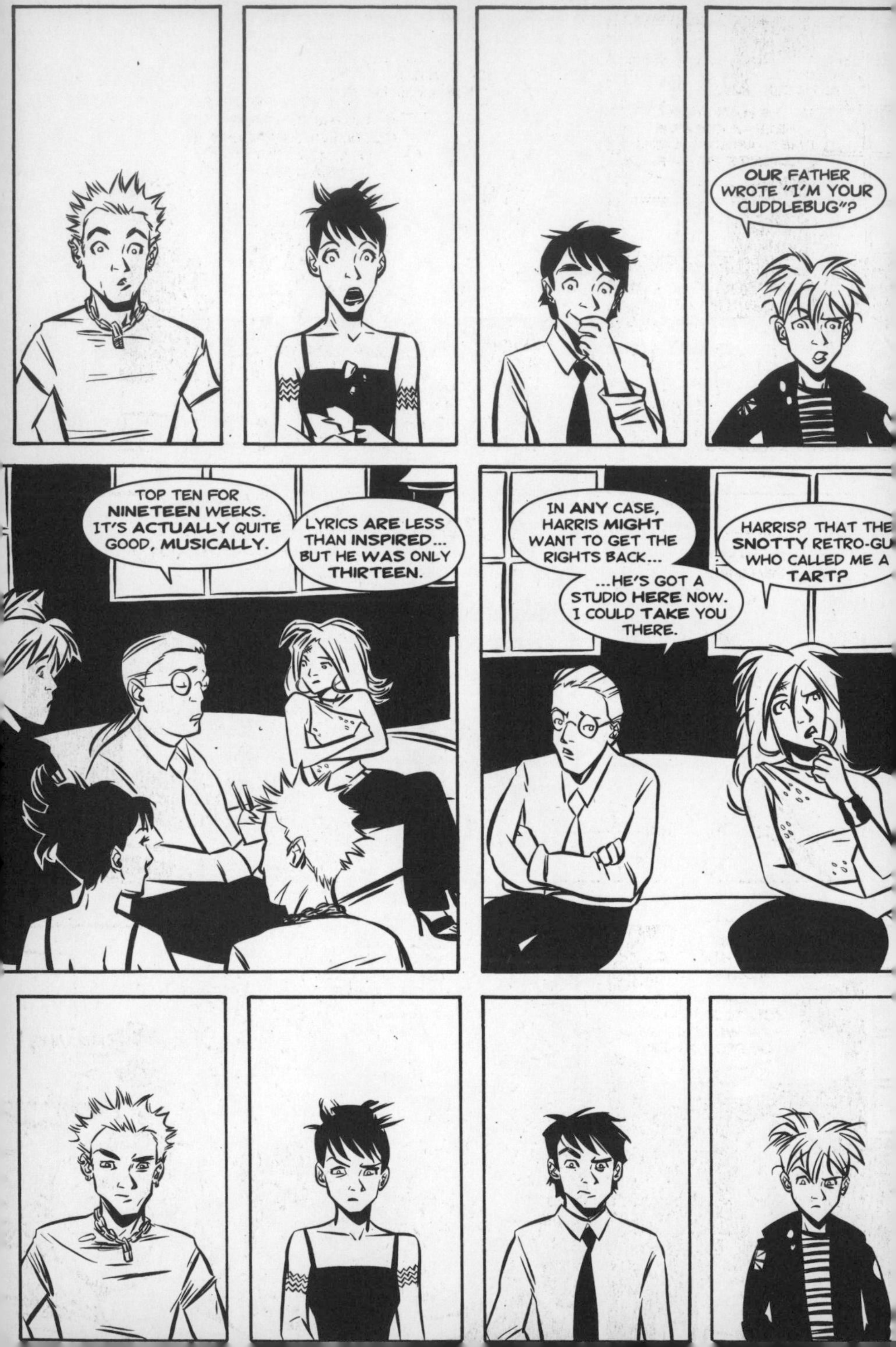
OUR FATHER WROTE "I'M YOUR CUDDLEBUG"?
TOP TEN FOR NINETEEN WEEKS. IT'S ACTUALLY QUITE GOOD, MUSICALLY.
LYRICS ARE LESS THAN INSPIRED... BUT HE WAS ONLY THIRTEEN.
IN ANY CASE, HARRIS MIGHT WANT TO GET THE RIGHTS BACK...
...HE'S GOT A STUDIO HERE NOW. I COULD TAKE YOU THERE.
HARRIS? THAT THE SNOTTY RETRO-GU WHO CALLED ME A TART?

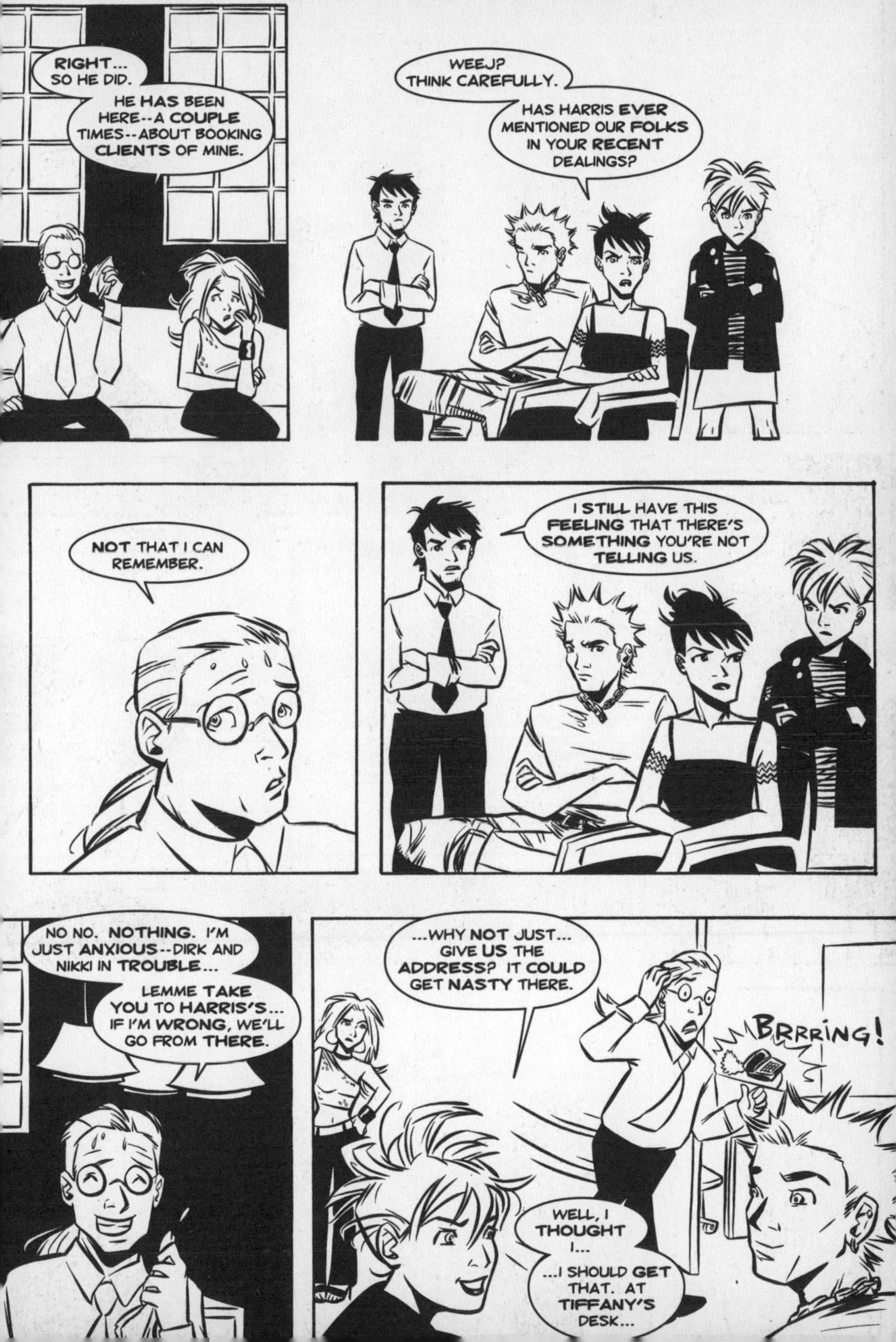

RIGHT... SO HE DID.
HE HAS BEEN HERE--A COUPLE TIMES--ABOUT BOOKING CLIENTS OF MINE.
WEEJ? THINK CAREFULLY.
HAS HARRIS EVER MENTIONED OUR FOLKS IN YOUR RECENT DEALINGS?
NOT THAT I CAN REMEMBER.
I STILL HAVE THIS FEELING THAT THERE'S SOMETHING YOU'RE NOT TELLING US.
NO NO. NOTHING. I'M JUST ANXIOUS--DIRK AND NIKKI IN TROUBLE...
LEMME TAKE YOU TO HARRIS'S... IF I'M WRONG, WE'LL GO FROM THERE.
...WHY NOT JUST... GIVE US THE ADDRESS? IT COULD GET NASTY THERE.
BRRRING!
WELL, I THOUGHT I...
...I SHOULD GET THAT. AT TIFFANY'S DESK...

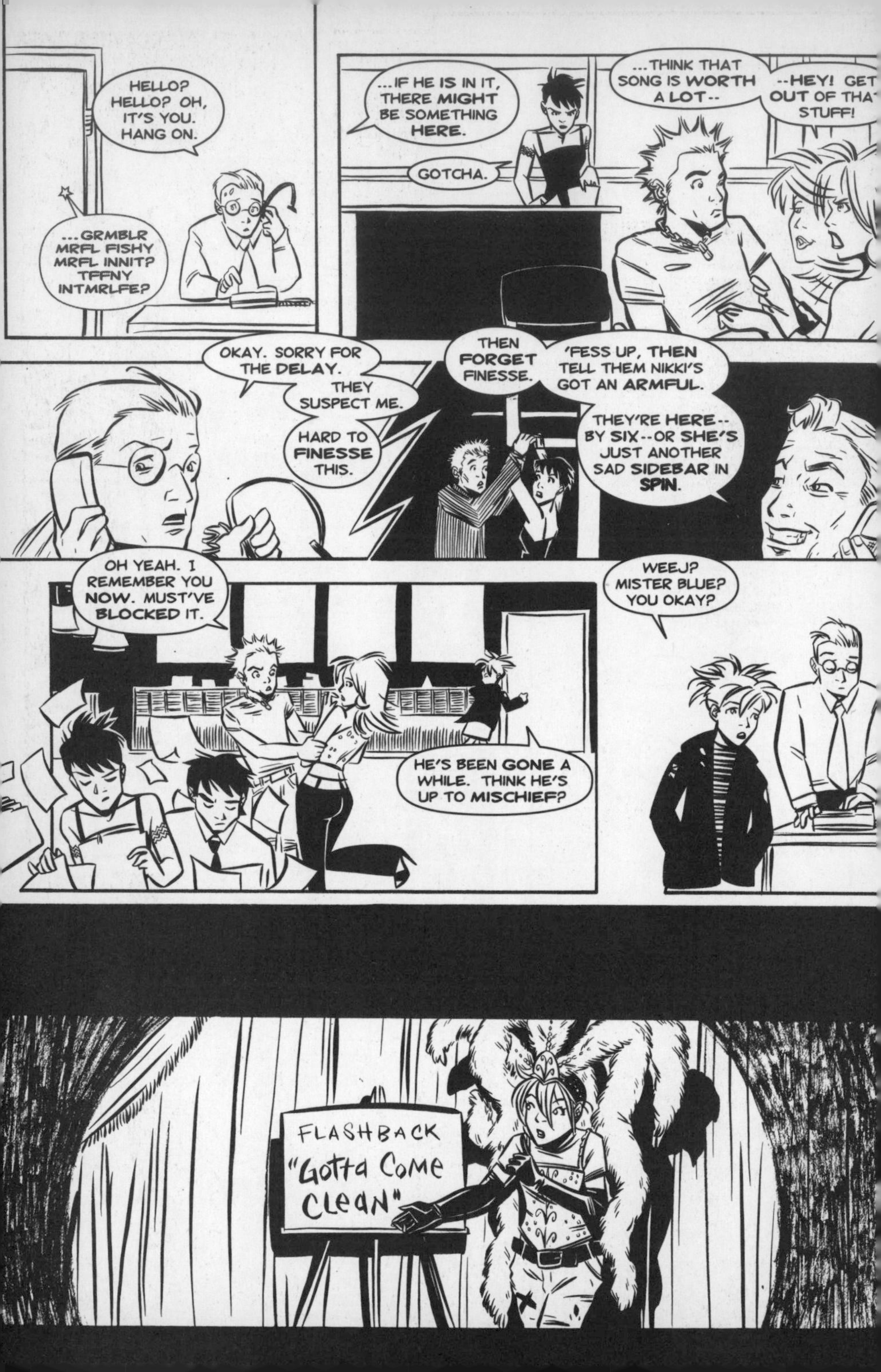
HELLO? HELLO? OH, IT'S YOU. HANG ON.
...GRMBLR MRFL FISHY MRFL INNIT? TFFNY INTMRLFE?
...IF HE IS IN IT, THERE MIGHT BE SOMETHING HERE.
GOTCHA.
...THINK THAT SONG IS WORTH A LOT--
--HEY! GET OUT OF THAT STUFF!
OKAY. SORRY FOR THE DELAY.
THEY SUSPECT ME.
HARD TO FINESSE THIS.
THEN FORGET FINESSE.
'FESS UP, THEN TELL THEM NIKKI'S GOT AN ARMFUL.
THEY'RE HERE--BY SIX--OR SHE'S JUST ANOTHER SAD SIDEBAR IN SPIN.
OH YEAH. I REMEMBER YOU NOW. MUST'VE BLOCKED IT.
HE'S BEEN GONE A WHILE. THINK HE'S UP TO MISCHIEF?
WEEJ? MISTER BLUE? YOU OKAY?
FLASHBACK
"Gotta Come Clean"

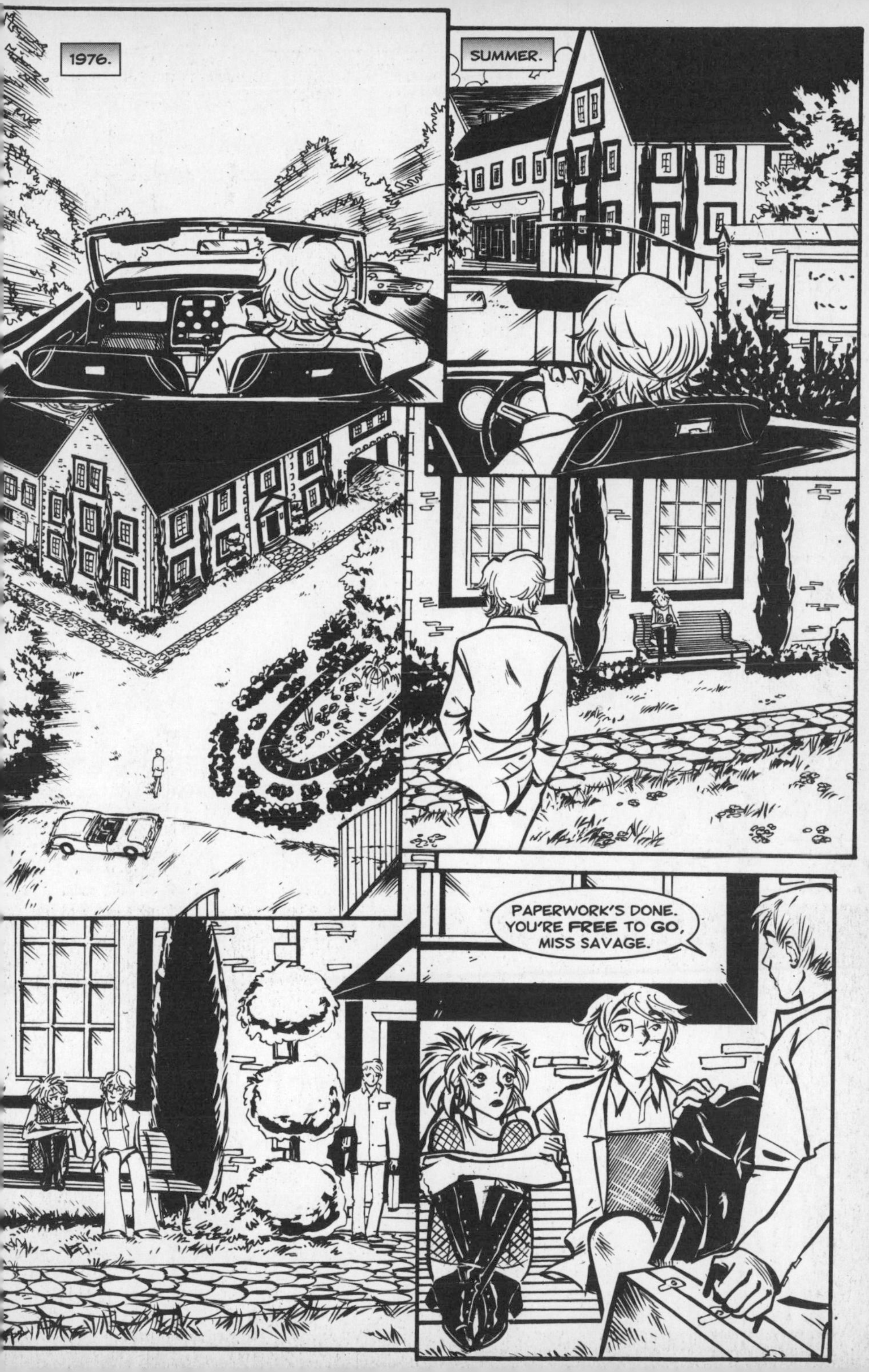
1976.
SUMMER.
PAPERWORK'S DONE. YOU'RE FREE TO GO, MISS SAVAGE.

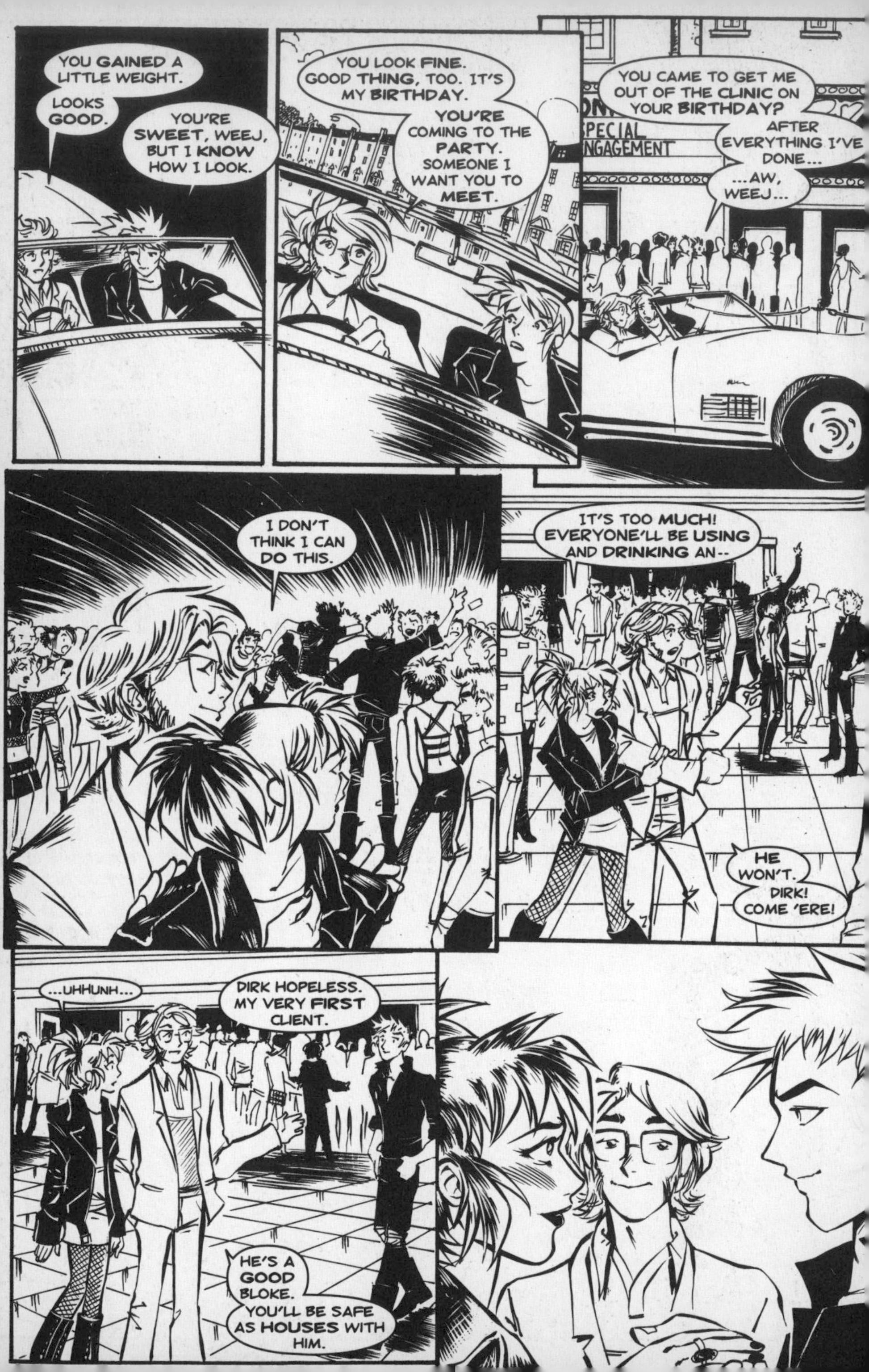

YOU GAINED A LITTLE WEIGHT.
LOOKS GOOD.
YOU'RE SWEET, WEEJ, BUT I KNOW HOW I LOOK.
YOU LOOK FINE. GOOD THING, TOO. IT'S MY BIRTHDAY.
YOU'RE COMING TO THE PARTY. SOMEONE I WANT YOU TO MEET.
SPECIAL ENGAGEMENT
YOU CAME TO GET ME OUT OF THE CLINIC ON YOUR BIRTHDAY?
AFTER EVERYTHING I'VE DONE...
...AW, WEEJ...
I DON'T THINK I CAN DO THIS.
IT'S TOO MUCH! EVERYONE'LL BE USING AND DRINKING AN--
HE WON'T.
DIRK! COME 'ERE!
...UHHUNH...
DIRK HOPELESS. MY VERY FIRST CLIENT.
HE'S A GOOD BLOKE.
YOU'LL BE SAFE AS HOUSES WITH HIM.

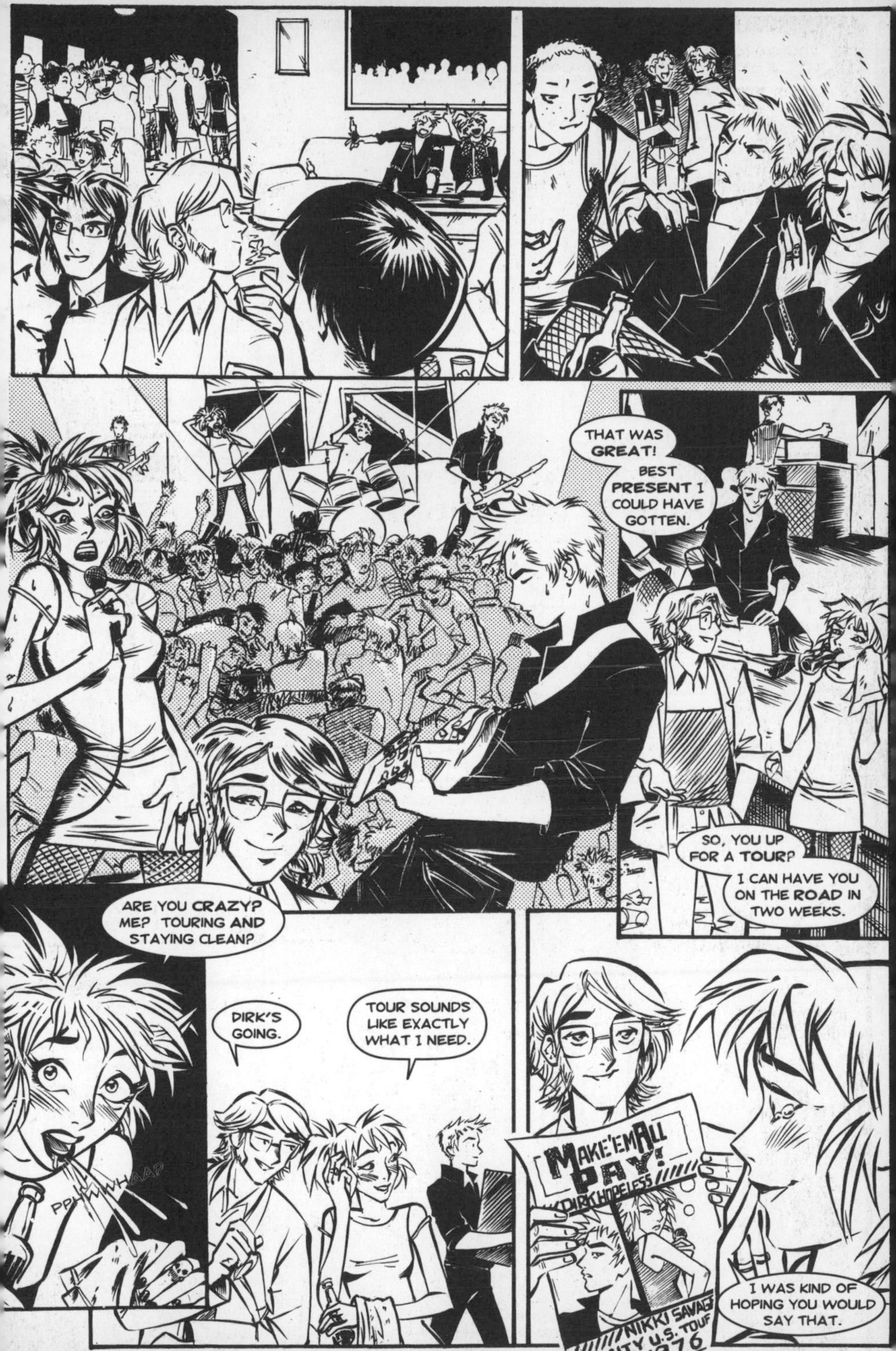
THAT WAS GREAT!
BEST PRESENT I COULD HAVE GOTTEN.
SO, YOU UP FOR A TOUR?
I CAN HAVE YOU ON THE ROAD IN TWO WEEKS.
ARE YOU CRAZY? ME? TOURING AND STAYING CLEAN?
PPHWHAAP
DIRK'S GOING.
TOUR SOUNDS LIKE EXACTLY WHAT I NEED.
MAKE 'EM ALL PAY!
DIRK HOPELESS
NIKKI SAVAGE
12 CITY U.S. TOUR
JULY 1976
I WAS KIND OF HOPING YOU WOULD SAY THAT.

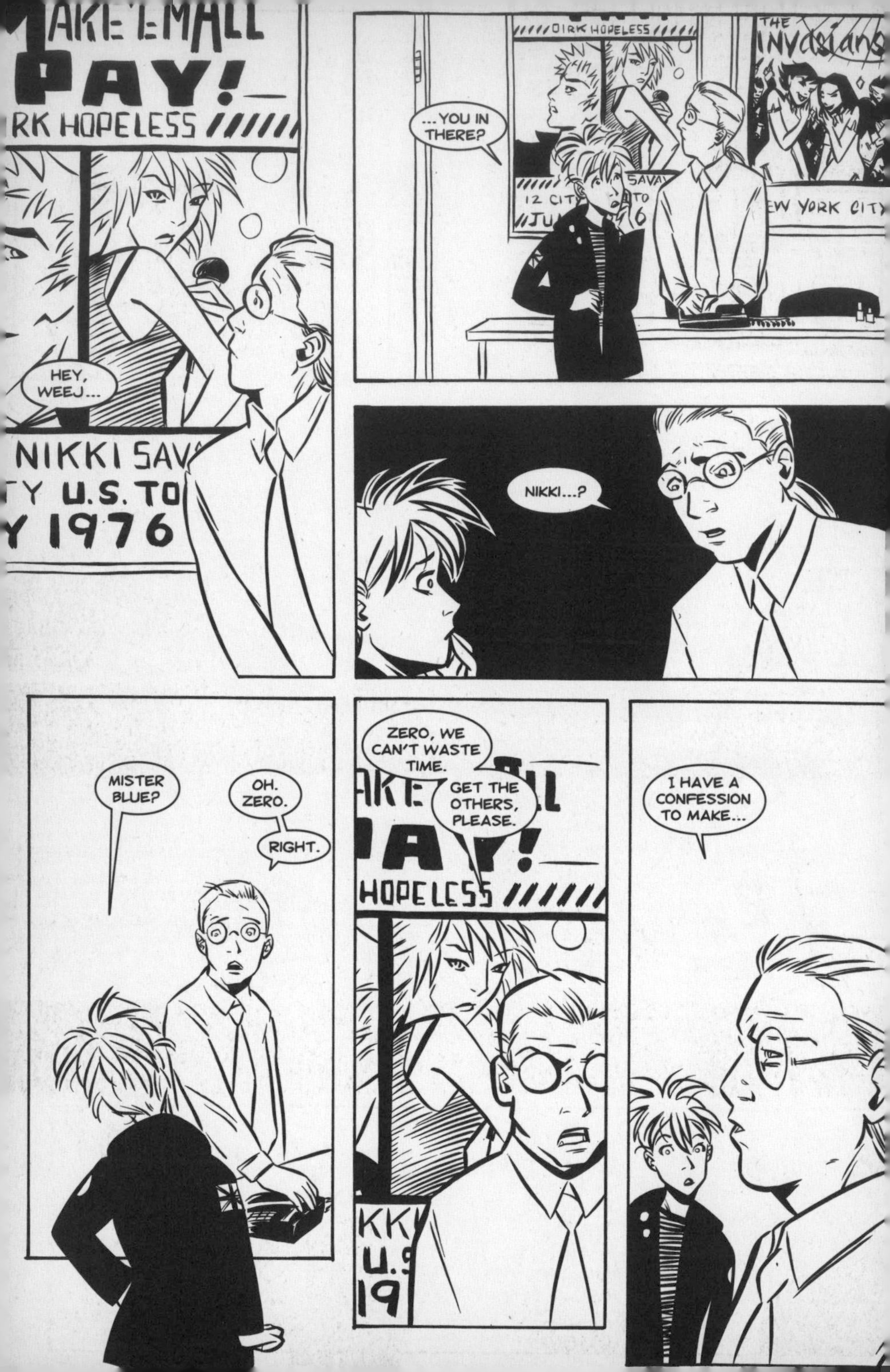
AKE 'EM ALL PAY!
RK HOPELESS
NIKKI SAV
TY U.S. TO
Y 1976
HEY, WEEJ...
DIRK HOPELESS
THE INVASIANS
NEW YORK CITY
...YOU IN THERE?
NIKKI...?
MISTER BLUE?
OH. ZERO.
RIGHT.
ZERO, WE CAN'T WASTE TIME.
GET THE OTHERS, PLEASE.
I HAVE A CONFESSION TO MAKE...

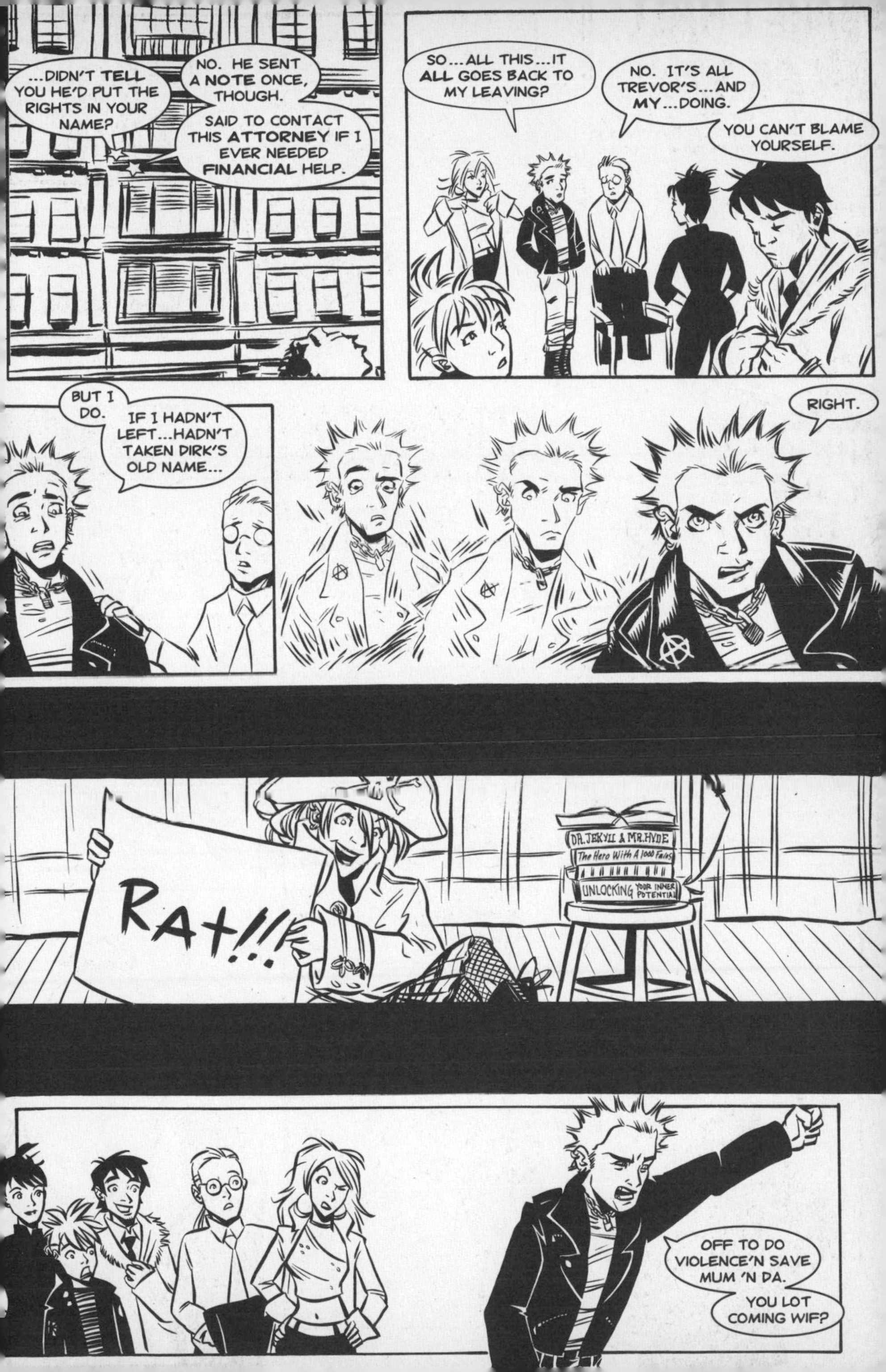
...DIDN'T TELL YOU HE'D PUT THE RIGHTS IN YOUR NAME?
NO. HE SENT A NOTE ONCE, THOUGH.
SAID TO CONTACT THIS ATTORNEY IF I EVER NEEDED FINANCIAL HELP.
SO... ALL THIS... IT ALL GOES BACK TO MY LEAVING?
NO. IT'S ALL TREVOR'S... AND MY... DOING.
YOU CAN'T BLAME YOURSELF.
BUT I DO.
IF I HADN'T LEFT... HADN'T TAKEN DIRK'S OLD NAME...
RIGHT.
RAT!!!
DR. JEKYLL & MR. HYDE
The Hero With A 1000 Faces
UNLOCKING YOUR INNER POTENTIAL
OFF TO DO VIOLENCE'N SAVE MUM 'N DA.
YOU LOT COMING WIF?

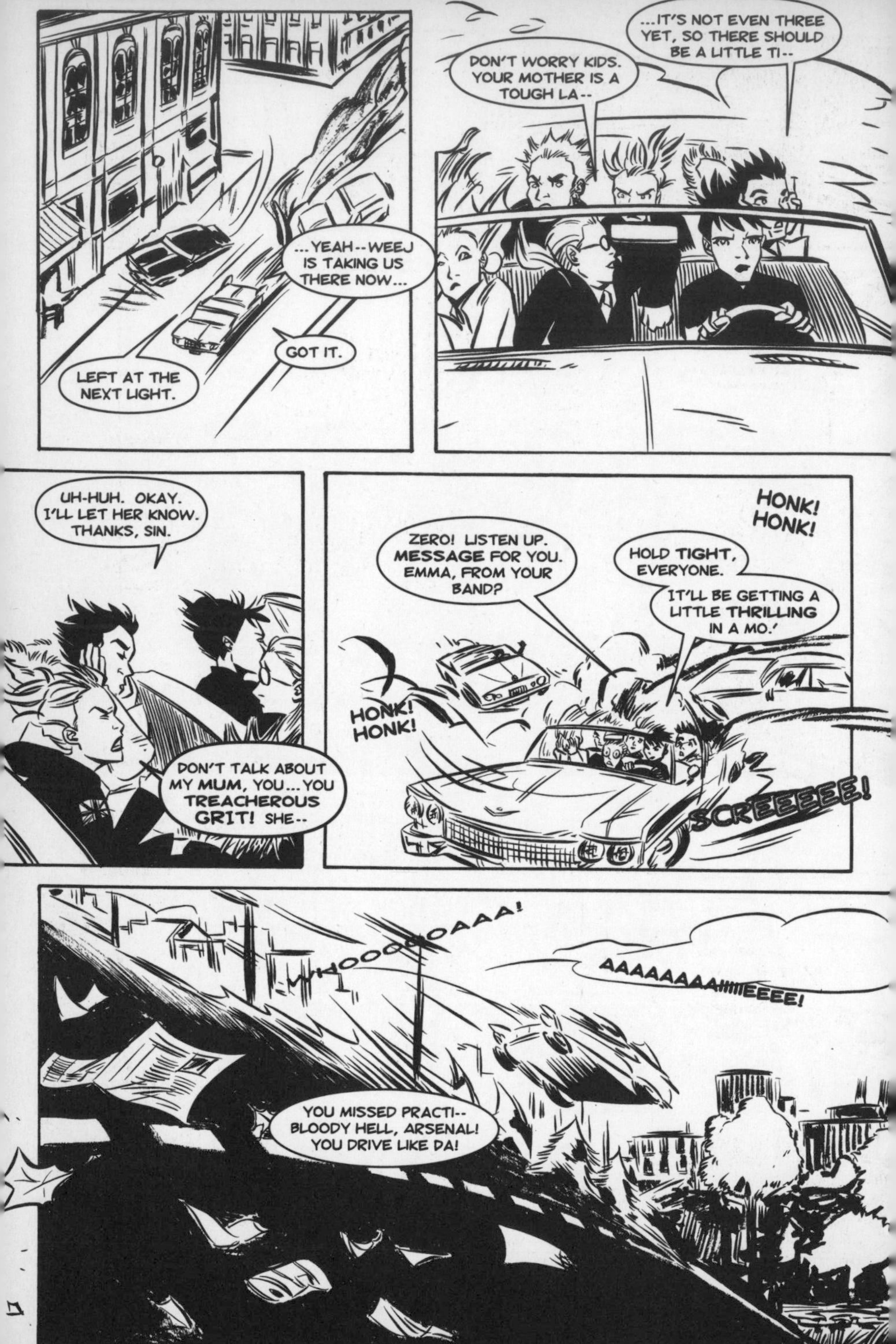
...YEAH--WEEJ IS TAKING US THERE NOW...
GOT IT.
LEFT AT THE NEXT LIGHT.
DON'T WORRY KIDS. YOUR MOTHER IS A TOUGH LA--
...IT'S NOT EVEN THREE YET, SO THERE SHOULD BE A LITTLE TI--
UH-HUH. OKAY. I'LL LET HER KNOW. THANKS, SIN.
DON'T TALK ABOUT MY MUM, YOU...YOU TREACHEROUS GRIT! SHE--
HONK! HONK!
ZERO! LISTEN UP. MESSAGE FOR YOU. EMMA, FROM YOUR BAND?
HOLD TIGHT, EVERYONE.
IT'LL BE GETTING A LITTLE THRILLING IN A MO.'
HONK! HONK!
SCREEEEEE!
AAAAAAAAIIIIIEEEE!
YOU MISSED PRACTI-- BLOODY HELL, ARSENAL! YOU DRIVE LIKE DA!

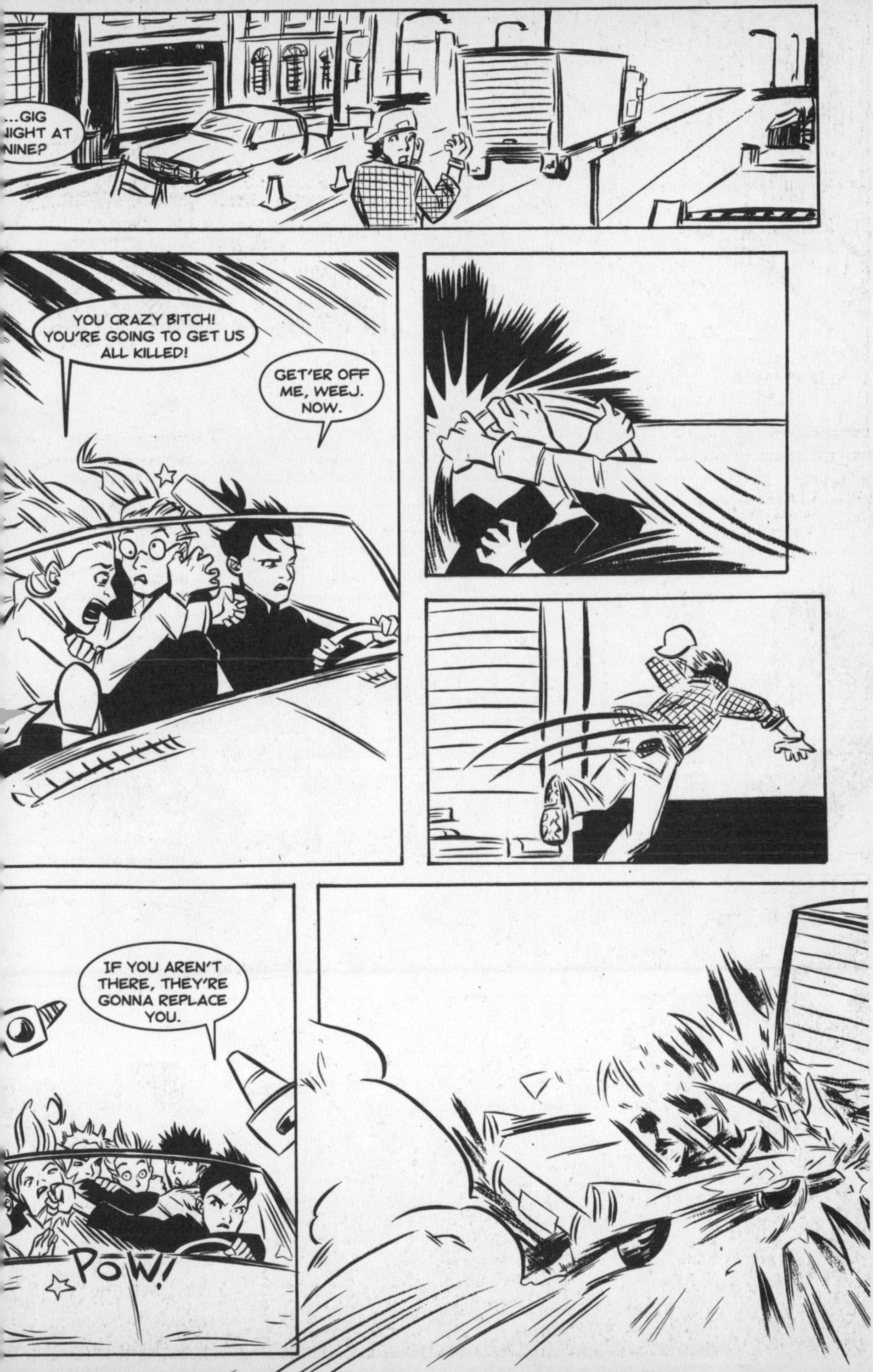
...GIG
NIGHT AT
NINE?
YOU CRAZY BITCH! YOU'RE GOING TO GET US ALL KILLED!
GET'ER OFF ME, WEEJ. NOW.
IF YOU AREN'T THERE, THEY'RE GONNA REPLACE YOU.
POW!

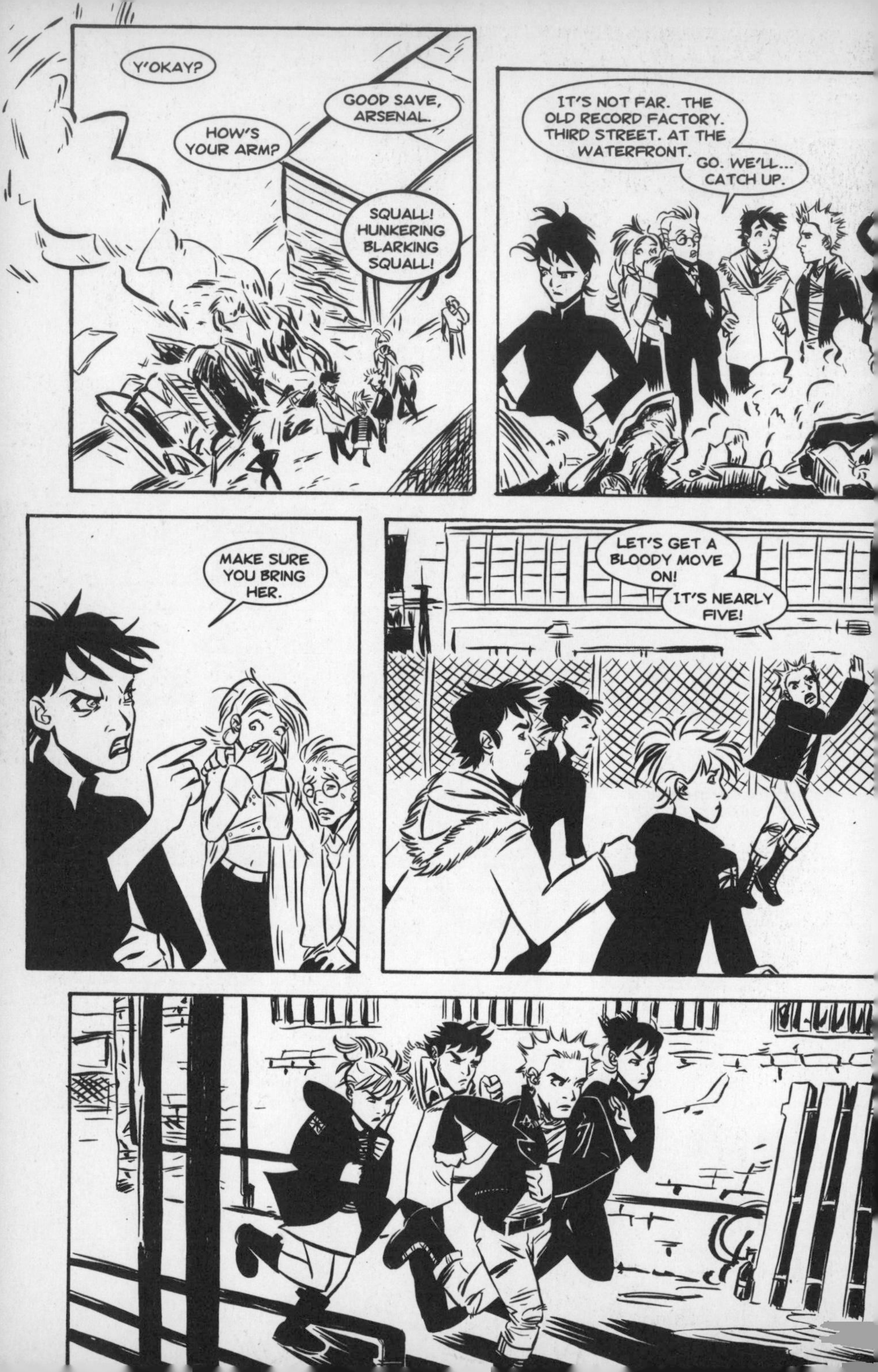
Y'OKAY?
GOOD SAVE, ARSENAL.
HOW'S YOUR ARM?
SQUALL! HUNKERING BLARKING SQUALL!
IT'S NOT FAR. THE OLD RECORD FACTORY. THIRD STREET. AT THE WATERFRONT.
GO. WE'LL... CATCH UP.
MAKE SURE YOU BRING HER.
LET'S GET A BLOODY MOVE ON!
IT'S NEARLY FIVE!

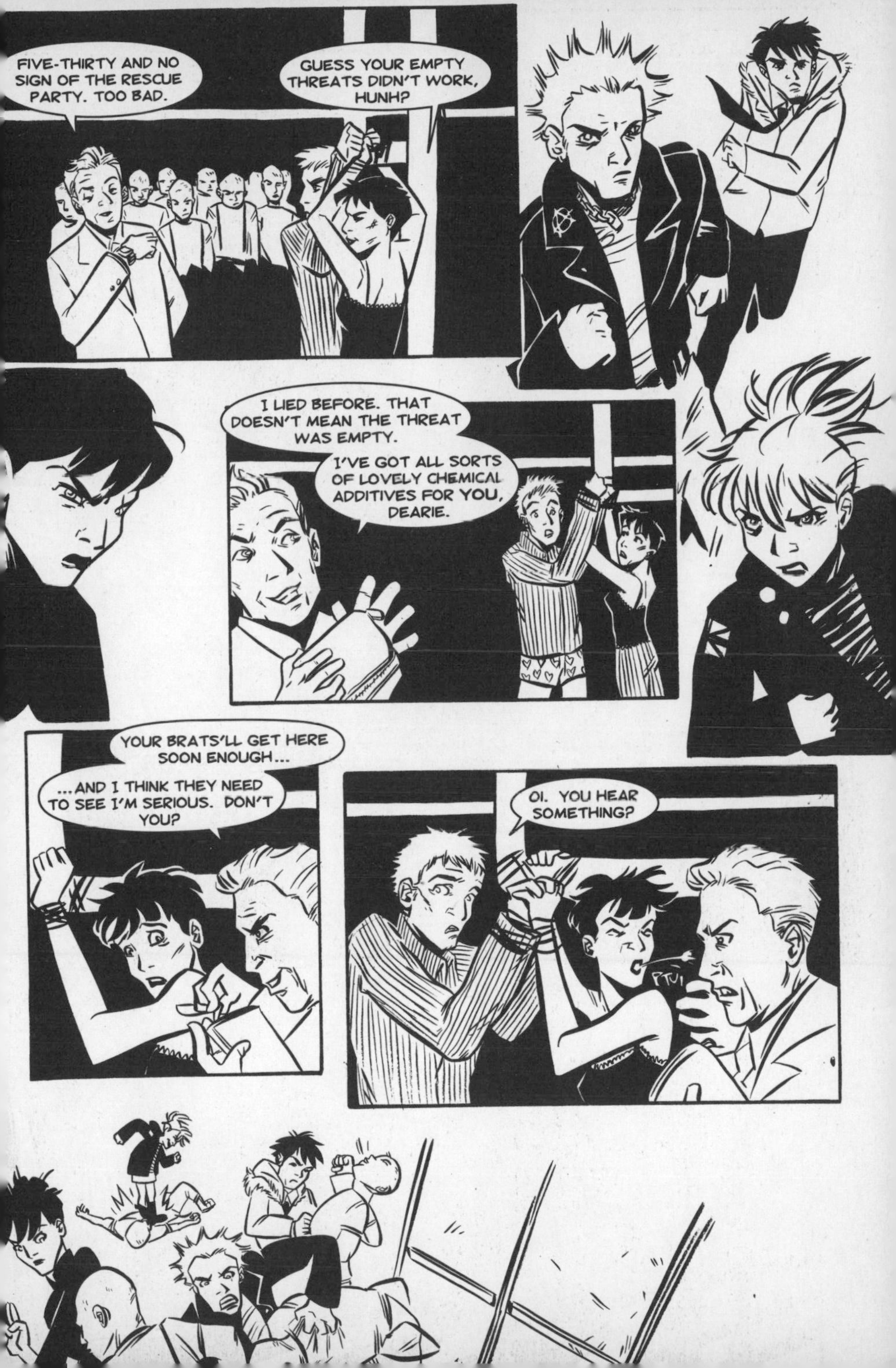
FIVE-THIRTY AND NO SIGN OF THE RESCUE PARTY. TOO BAD.
GUESS YOUR EMPTY THREATS DIDN'T WORK, HUNH?
I LIED BEFORE. THAT DOESN'T MEAN THE THREAT WAS EMPTY.
I'VE GOT ALL SORTS OF LOVELY CHEMICAL ADDITIVES FOR YOU, DEARIE.
YOUR BRATS'LL GET HERE SOON ENOUGH...
...AND I THINK THEY NEED TO SEE I'M SERIOUS. DON'T YOU?
OI. YOU HEAR SOMETHING?
PTU!

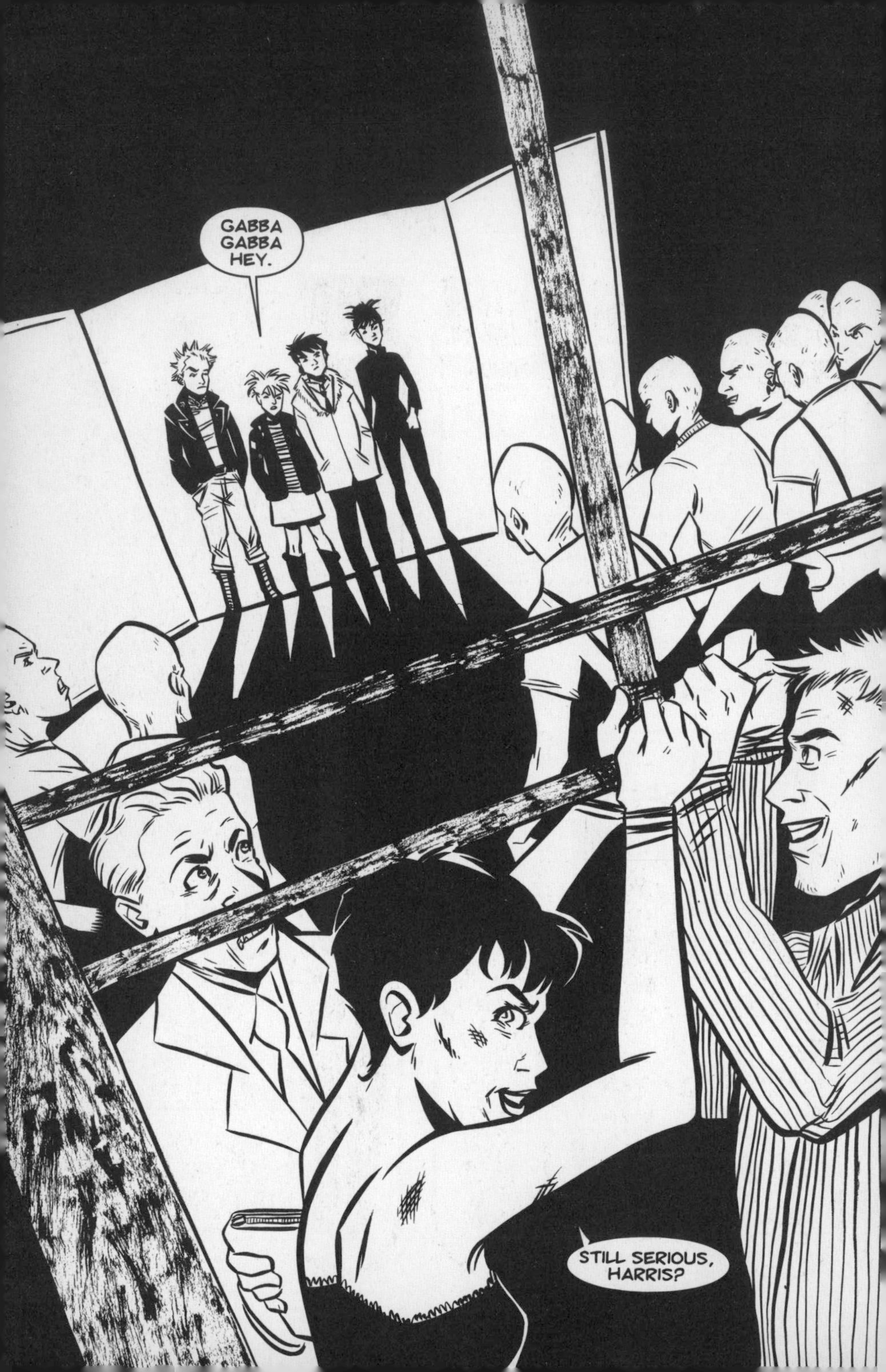
GABBA GABBA HEY.
STILL SERIOUS, HARRIS?

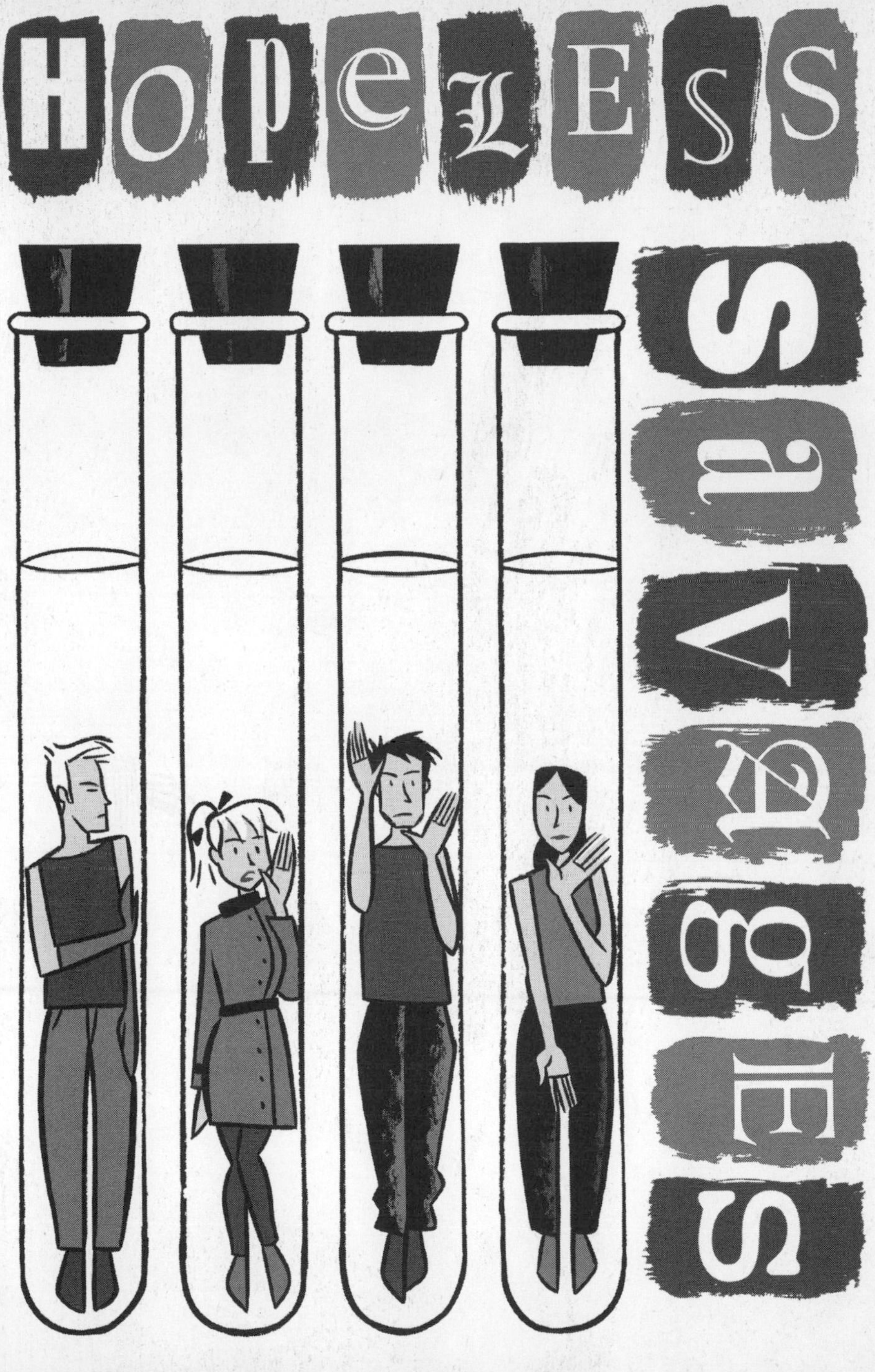
HOPELESS
SAVAGES

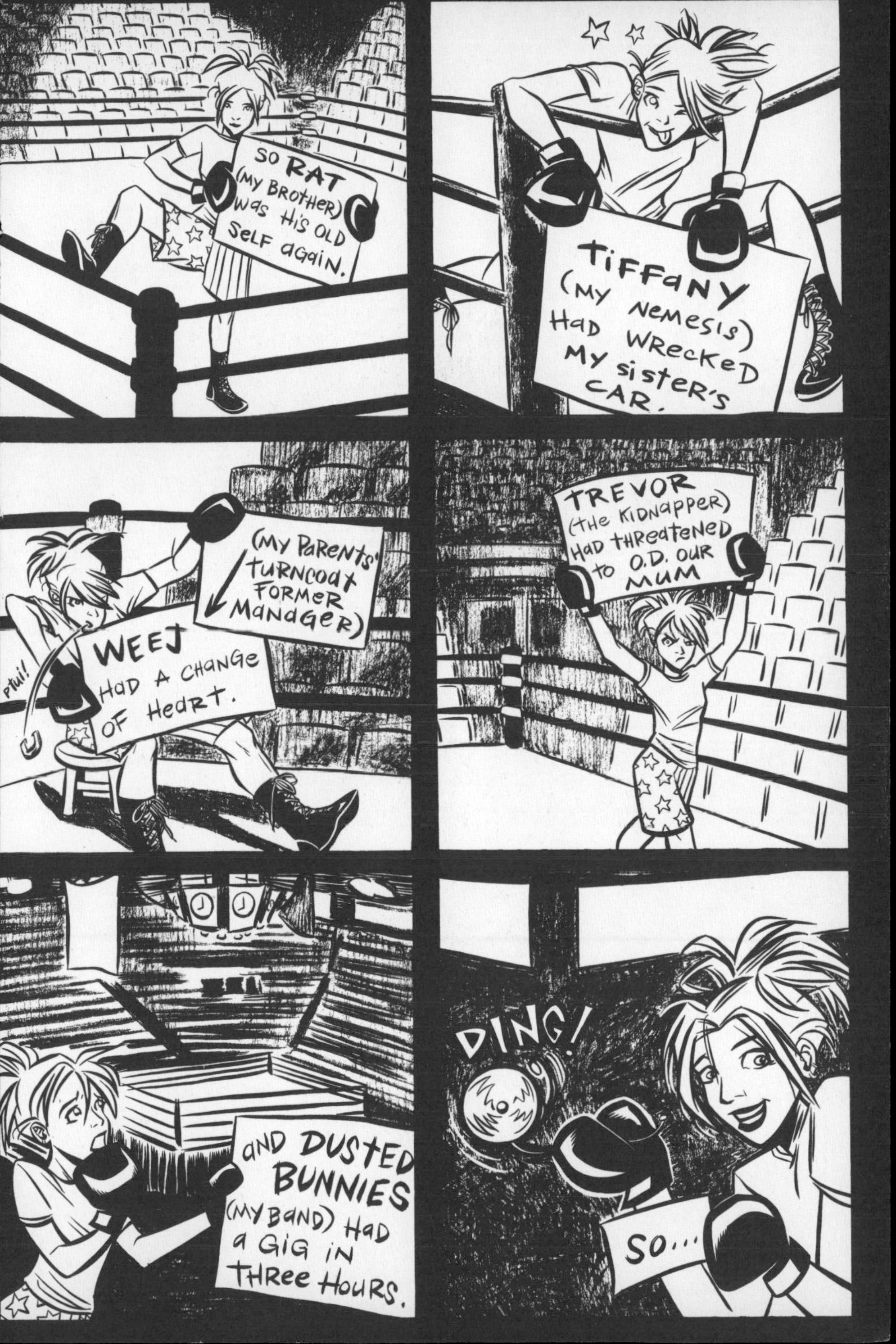

SO RAT (MY BROTHER) Was His OLD SELF again.
TiFFaNY (MY NeMeSiS) HaD WRecKED MY SiSTER'S CAR.
(MY ParenTs' TurNcoaT FormeR ManaGeR)
WEEJ HaD A CHanGe OF HeaRT.
pTui!
TREVOR (THe KIDNapper) HaD THReaTeNED to O.D. OUR MUM
aND DUSTED BUNNIES (MY BaND) HaD a GiG iN THRee HOURS.
DING!
So...

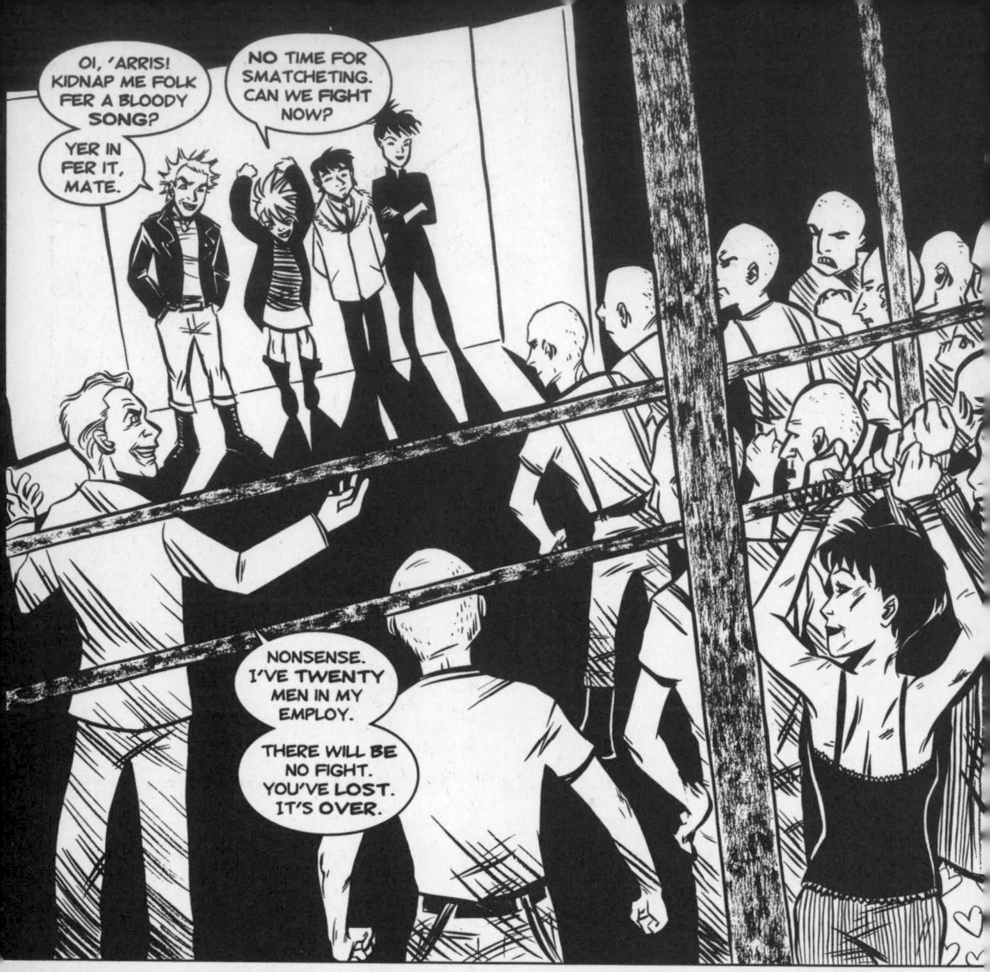
OI, 'ARRIS! KIDNAP ME FOLK FER A BLOODY SONG?
YER IN FER IT, MATE.
NO TIME FOR SMATCHETING. CAN WE FIGHT NOW?
NONSENSE. I'VE TWENTY MEN IN MY EMPLOY.
THERE WILL BE NO FIGHT. YOU'VE LOST. IT'S OVER.

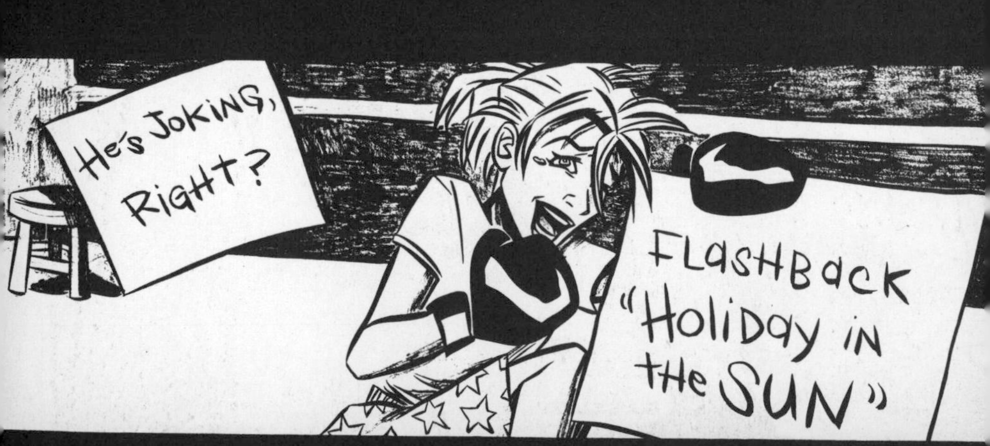
He's JoKiNG, RiGHT?
FLasHBack "HoliDay iN tHe SUN"

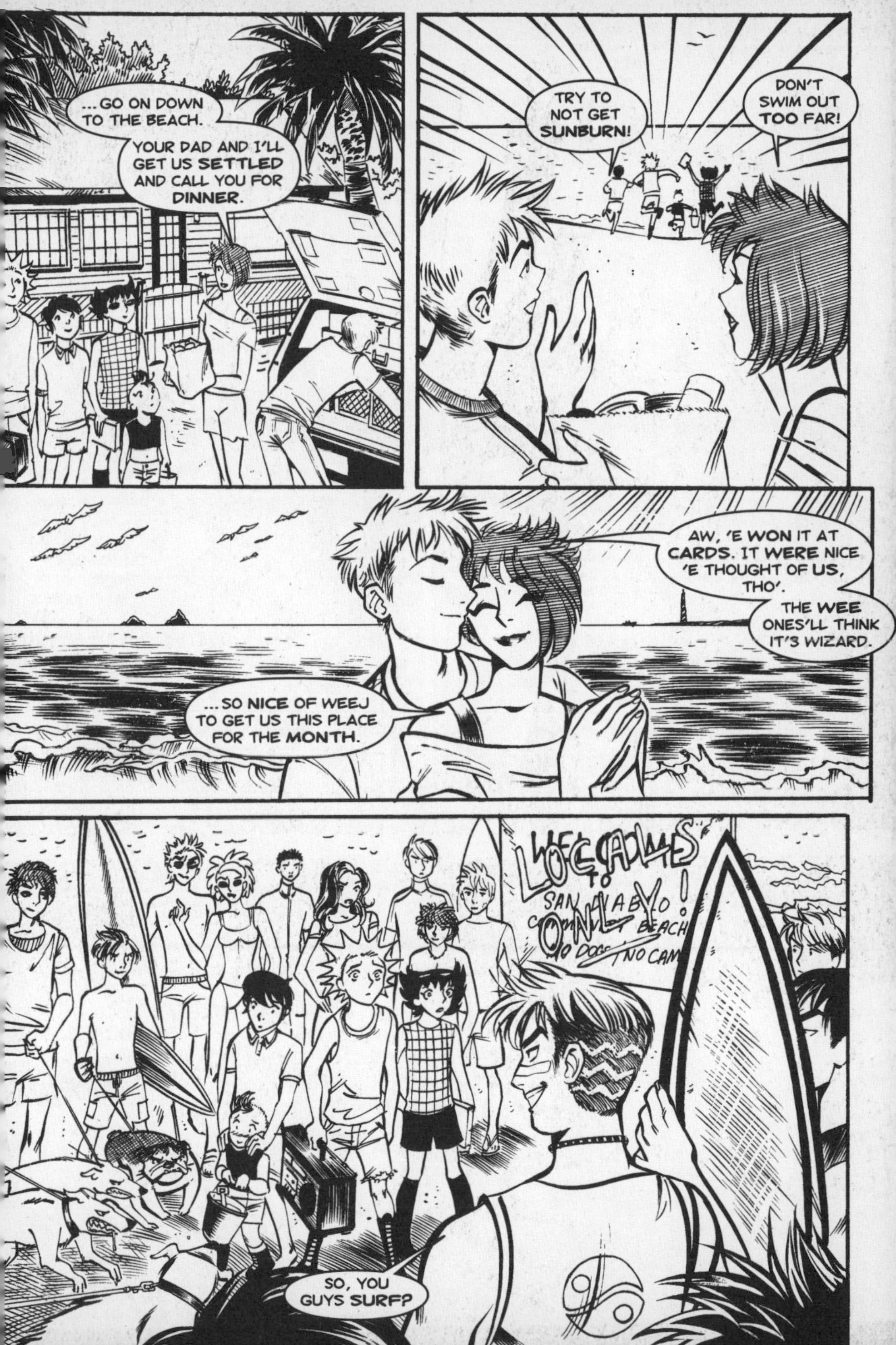
...GO ON DOWN TO THE BEACH.
YOUR DAD AND I'LL GET US SETTLED AND CALL YOU FOR DINNER.
TRY TO NOT GET SUNBURN!
DON'T SWIM OUT TOO FAR!
...SO NICE OF WEEJ TO GET US THIS PLACE FOR THE MONTH.
AW, 'E WON IT AT CARDS. IT WERE NICE 'E THOUGHT OF US, THO'.
THE WEE ONES'LL THINK IT'S WIZARD.
SO, YOU GUYS SURF?

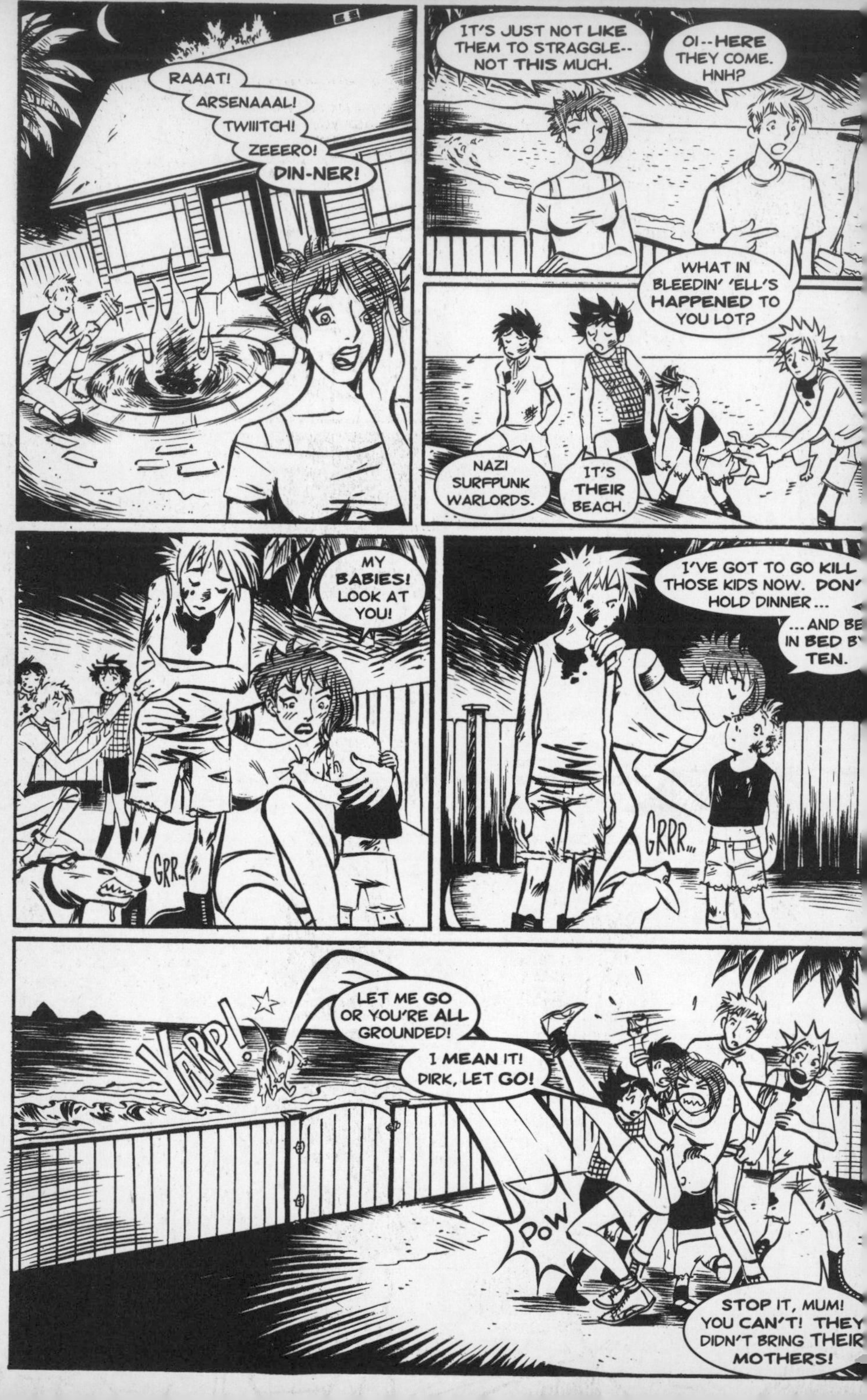

RAAAT!
ARSENAAAL!
TWIIITCH!
ZEEERO!
DIN-NER!
IT'S JUST NOT LIKE THEM TO STRAGGLE-- NOT THIS MUCH.
OI--HERE THEY COME. HNH?
WHAT IN BLEEDIN' 'ELL'S HAPPENED TO YOU LOT?
NAZI SURFPUNK WARLORDS.
IT'S THEIR BEACH.
MY BABIES! LOOK AT YOU!
GRR...
I'VE GOT TO GO KILL THOSE KIDS NOW. DON' HOLD DINNER...
...AND BE IN BED B' TEN.
GRRR...
YARP!
LET ME GO OR YOU'RE ALL GROUNDED!
I MEAN IT! DIRK, LET GO!
POW
STOP IT, MUM! YOU CAN'T! THEY DIDN'T BRING THEIR MOTHERS!

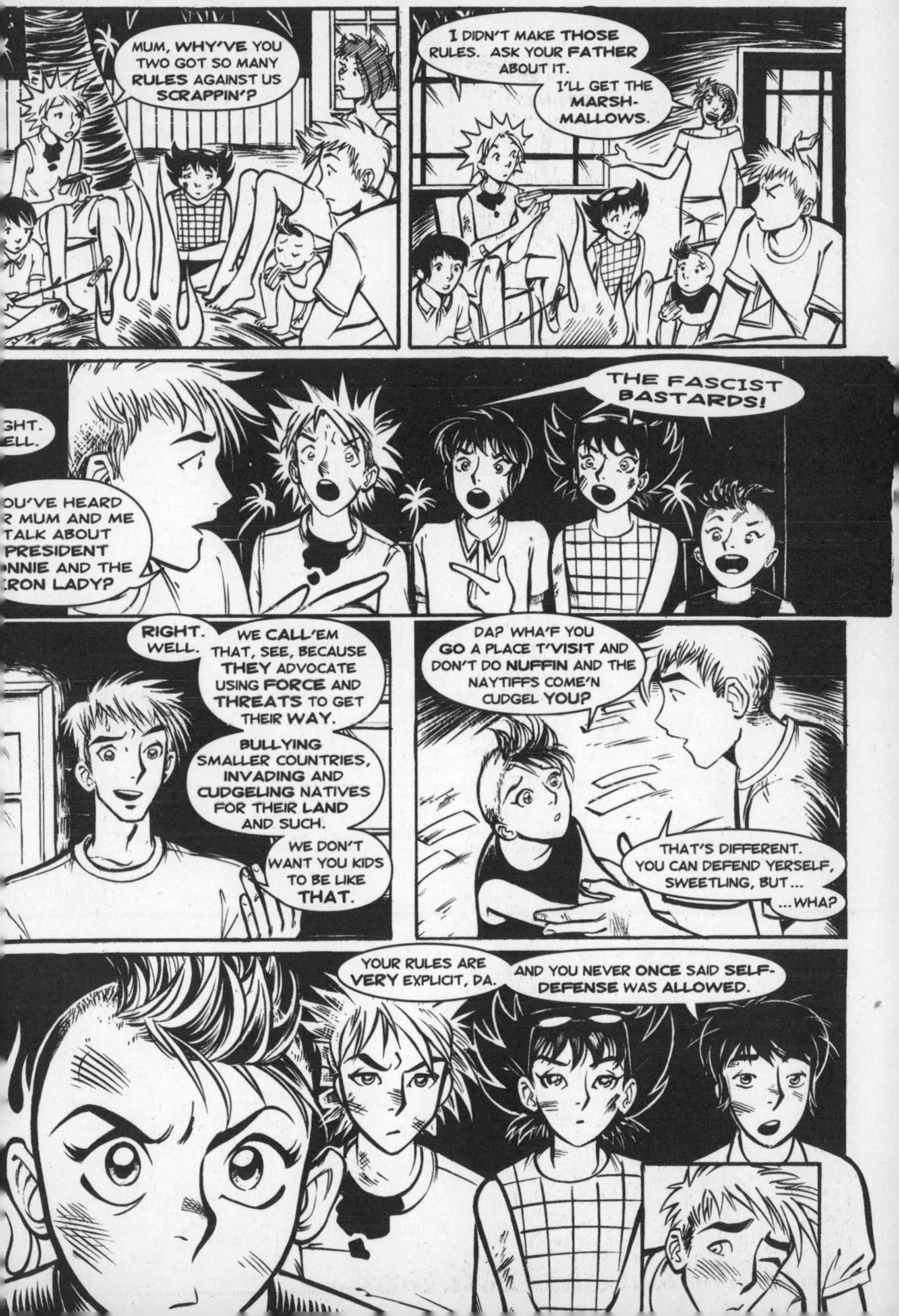

MUM, WHY'VE YOU TWO GOT SO MANY RULES AGAINST US SCRAPPIN'?
I DIDN'T MAKE THOSE RULES. ASK YOUR FATHER ABOUT IT.
I'LL GET THE MARSH-MALLOWS.
GHT. ELL.
OU'VE HEARD R MUM AND ME TALK ABOUT PRESIDENT ONNIE AND THE RON LADY?
THE FASCIST BASTARDS!
RIGHT. WELL.
WE CALL'EM THAT, SEE, BECAUSE THEY ADVOCATE USING FORCE AND THREATS TO GET THEIR WAY.
BULLYING SMALLER COUNTRIES, INVADING AND CUDGELING NATIVES FOR THEIR LAND AND SUCH.
WE DON'T WANT YOU KIDS TO BE LIKE THAT.
DA? WHA'F YOU GO A PLACE T'VISIT AND DON'T DO NUFFIN AND THE NAYTIFFS COME'N CUDGEL YOU?
THAT'S DIFFERENT. YOU CAN DEFEND YERSELF, SWEETLING, BUT...
...WHA?
YOUR RULES ARE VERY EXPLICIT, DA.
AND YOU NEVER ONCE SAID SELF-DEFENSE WAS ALLOWED.

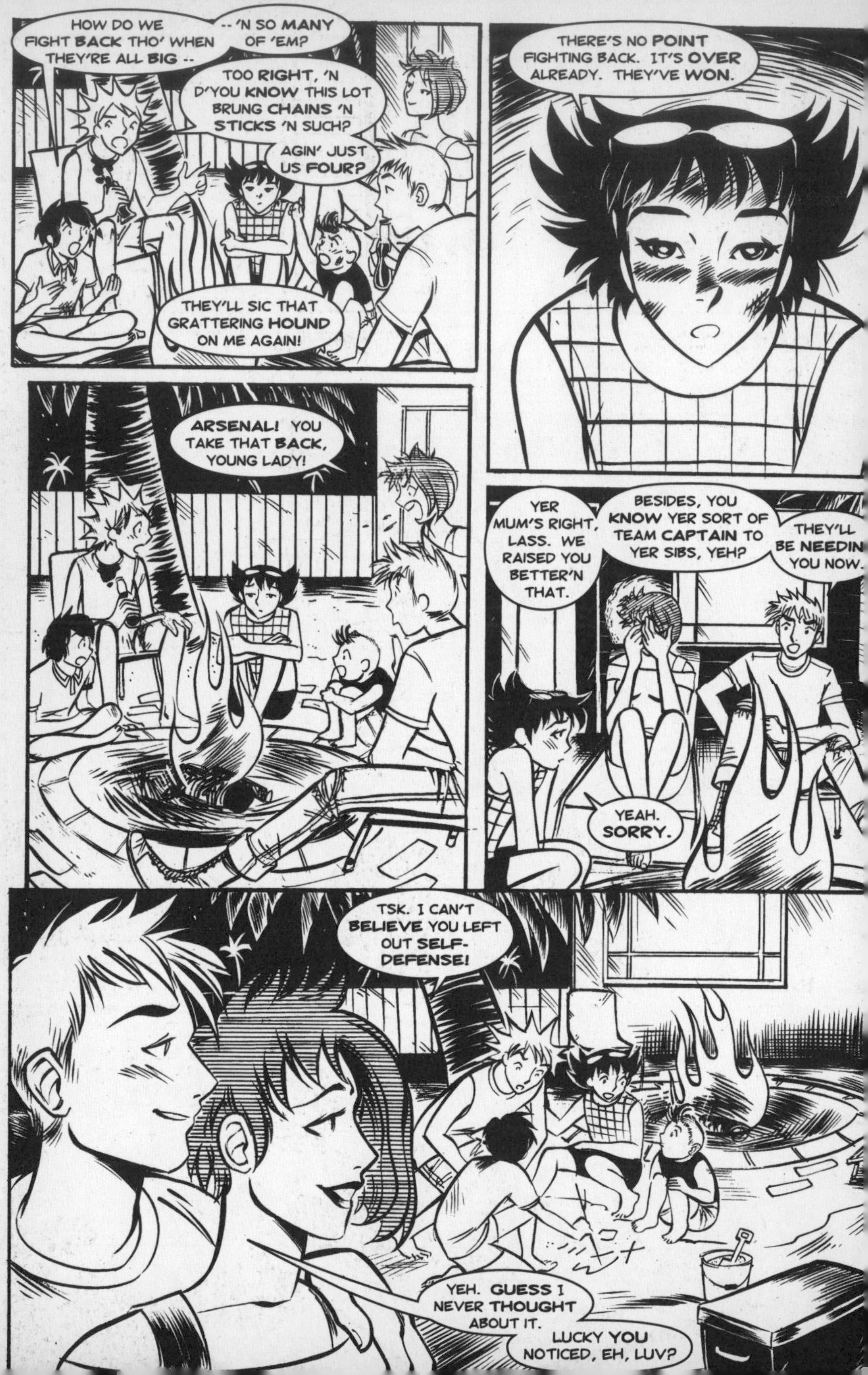
HOW DO WE FIGHT BACK THO' WHEN THEY'RE ALL BIG --
-- 'N SO MANY OF 'EM?
TOO RIGHT, 'N D'YOU KNOW THIS LOT BRUNG CHAINS 'N STICKS 'N SUCH?
AGIN' JUST US FOUR?
THEY'LL SIC THAT GRATTERING HOUND ON ME AGAIN!
THERE'S NO POINT FIGHTING BACK. IT'S OVER ALREADY. THEY'VE WON.
ARSENAL! YOU TAKE THAT BACK, YOUNG LADY!
YER MUM'S RIGHT, LASS. WE RAISED YOU BETTER'N THAT.
BESIDES, YOU KNOW YER SORT OF TEAM CAPTAIN TO YER SIBS, YEH?
THEY'LL BE NEEDIN YOU NOW.
YEAH. SORRY.
TSK. I CAN'T BELIEVE YOU LEFT OUT SELF-DEFENSE!
YEH. GUESS I NEVER THOUGHT ABOUT IT.
LUCKY YOU NOTICED, EH, LUV?

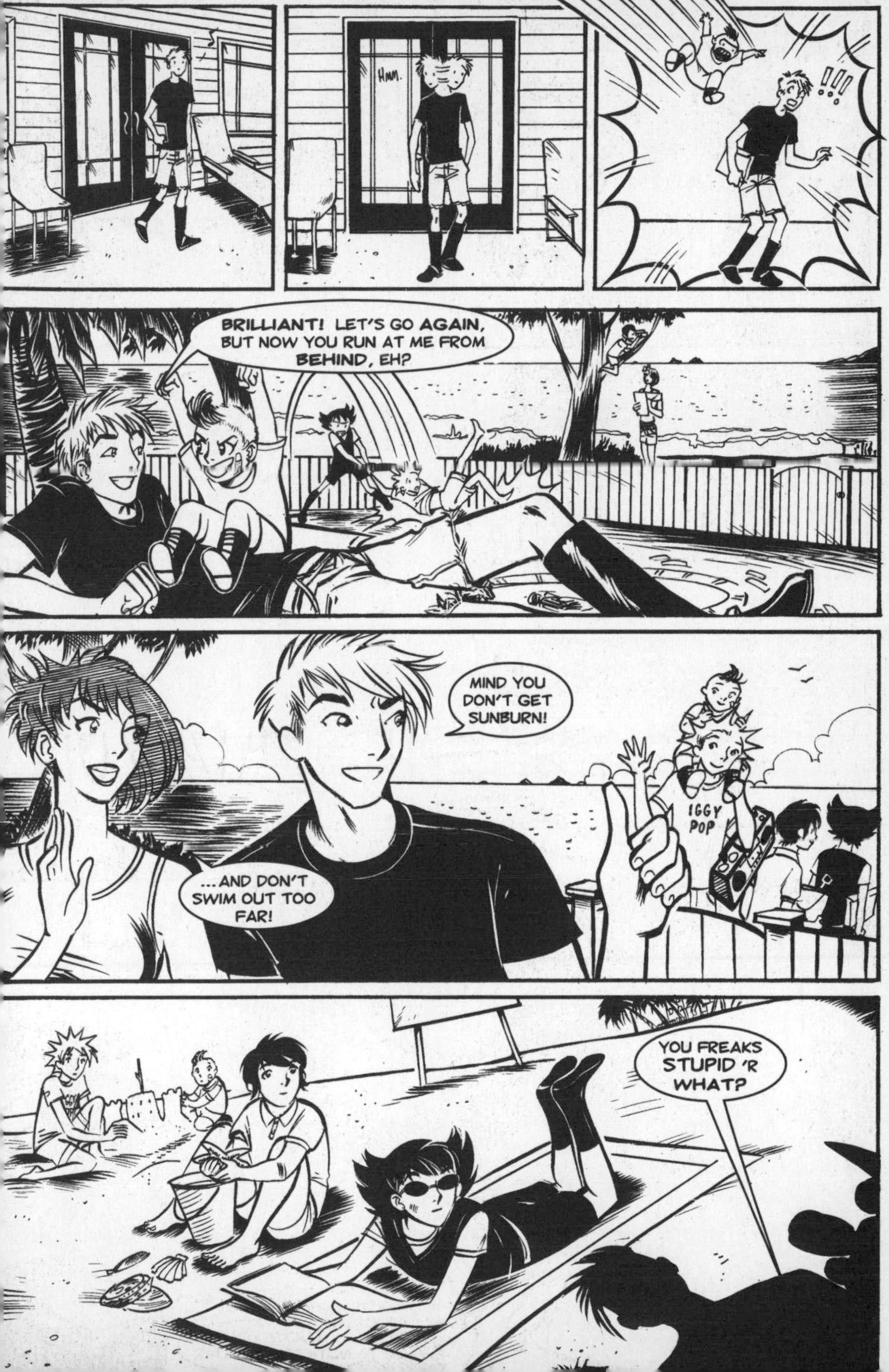
HMM.
!!!
BRILLIANT! LET'S GO AGAIN, BUT NOW YOU RUN AT ME FROM BEHIND, EH?
MIND YOU DON'T GET SUNBURN!
...AND DON'T SWIM OUT TOO FAR!
IGGY POP
YOU FREAKS STUPID 'R WHAT?

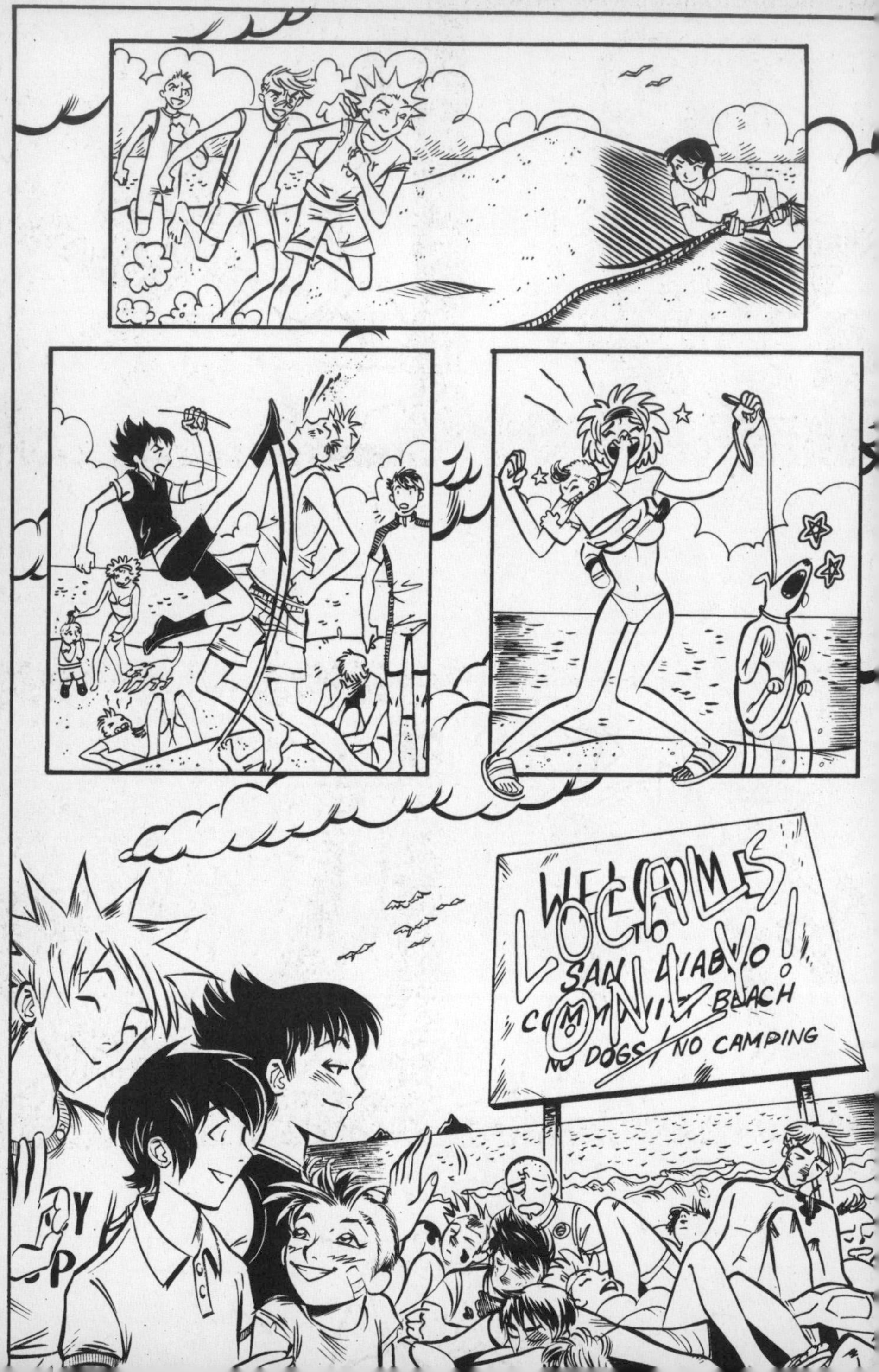
LOCALS ONLY!
NO DOGS / NO CAMPING

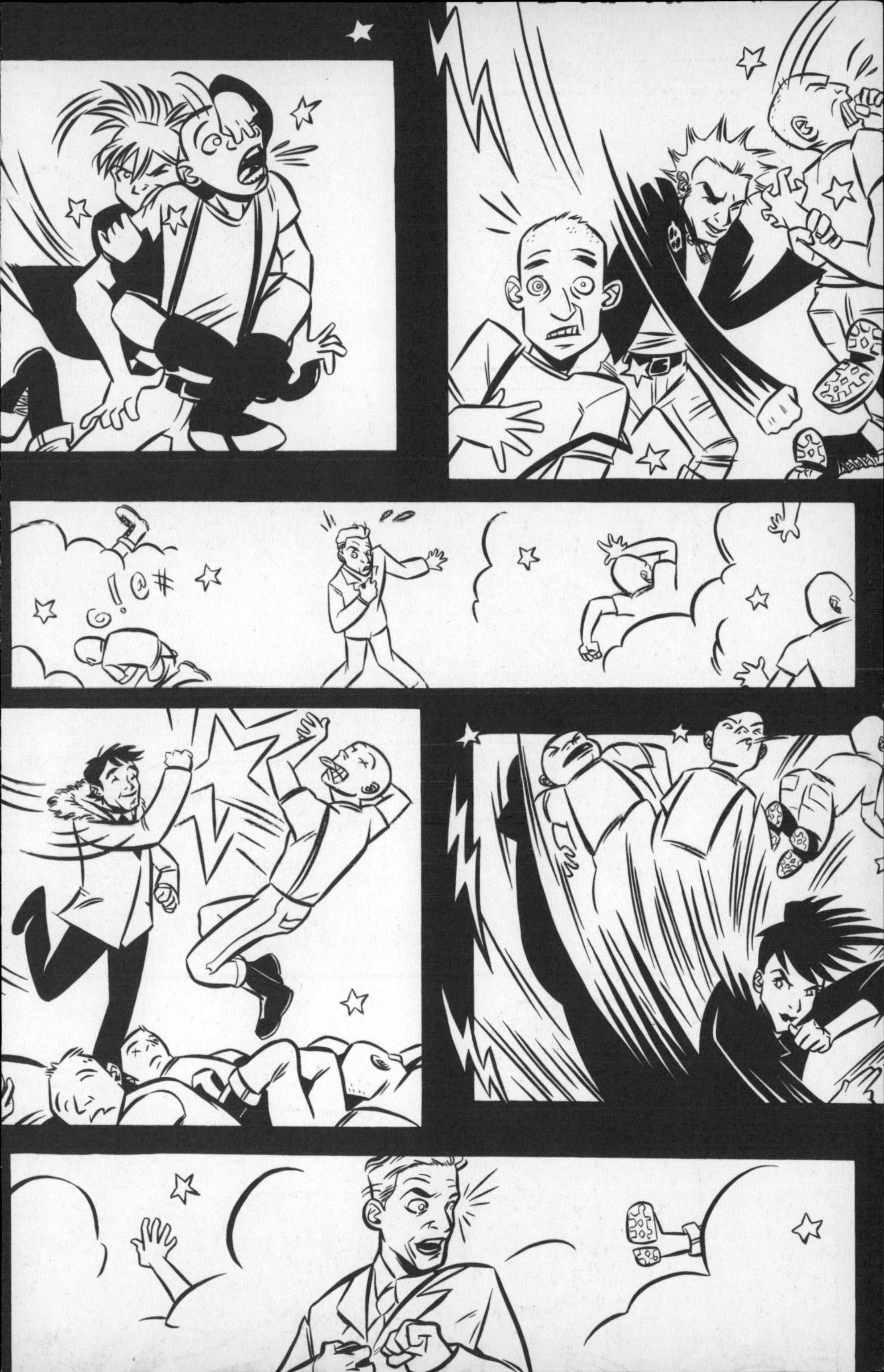
!@#

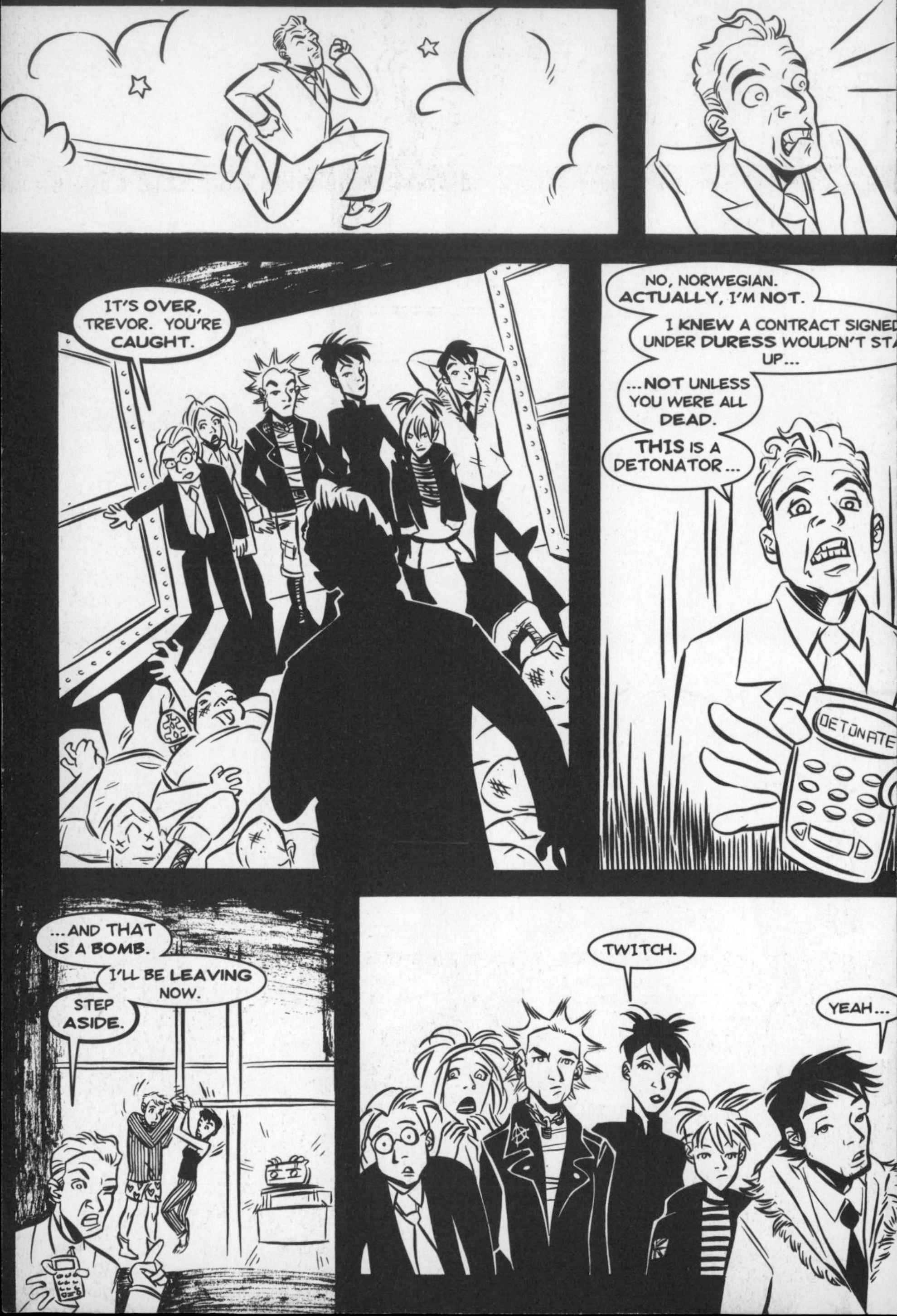
IT'S OVER, TREVOR. YOU'RE CAUGHT.
NO, NORWEGIAN. ACTUALLY, I'M NOT.
I KNEW A CONTRACT SIGNED UNDER DURESS WOULDN'T ST
UP...
...NOT UNLESS YOU WERE ALL DEAD.
THIS IS A DETONATOR...
DETONATE
...AND THAT IS A BOMB.
I'LL BE LEAVING NOW.
STEP ASIDE.
TWITCH.
YEAH...

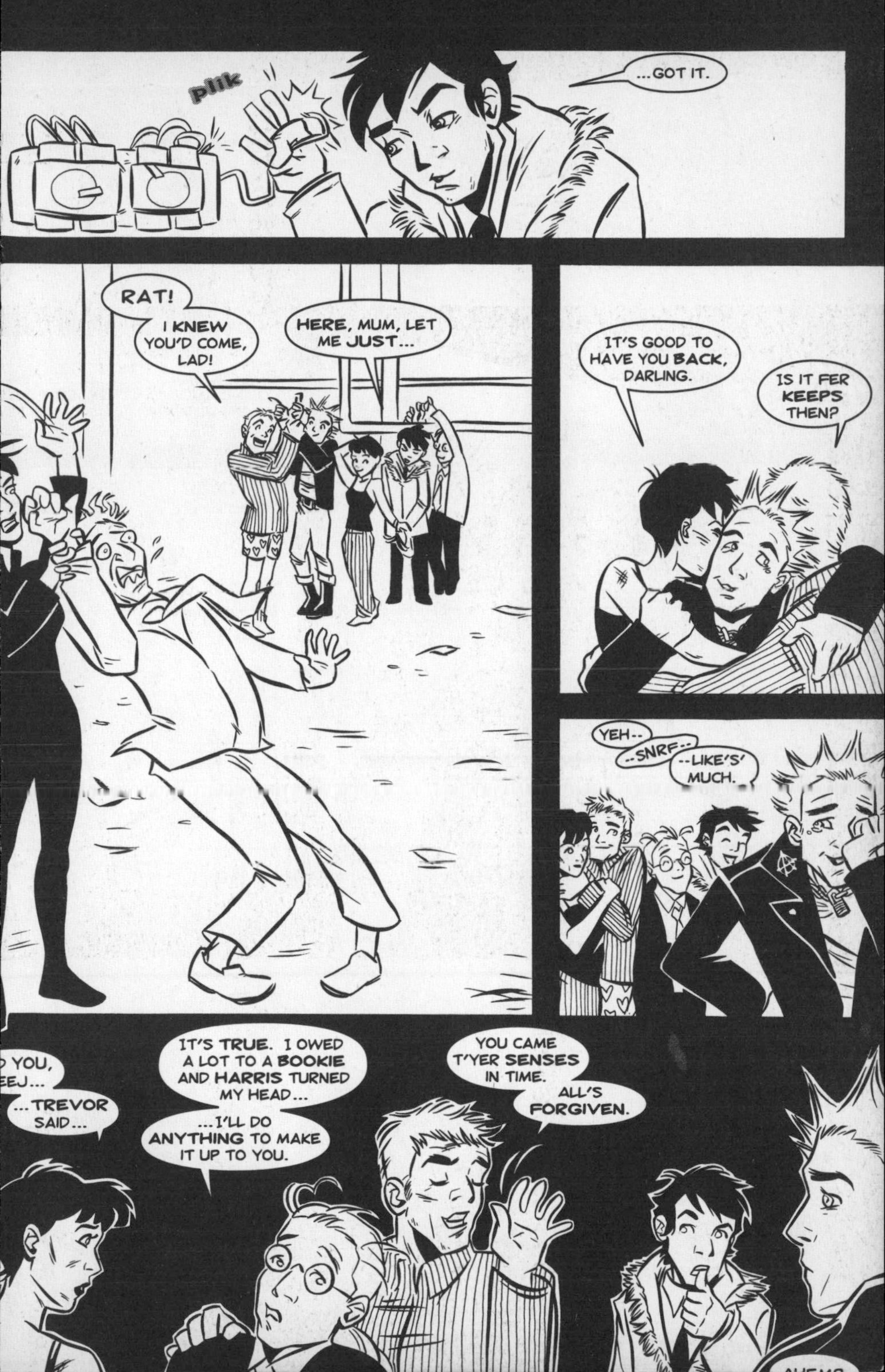
plik
...GOT IT.
RAT!
I KNEW YOU'D COME, LAD!
HERE, MUM, LET ME JUST...
IT'S GOOD TO HAVE YOU BACK, DARLING.
IS IT FER KEEPS THEN?
YEH--
--SNRF--
--LIKE'S' MUCH.
...TREVOR SAID...
IT'S TRUE. I OWED A LOT TO A BOOKIE AND HARRIS TURNED MY HEAD...
...I'LL DO ANYTHING TO MAKE IT UP TO YOU.
YOU CAME T'YER SENSES IN TIME.
ALL'S FORGIVEN.

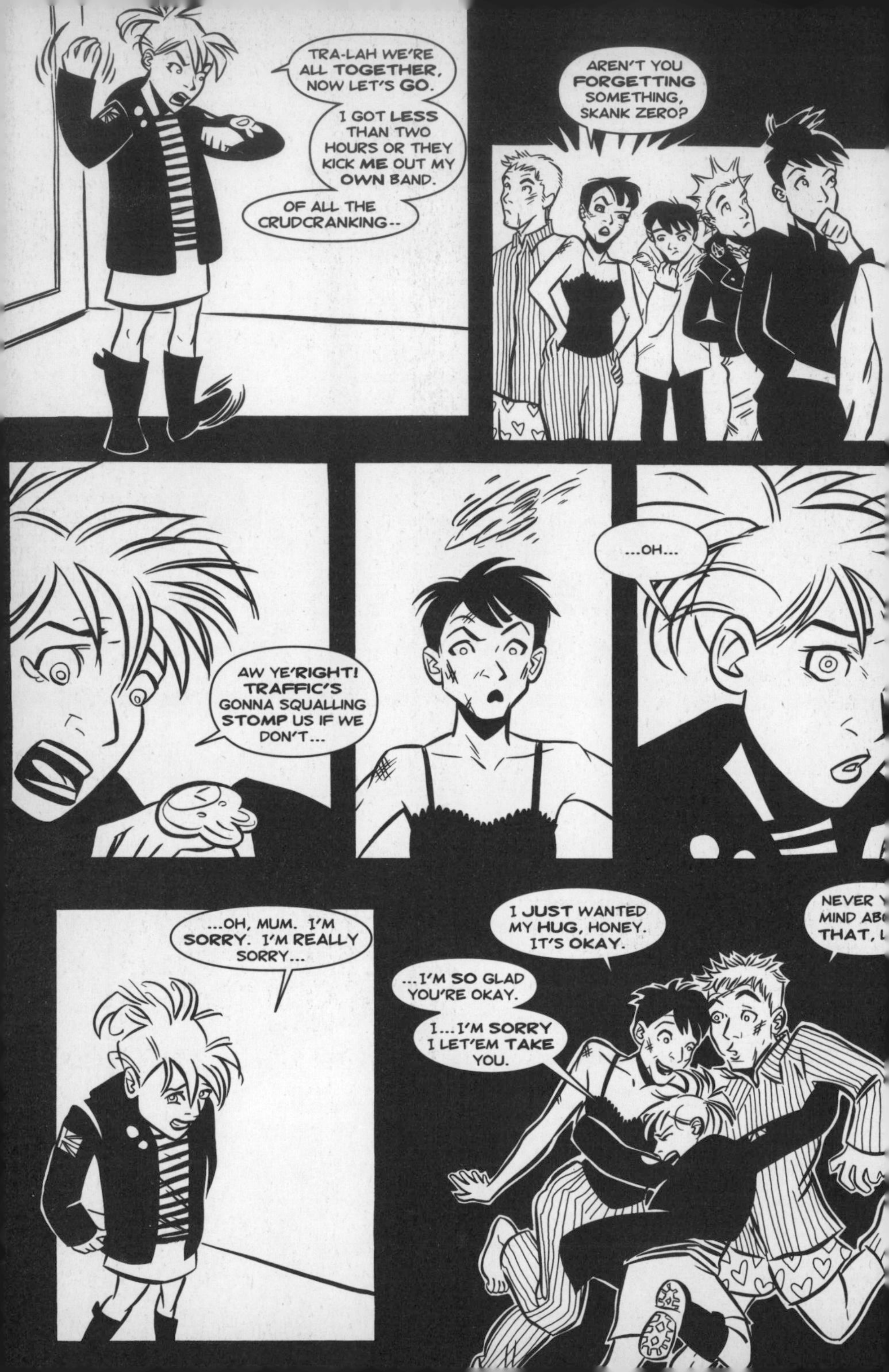
TRA-LAH WE'RE ALL TOGETHER, NOW LET'S GO.
I GOT LESS THAN TWO HOURS OR THEY KICK ME OUT MY OWN BAND.
OF ALL THE CRUDCRANKING--
AREN'T YOU FORGETTING SOMETHING, SKANK ZERO?
AW YE'RIGHT! TRAFFIC'S GONNA SQUALLING STOMP US IF WE DON'T...
...OH...
...OH, MUM. I'M SORRY. I'M REALLY SORRY...
I JUST WANTED MY HUG, HONEY. IT'S OKAY.
...I'M SO GLAD YOU'RE OKAY.
I...I'M SORRY I LET'EM TAKE YOU.

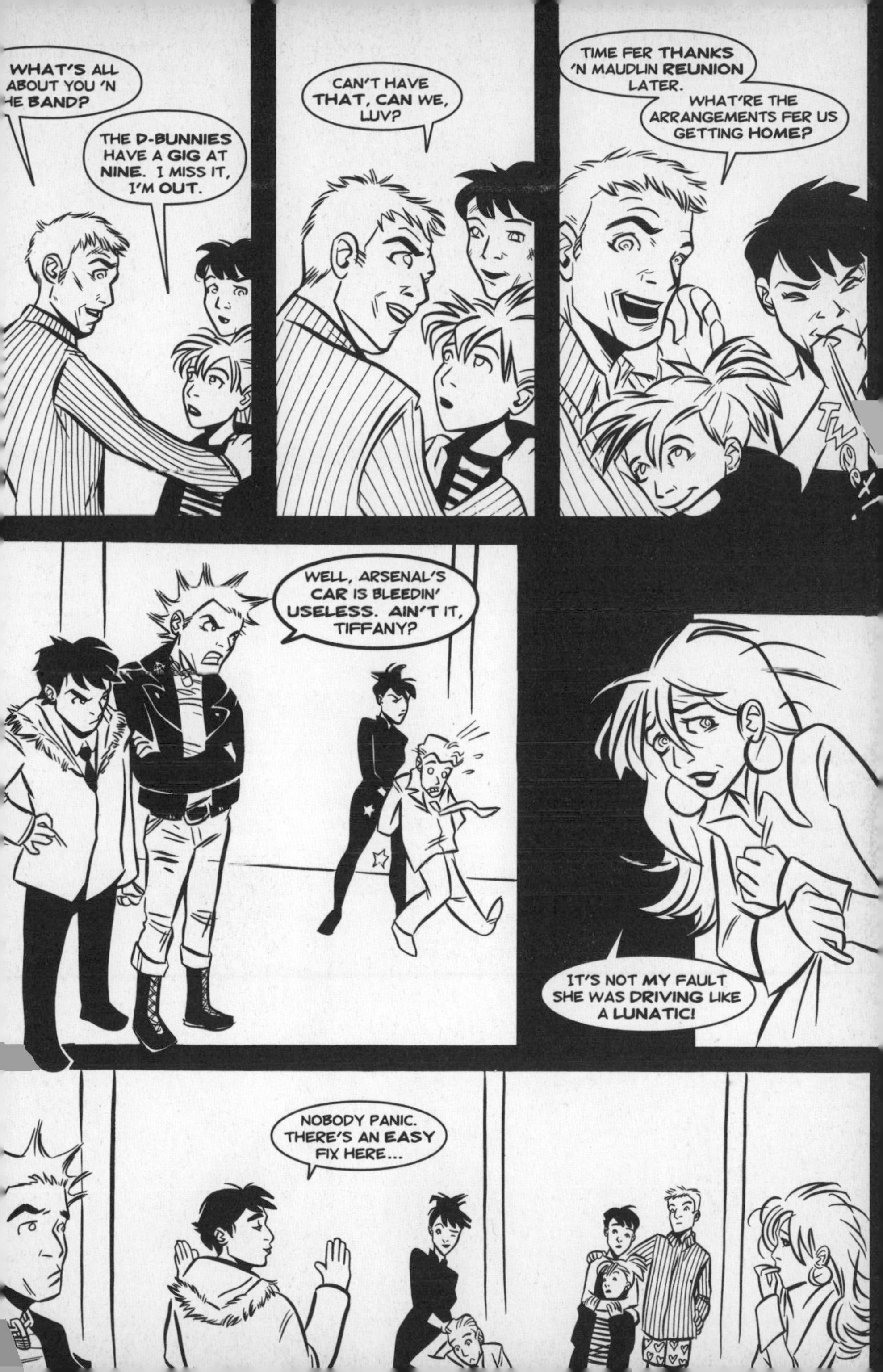
WHAT'S ALL ABOUT YOU 'N HE BAND?
THE D-BUNNIES HAVE A GIG AT NINE. I MISS IT, I'M OUT.
CAN'T HAVE THAT, CAN WE, LUV?
TIME FER THANKS 'N MAUDLIN REUNION LATER.
WHAT'RE THE ARRANGEMENTS FER US GETTING HOME?
TWEET
WELL, ARSENAL'S CAR IS BLEEDIN' USELESS. AIN'T IT, TIFFANY?
IT'S NOT MY FAULT SHE WAS DRIVING LIKE A LUNATIC!
NOBODY PANIC. THERE'S AN EASY FIX HERE...

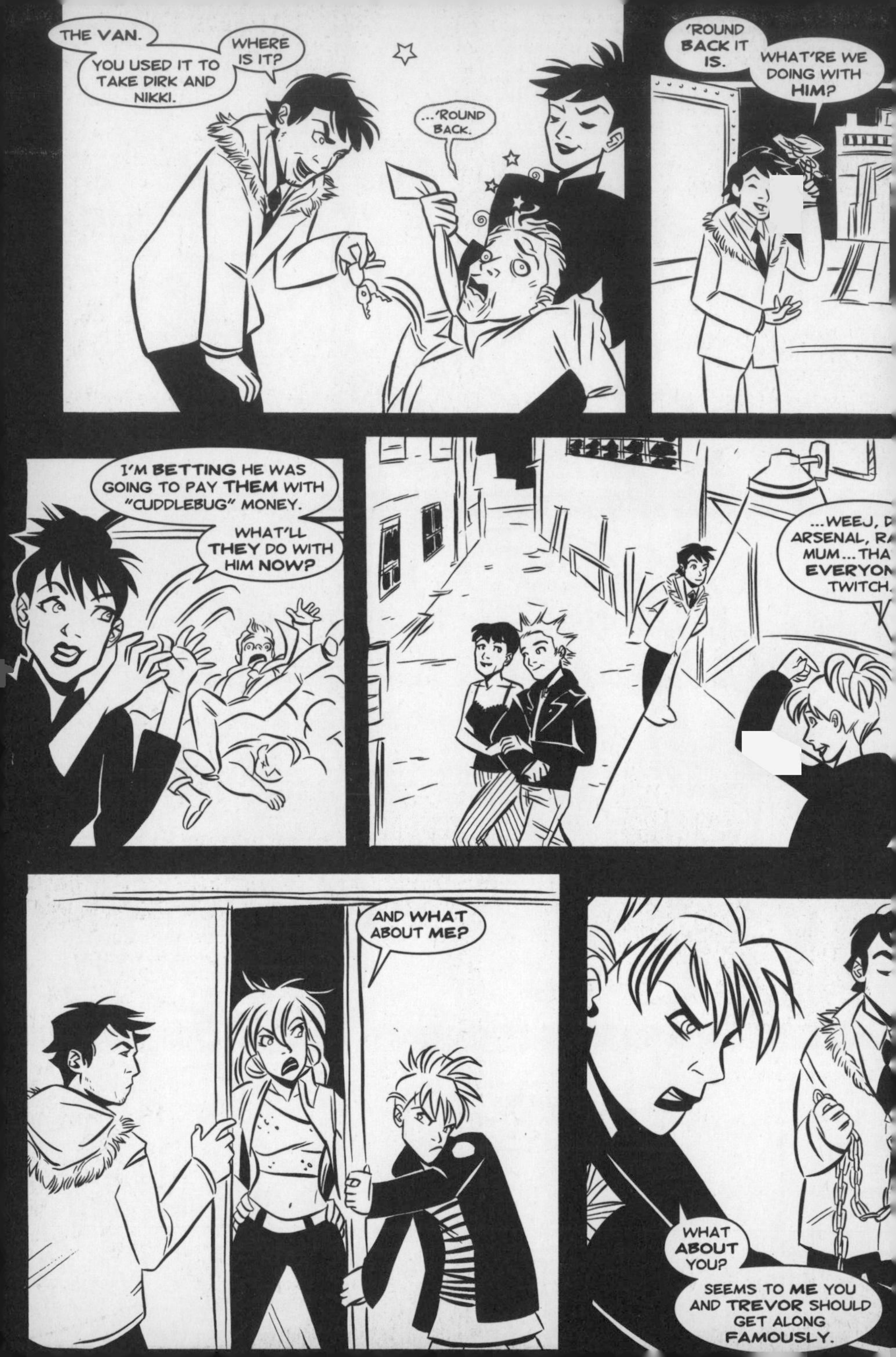
THE VAN.
YOU USED IT TO TAKE DIRK AND NIKKI.
WHERE IS IT?
...'ROUND BACK.
'ROUND BACK IT IS.
WHAT'RE WE DOING WITH HIM?
I'M BETTING HE WAS GOING TO PAY THEM WITH "CUDDLEBUG" MONEY.
WHAT'LL THEY DO WITH HIM NOW?
AND WHAT ABOUT ME?
WHAT ABOUT YOU?
SEEMS TO ME YOU AND TREVOR SHOULD GET ALONG FAMOUSLY.

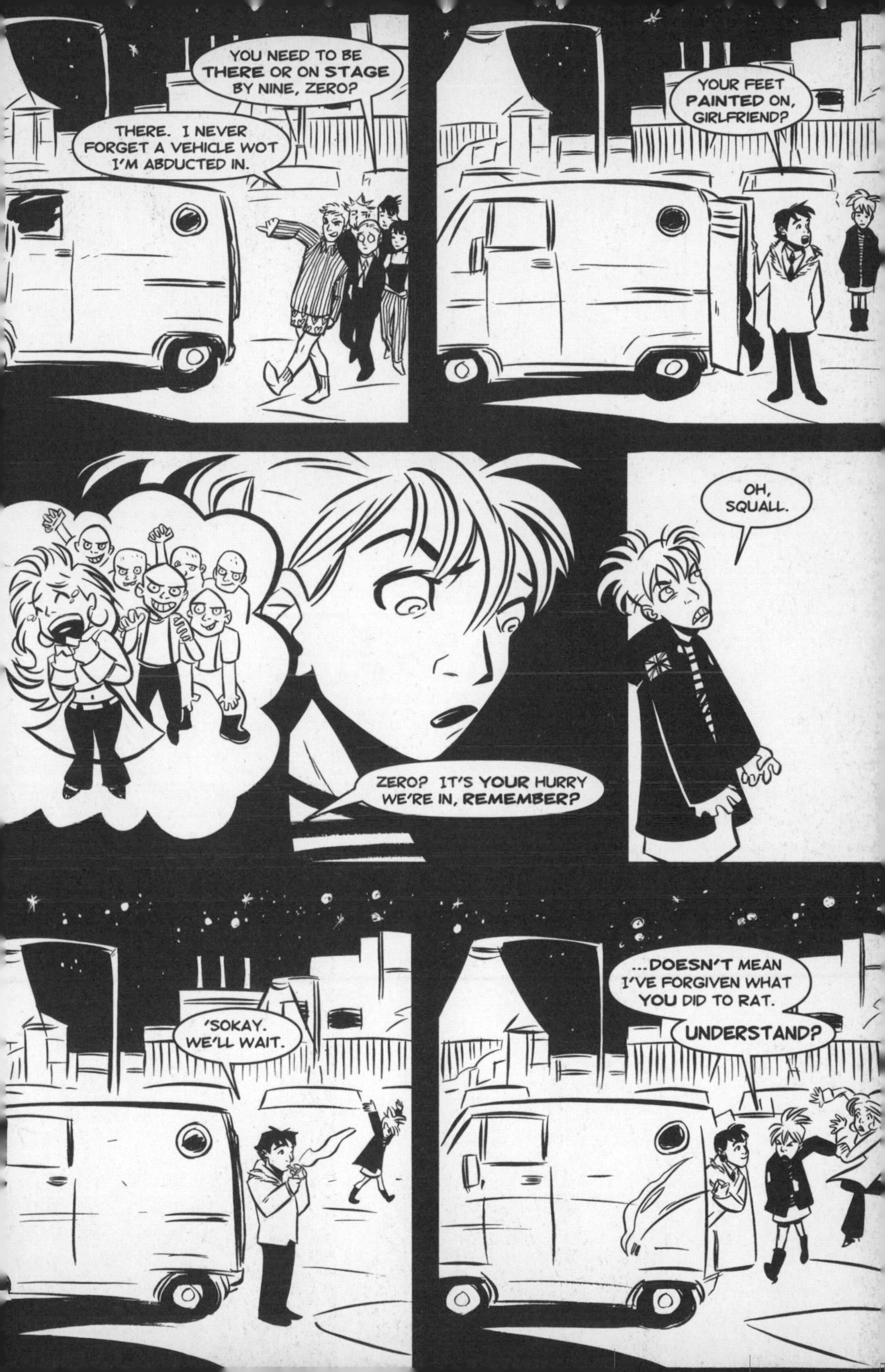
YOU NEED TO BE THERE OR ON STAGE BY NINE, ZERO?
THERE. I NEVER FORGET A VEHICLE WOT I'M ABDUCTED IN.
YOUR FEET PAINTED ON, GIRLFRIEND?
ZERO? IT'S YOUR HURRY WE'RE IN, REMEMBER?
OH, SQUALL.
'SOKAY. WE'LL WAIT.
...DOESN'T MEAN I'VE FORGIVEN WHAT YOU DID TO RAT.
UNDERSTAND?

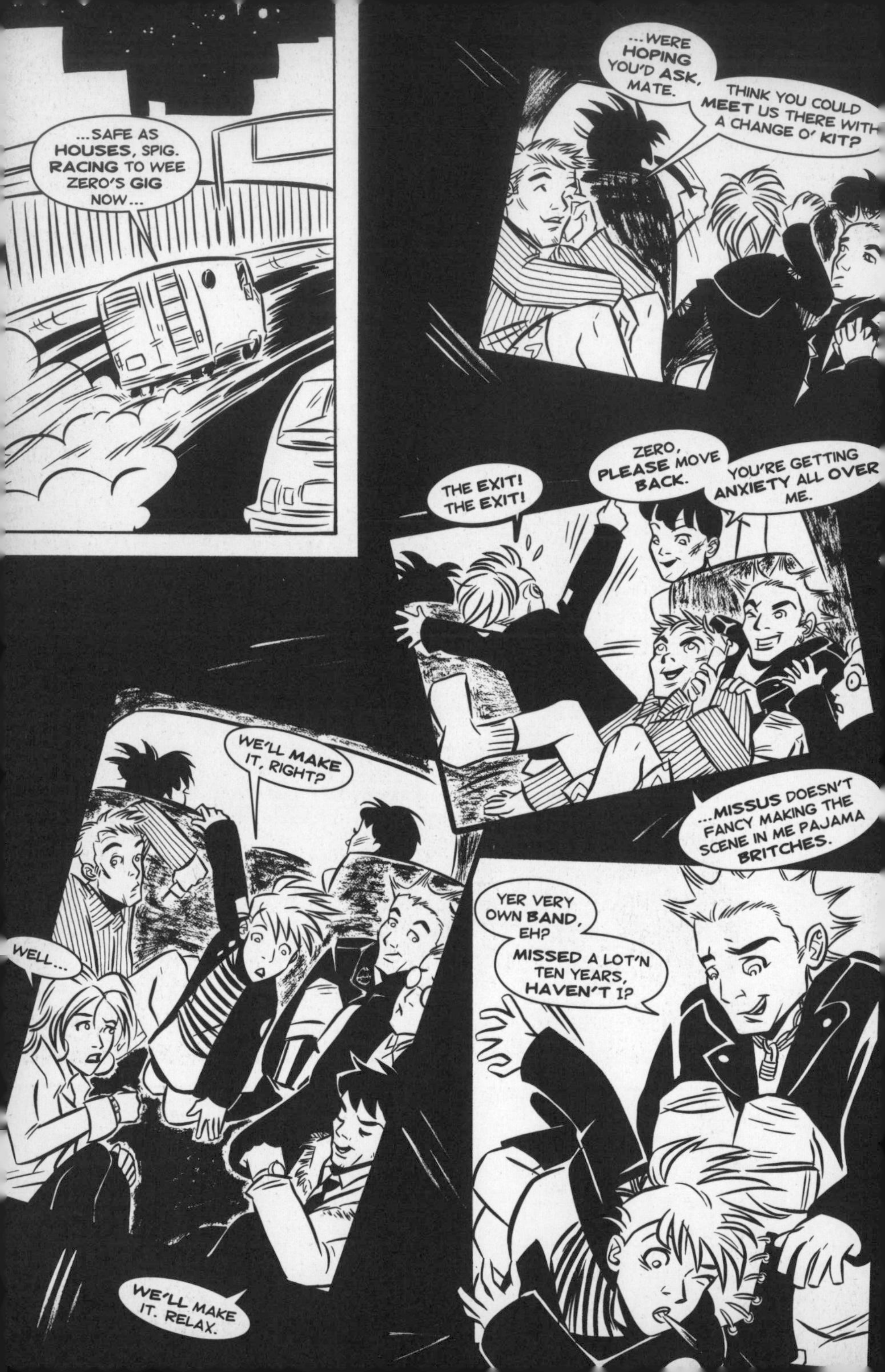
...SAFE AS HOUSES, SPIG. RACING TO WEE ZERO'S GIG NOW...
...WERE HOPING YOU'D ASK, MATE.
THINK YOU COULD MEET US THERE WITH A CHANGE O' KIT?
THE EXIT! THE EXIT!
ZERO, PLEASE MOVE BACK.
YOU'RE GETTING ANXIETY ALL OVER ME.
WE'LL MAKE IT, RIGHT?
WELL...
WE'LL MAKE IT. RELAX.
...MISSUS DOESN'T FANCY MAKING THE SCENE IN ME PAJAMA BRITCHES.
YER VERY OWN BAND, EH?
MISSED A LOT'N TEN YEARS, HAVEN'T I?

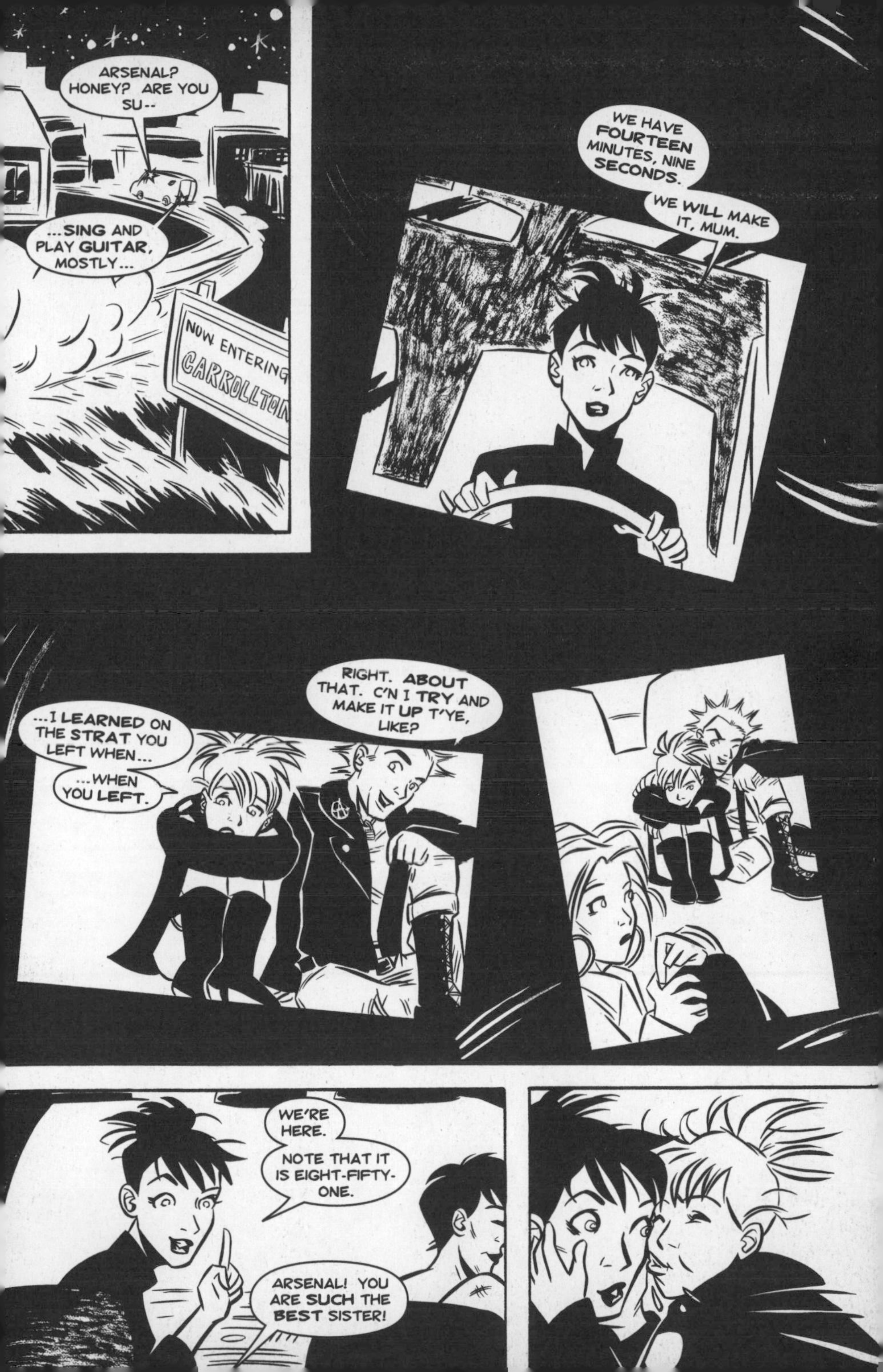
ARSENAL? HONEY? ARE YOU SU--
...SING AND PLAY GUITAR, MOSTLY...
NOW ENTERING CARROLLTON
WE HAVE FOURTEEN MINUTES, NINE SECONDS.
WE WILL MAKE IT, MUM.
...I LEARNED ON THE STRAT YOU LEFT WHEN...
...WHEN YOU LEFT.
RIGHT. ABOUT THAT. C'N I TRY AND MAKE IT UP T'YE, LIKE?
WE'RE HERE.
NOTE THAT IT IS EIGHT-FIFTY-ONE.
ARSENAL! YOU ARE SUCH THE BEST SISTER!

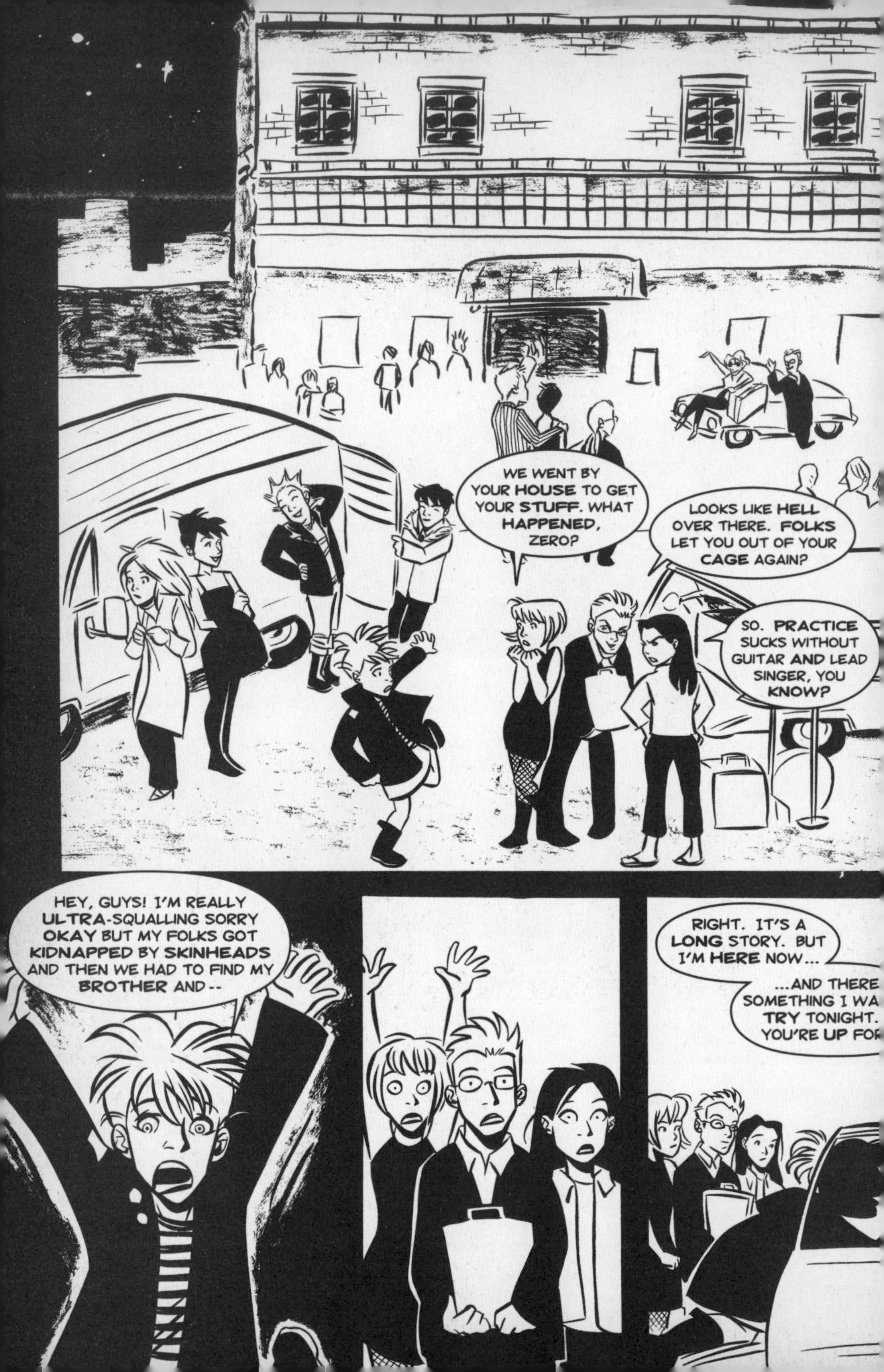
WE WENT BY YOUR HOUSE TO GET YOUR STUFF. WHAT HAPPENED, ZERO?
LOOKS LIKE HELL OVER THERE. FOLKS LET YOU OUT OF YOUR CAGE AGAIN?
SO. PRACTICE SUCKS WITHOUT GUITAR AND LEAD SINGER, YOU KNOW?
HEY, GUYS! I'M REALLY ULTRA-SQUALLING SORRY OKAY BUT MY FOLKS GOT KIDNAPPED BY SKINHEADS AND THEN WE HAD TO FIND MY BROTHER AND --
RIGHT. IT'S A LONG STORY. BUT I'M HERE NOW...
...AND THERE SOMETHING I WA TRY TONIGHT. YOU'RE UP FOR

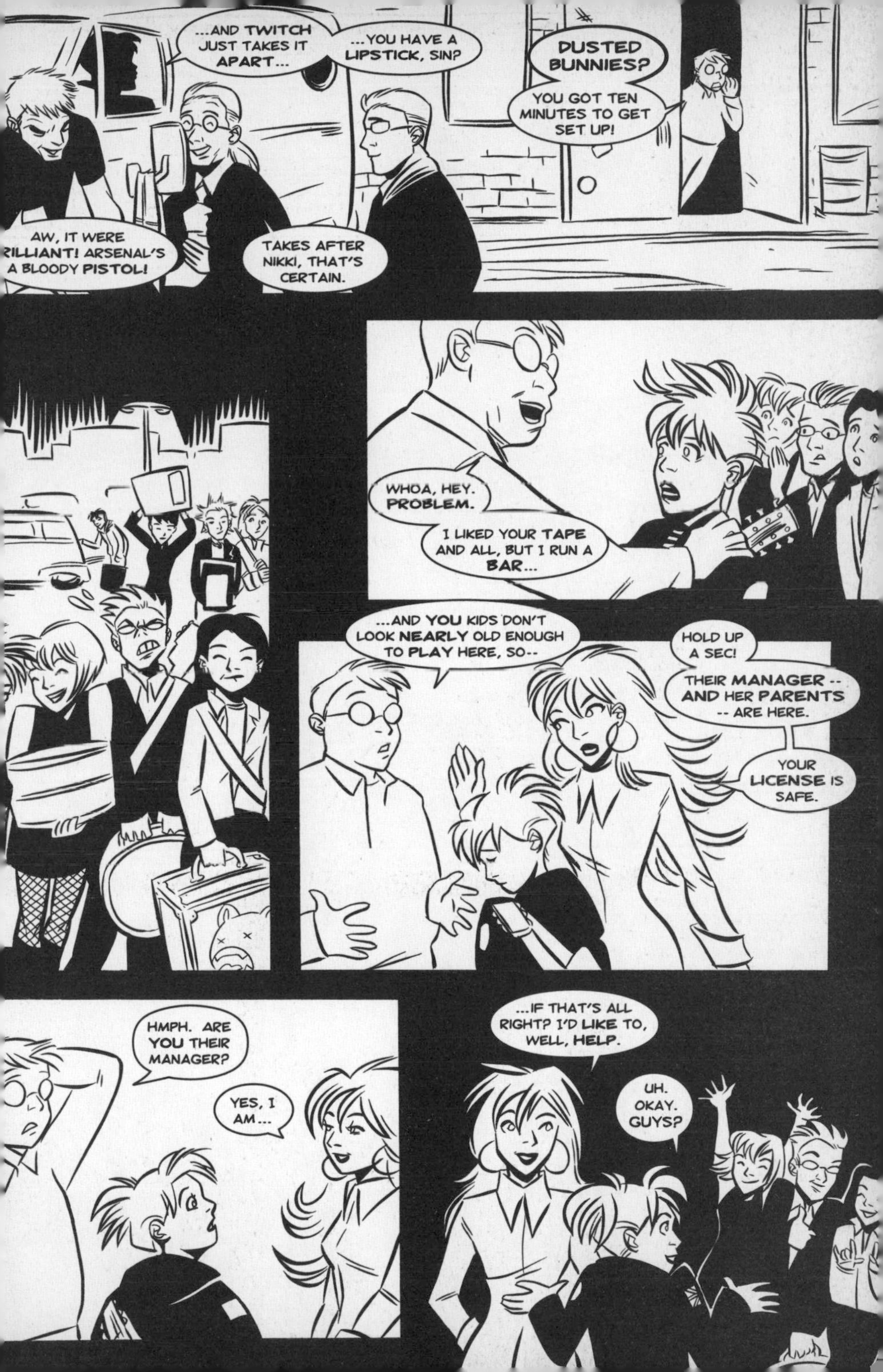

AW, IT WERE
RILLIANT! ARSENAL'S A BLOODY PISTOL!
...AND TWITCH JUST TAKES IT APART...
TAKES AFTER NIKKI, THAT'S CERTAIN.
...YOU HAVE A LIPSTICK, SIN?
DUSTED BUNNIES?
YOU GOT TEN MINUTES TO GET SET UP!
WHOA, HEY. PROBLEM.
I LIKED YOUR TAPE AND ALL, BUT I RUN A BAR...
...AND YOU KIDS DON'T LOOK NEARLY OLD ENOUGH TO PLAY HERE, SO--
HOLD UP A SEC!
THEIR MANAGER -- AND HER PARENTS -- ARE HERE.
YOUR LICENSE IS SAFE.
HMPH. ARE YOU THEIR MANAGER?
YES, I AM...
...IF THAT'S ALL RIGHT? I'D LIKE TO, WELL, HELP.
UH. OKAY. GUYS?

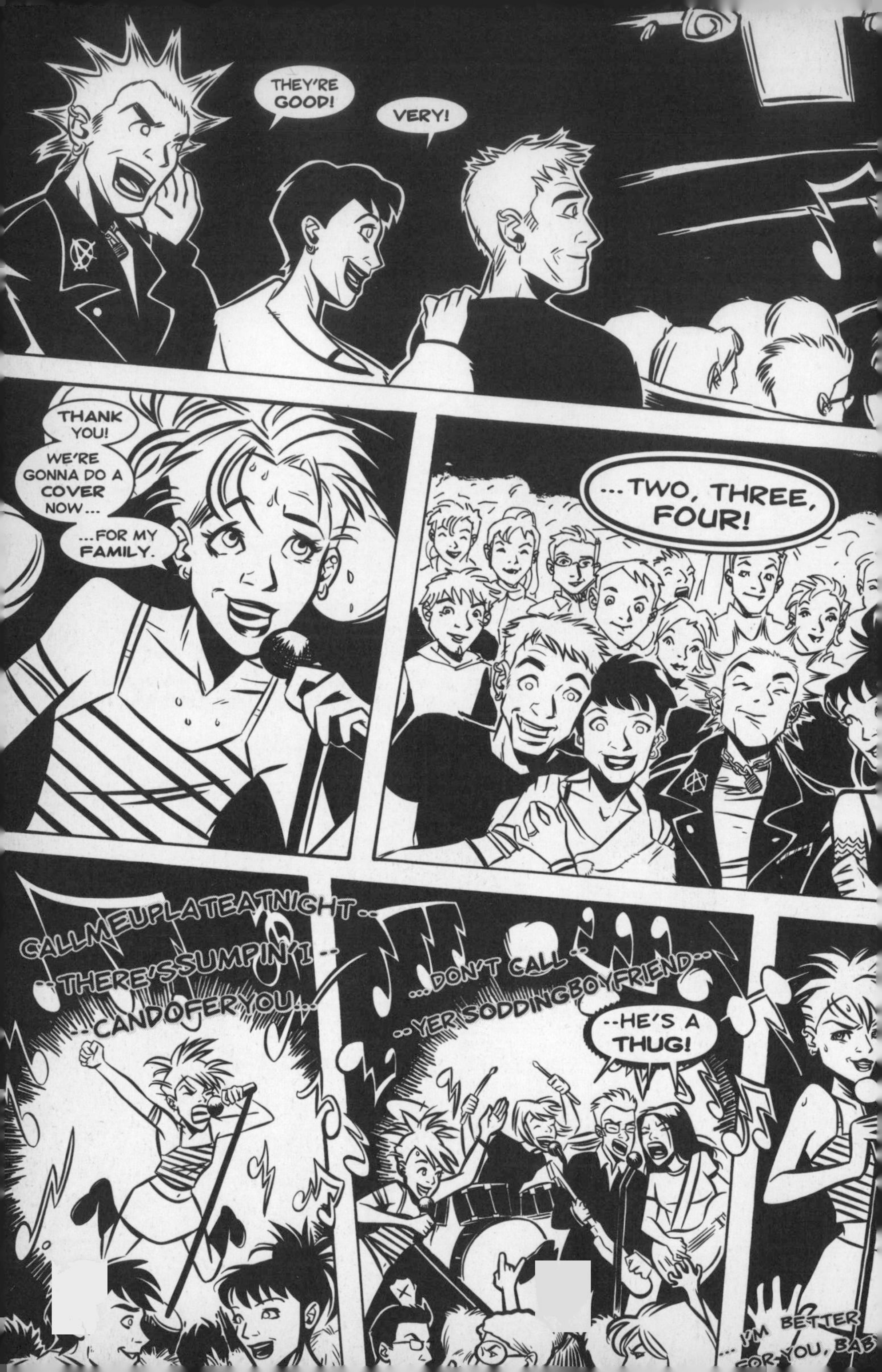
THEY'RE GOOD!
VERY!
THANK YOU!
WE'RE GONNA DO A COVER NOW...
...FOR MY FAMILY.
...TWO, THREE, FOUR!
CALLMEUPLATEATNIGHT--
--THERE'SSUMPIN'I--
--CANDOFERYOU...
...DON'T CALL--
--YER SODDINGBOYFRIEND--
--HE'S A THUG!
...I'M BETTER FOR YOU, BAB

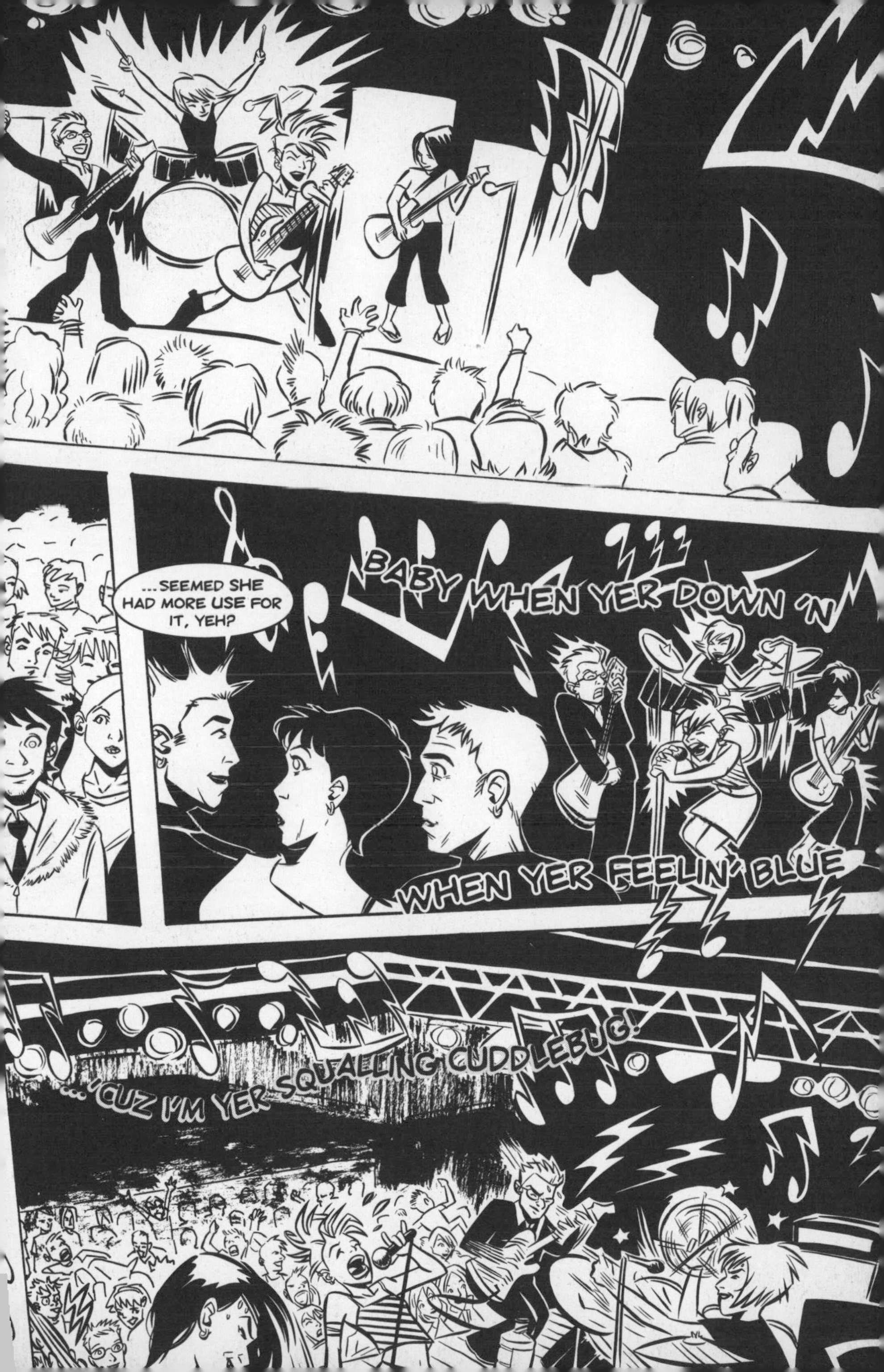
...SEEMED SHE HAD MORE USE FOR IT, YEH?
BABY WHEN YER DOWN 'N
WHEN YER FEELIN' BLUE
...'CUZ I'M YER SQUALLING CUDDLEBUG!

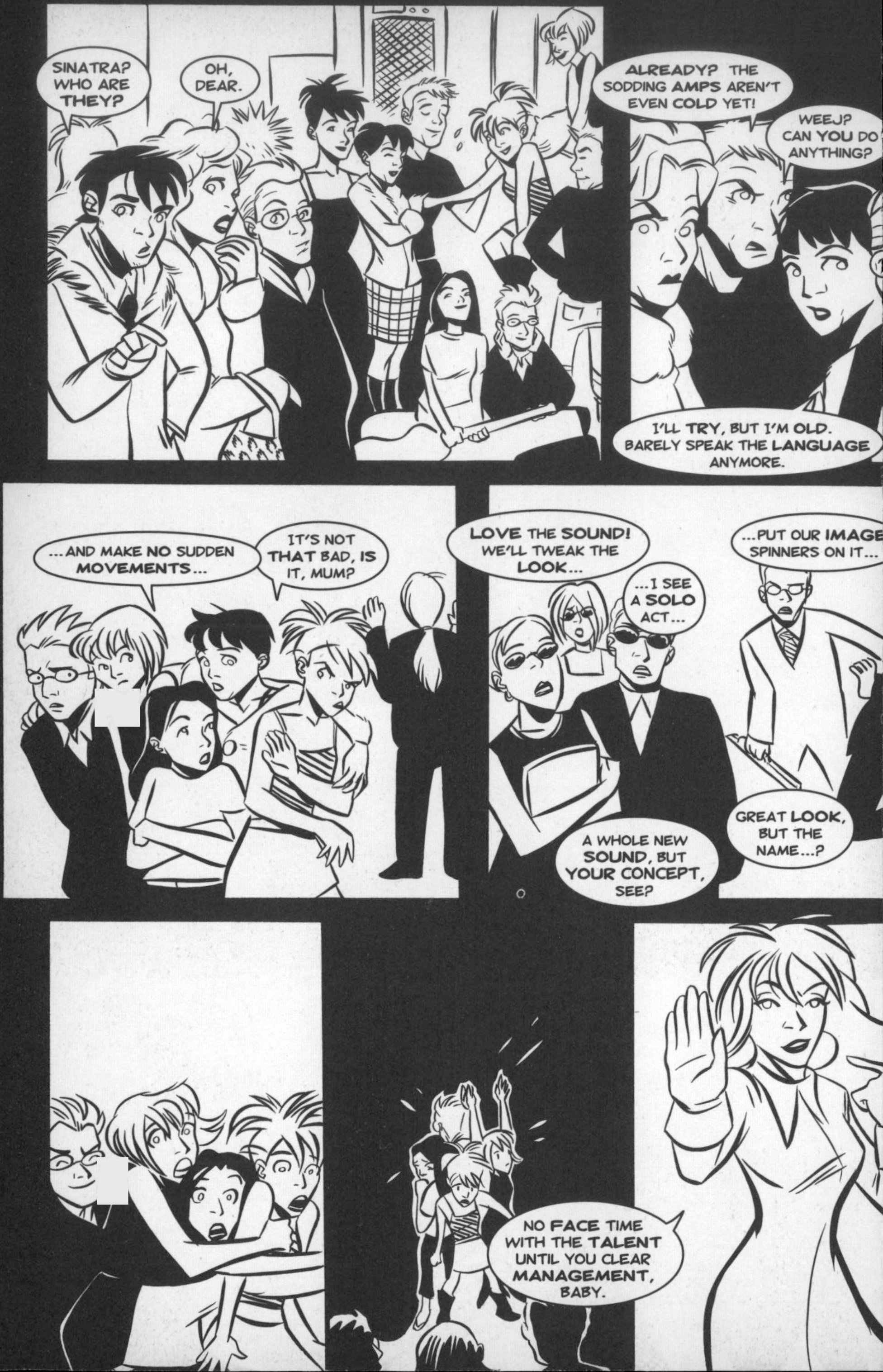

SINATRA? WHO ARE THEY?
OH, DEAR.
ALREADY? THE SODDING AMPS AREN'T EVEN COLD YET!
WEEJ? CAN YOU DO ANYTHING?
I'LL TRY, BUT I'M OLD. BARELY SPEAK THE LANGUAGE ANYMORE.
...AND MAKE NO SUDDEN MOVEMENTS...
IT'S NOT THAT BAD, IS IT, MUM?
LOVE THE SOUND! WE'LL TWEAK THE LOOK...
...I SEE A SOLO ACT...
...PUT OUR IMAGE SPINNERS ON IT...
A WHOLE NEW SOUND, BUT YOUR CONCEPT, SEE?
GREAT LOOK, BUT THE NAME...?
NO FACE TIME WITH THE TALENT UNTIL YOU CLEAR MANAGEMENT, BABY.

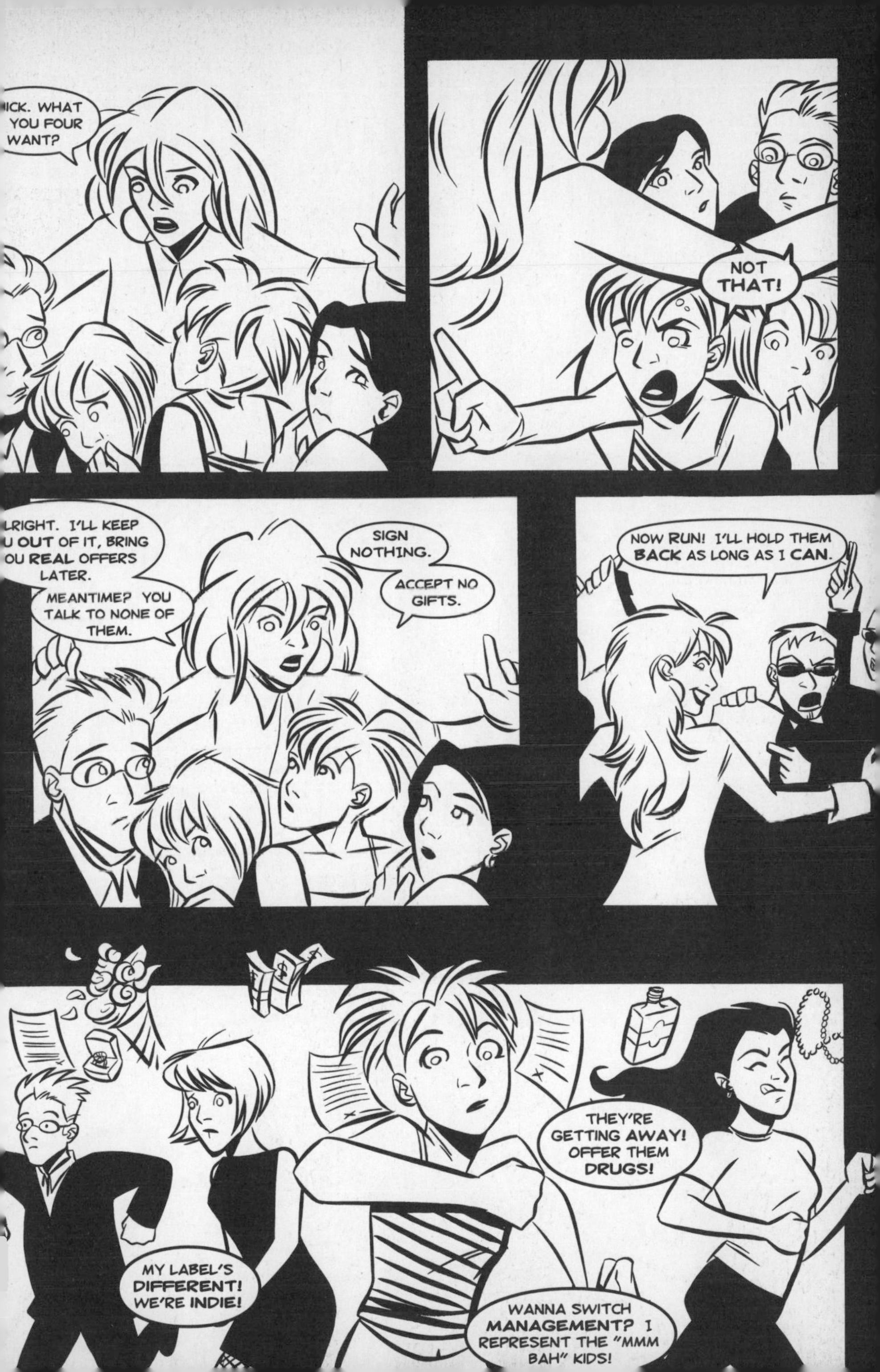

ICK. WHAT YOU FOUR WANT?
NOT THAT!
LRIGHT. I'LL KEEP U OUT OF IT, BRING OU REAL OFFERS LATER.
MEANTIME? YOU TALK TO NONE OF THEM.
SIGN NOTHING.
ACCEPT NO GIFTS.
NOW RUN! I'LL HOLD THEM BACK AS LONG AS I CAN.
THEY'RE GETTING AWAY! OFFER THEM DRUGS!
MY LABEL'S DIFFERENT! WE'RE INDIE!
WANNA SWITCH MANAGEMENT? I REPRESENT THE "MMM BAH" KIDS!

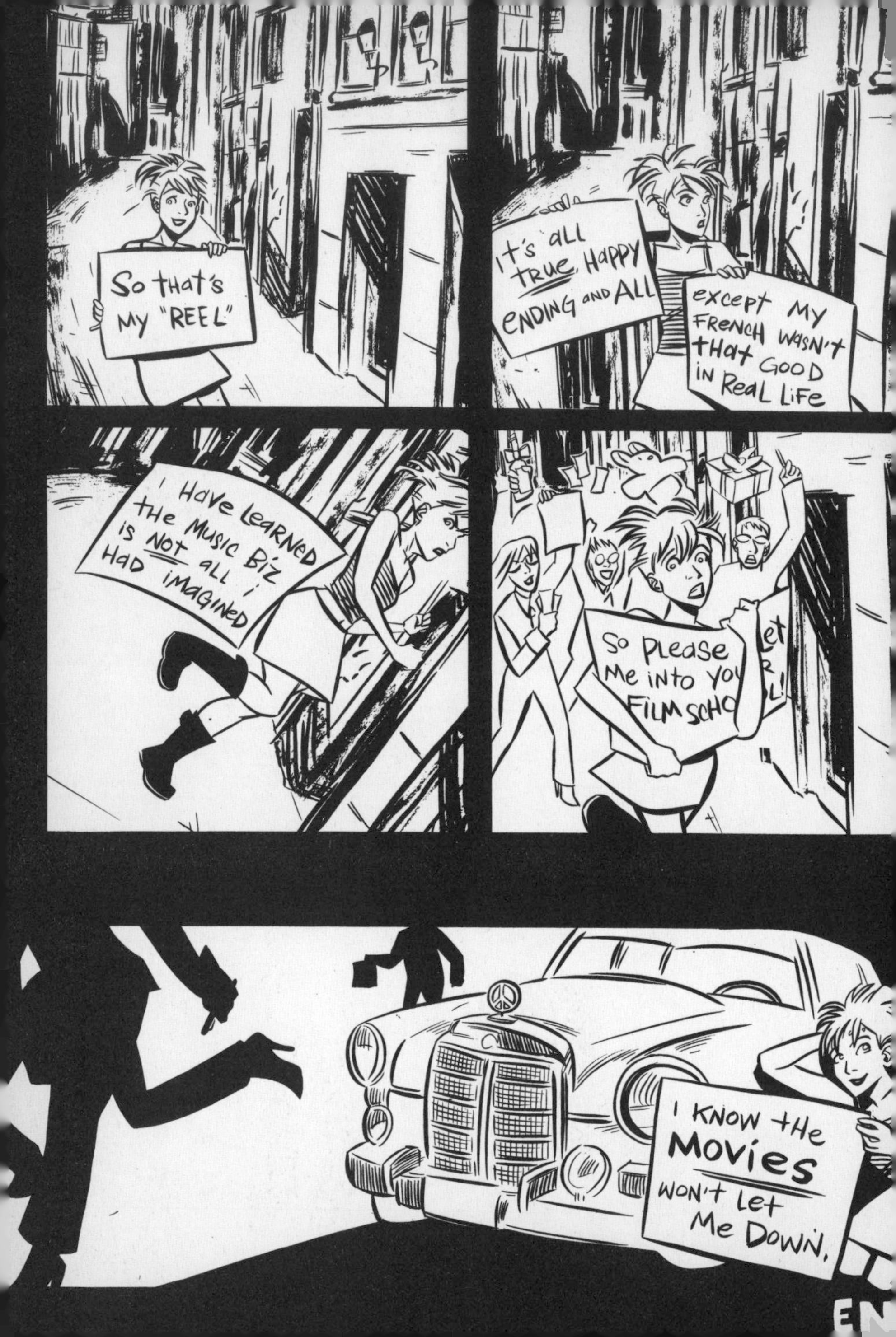
So that's my "REEL"
It's all TRUE, Happy ending and all
except my French wasn't that good in Real Life
I have learned the Music Biz is NOT all I had imagined
So Please Me into Yo FILM SCHO
I know the Movies won't let Me Down.

GALLERY

The following pages contain Christine Norrie's developmental sketches done in preparation for the series. Many of these were also used as design elements throughout this collection.

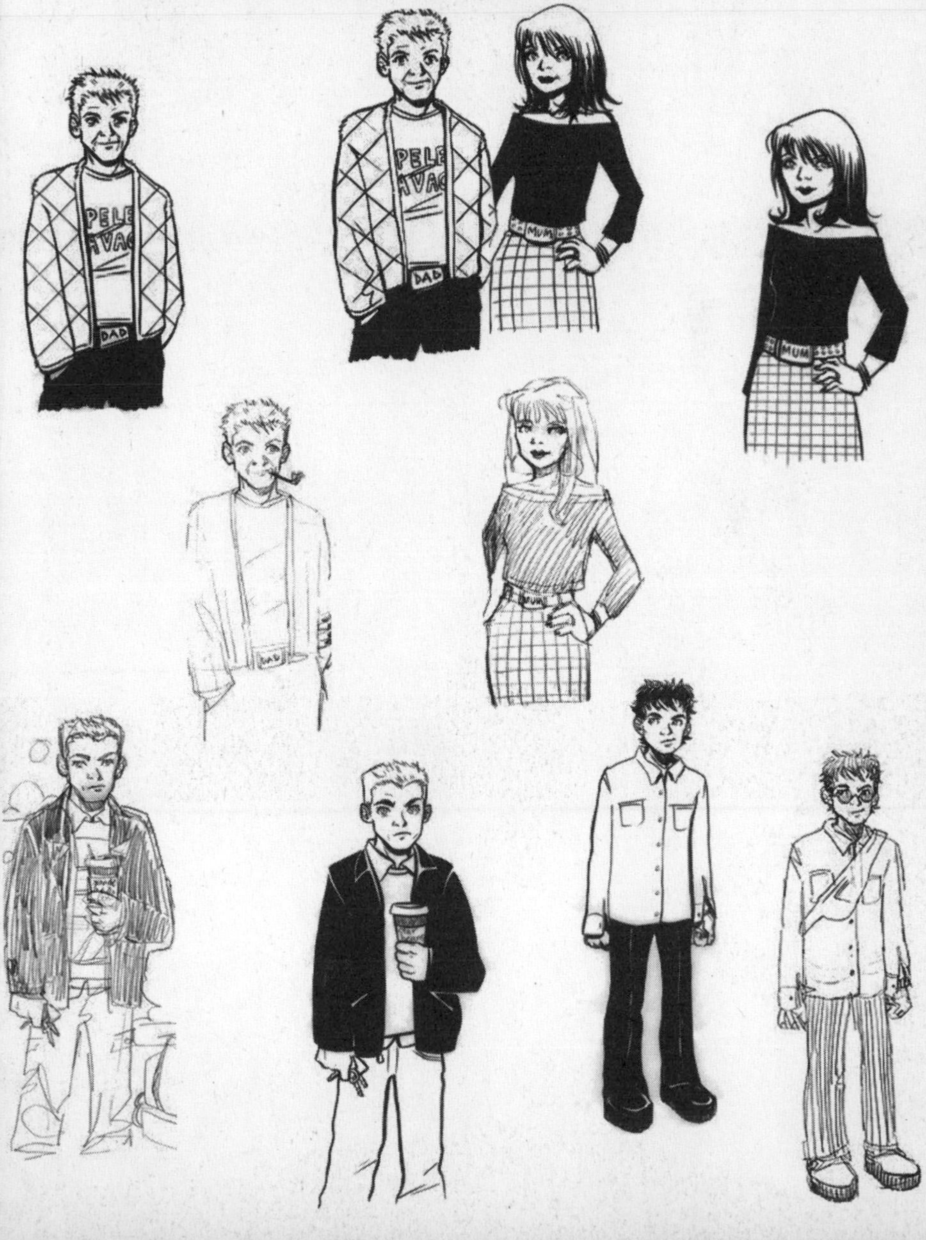
DAD
MUM

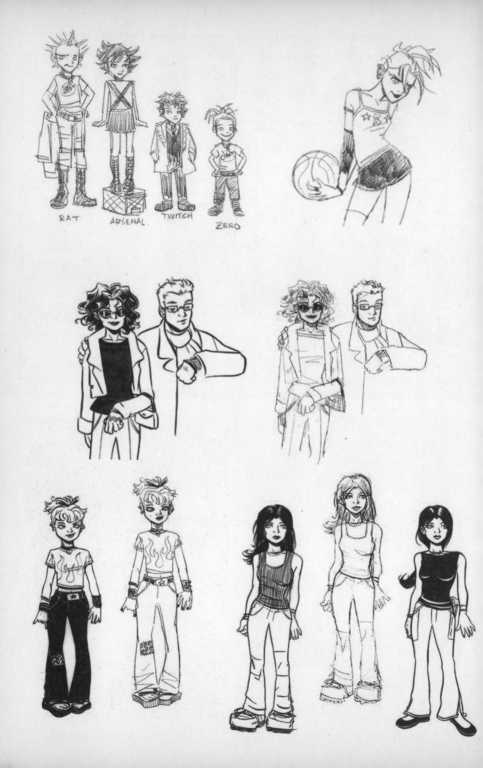

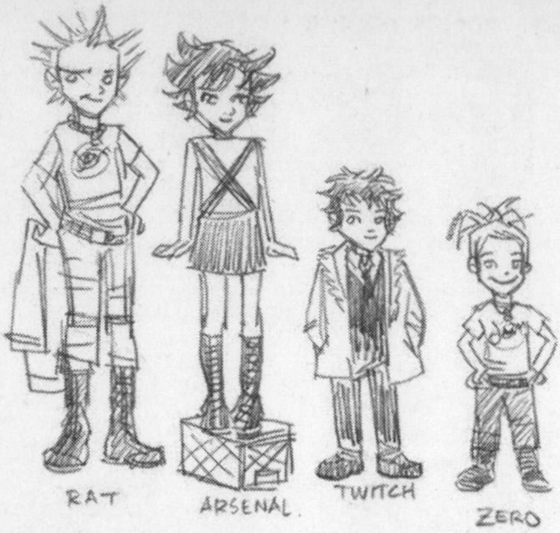
RAT
ARSENAL
TWITCH
ZERO

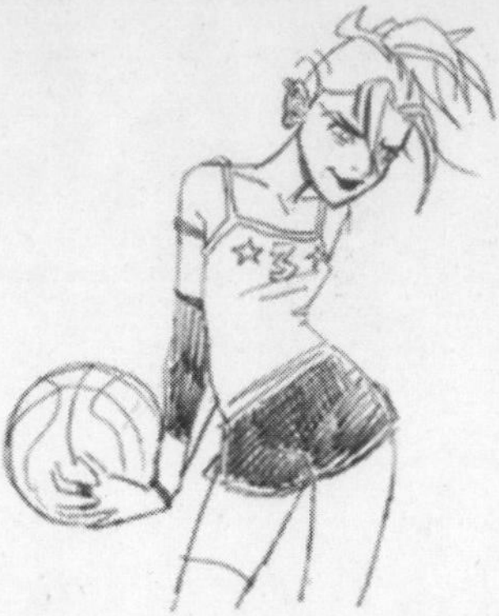

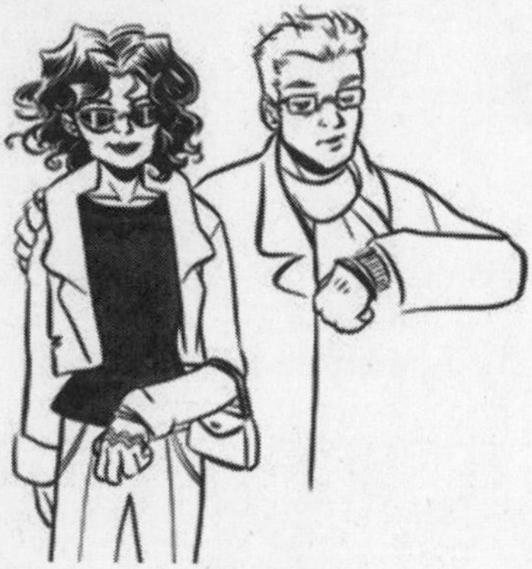

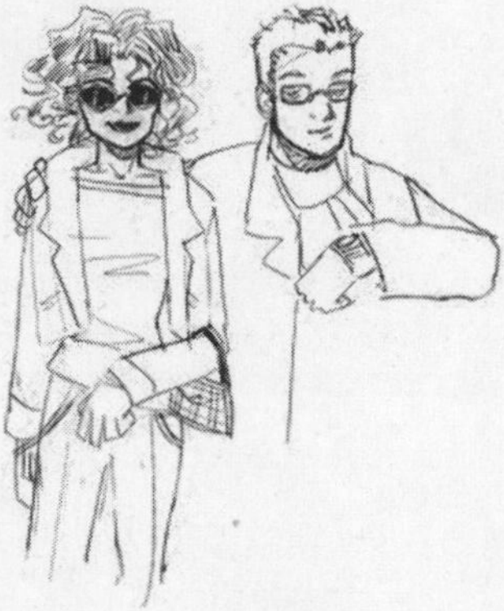

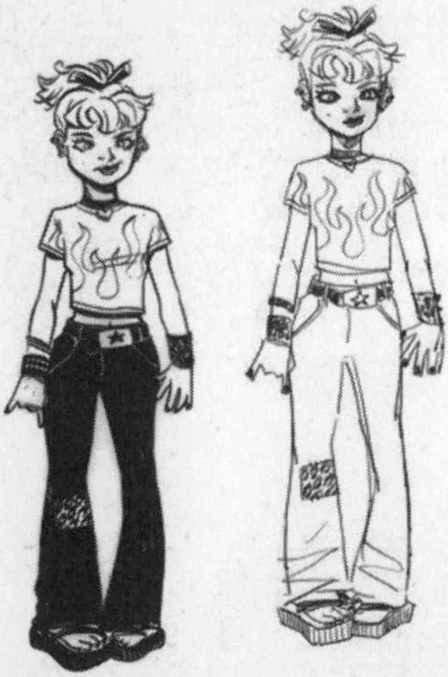

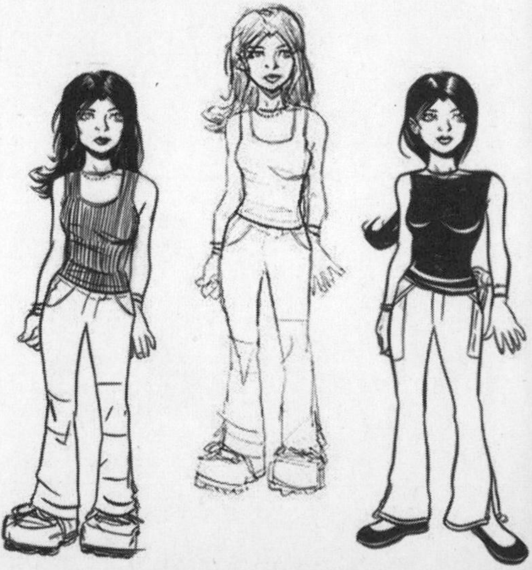

Thumbnail layouts by Clugston-Major and Norrie.

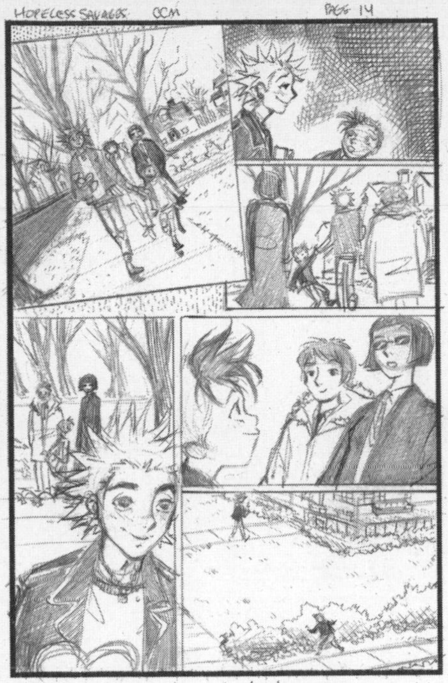
HOPELESS SAVAGES CCM PAGE 14

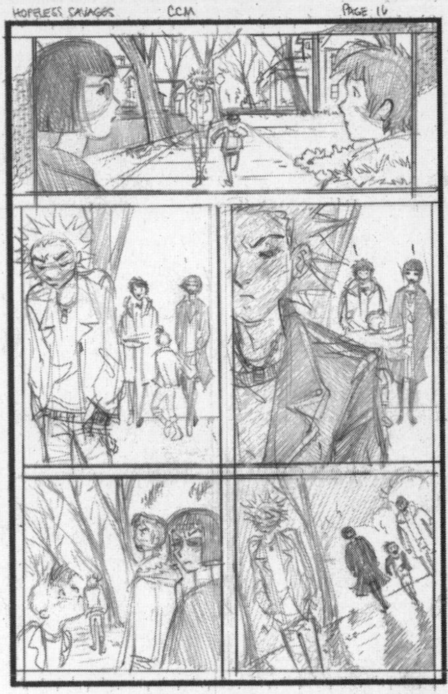
HOPELESS SAVAGES CCM PAGE 16

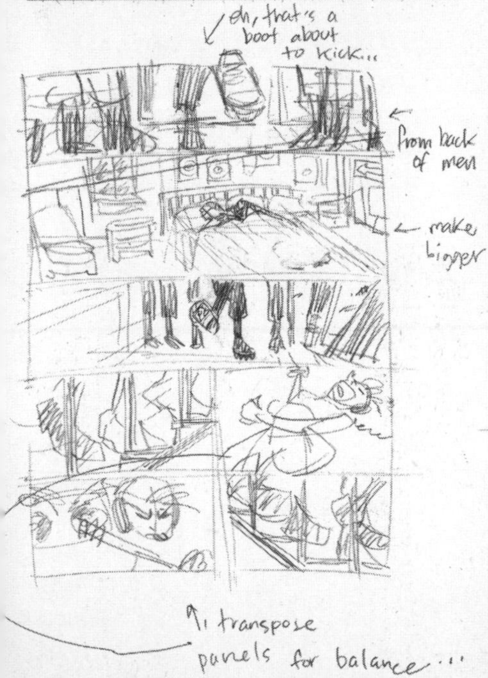
oh, that's a boot about to kick..
from back of men
make bigger
↑, transpose panels for balance...
(hope that's ok)

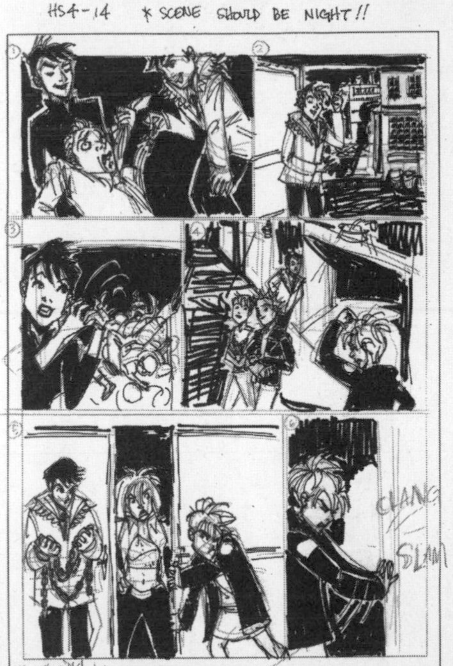
HS4-14 * SCENE SHOULD BE NIGHT!!
CLANG
SLAM
outer box: 6.875x10.25 is full bleed / inner box is bounding box for text

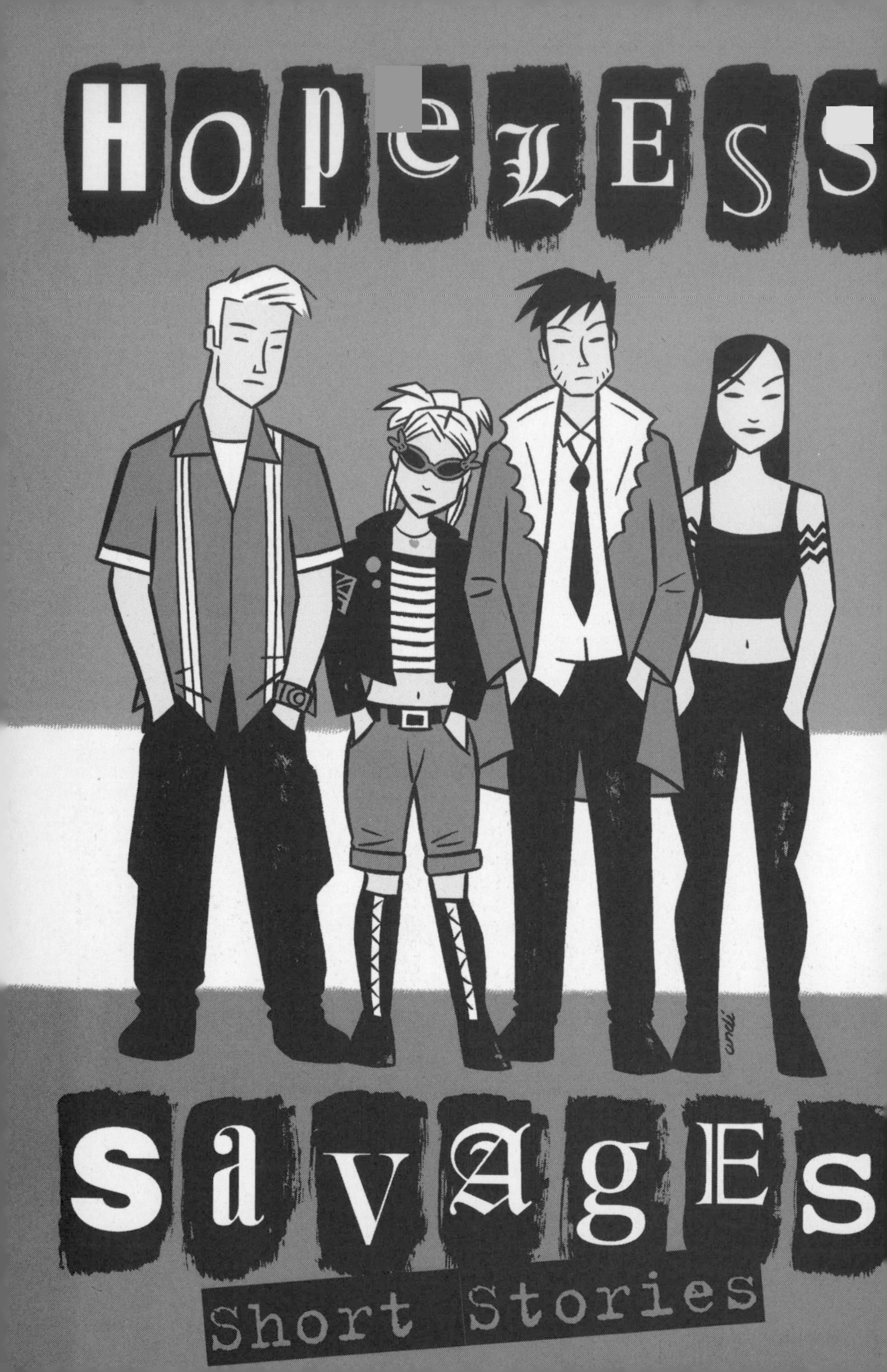
Hopeless
Savages
Short Stories

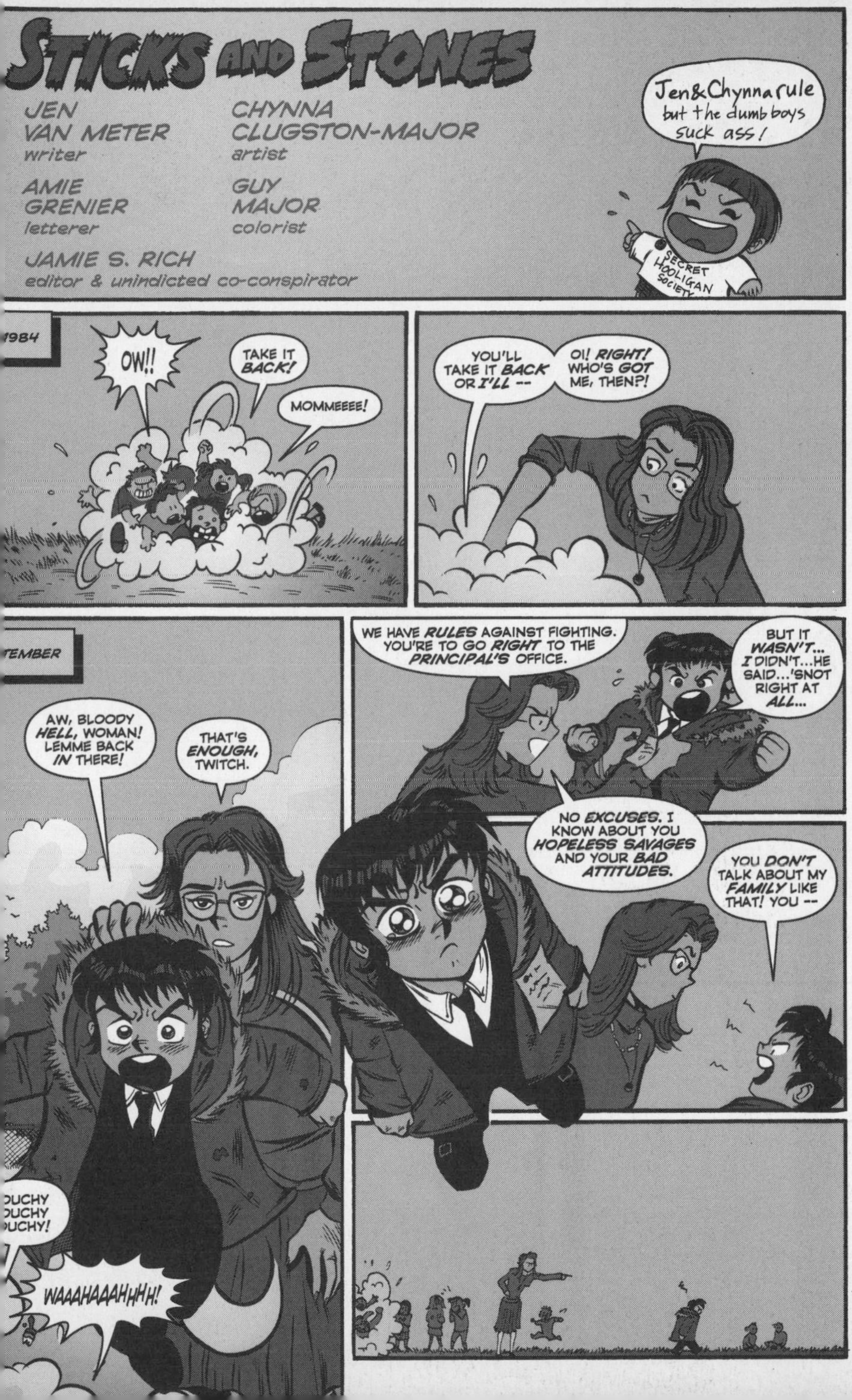
STICKS AND STONES
JEN VAN METER writer
CHYNNA CLUGSTON-MAJOR artist
AMIE GRENIER letterer
GUY MAJOR colorist
JAMIE S. RICH editor & unindicted co-conspirator
Jen&Chynna rule but the dumb boys suck ass!
SECRET HOOLIGAN SOCIETY
1984
OW!!
TAKE IT BACK!
MOMMEEEE!
YOU'LL TAKE IT BACK OR I'LL --
OI! RIGHT! WHO'S GOT ME, THEN?!
TEMBER
AW, BLOODY HELL, WOMAN! LEMME BACK IN THERE!
THAT'S ENOUGH, TWITCH.
OUCHY OUCHY OUCHY!
WAAAHAAAHHHH!
WE HAVE RULES AGAINST FIGHTING. YOU'RE TO GO RIGHT TO THE PRINCIPAL'S OFFICE.
BUT IT WASN'T... I DIDN'T...HE SAID...'SNOT RIGHT AT ALL...
NO EXCUSES. I KNOW ABOUT YOU HOPELESS SAVAGES AND YOUR BAD ATTITUDES.
YOU DON'T TALK ABOUT MY FAMILY LIKE THAT! YOU --

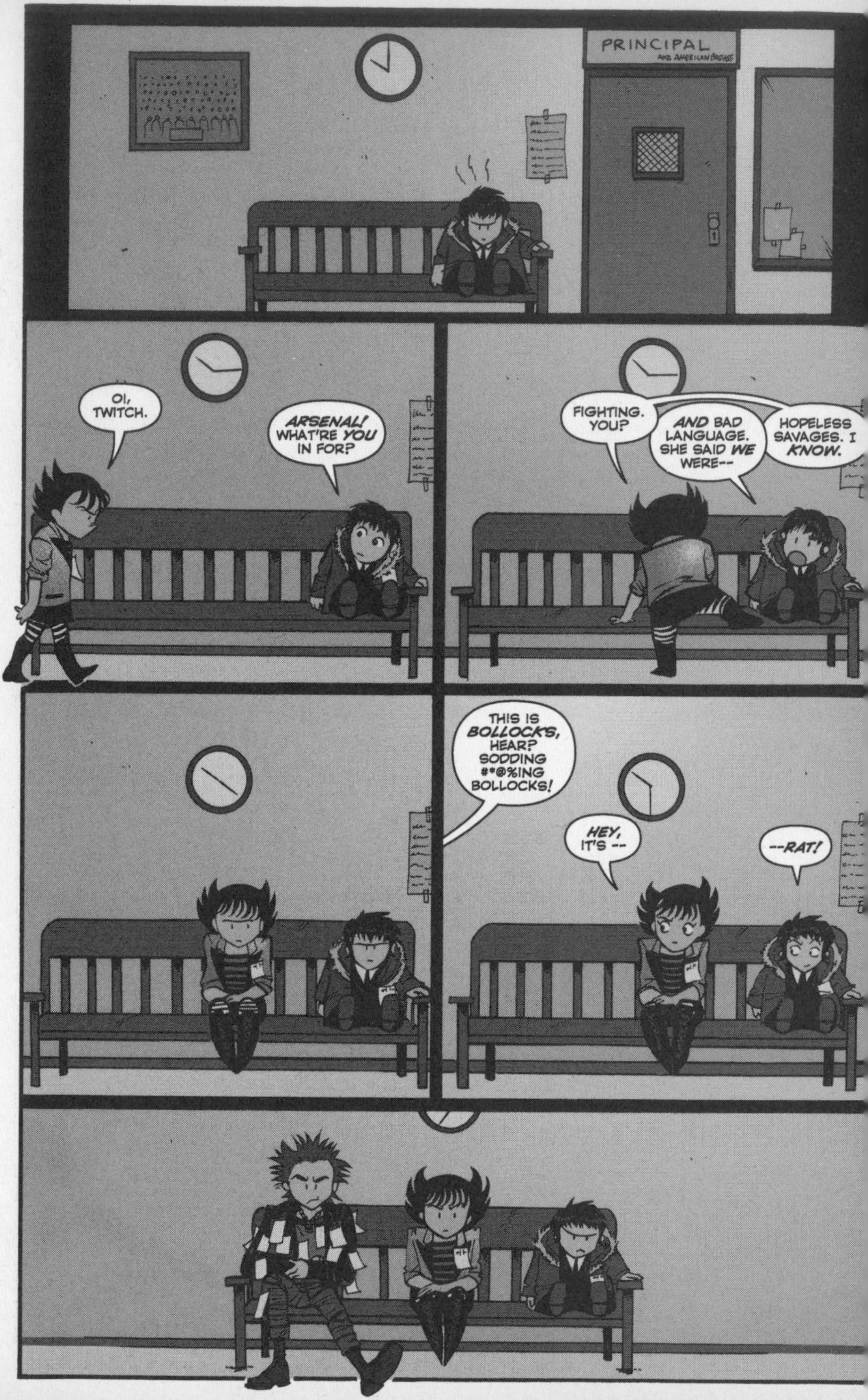

PRINCIPAL
AND AMERICAN BRASS
OI, TWITCH.
ARSENAL! WHAT'RE YOU IN FOR?
FIGHTING. YOU?
AND BAD LANGUAGE. SHE SAID WE WERE--
HOPELESS SAVAGES. I KNOW.
THIS IS BOLLOCKS, HEAR? SODDING #*@%ING BOLLOCKS!
HEY, IT'S --
--RAT!

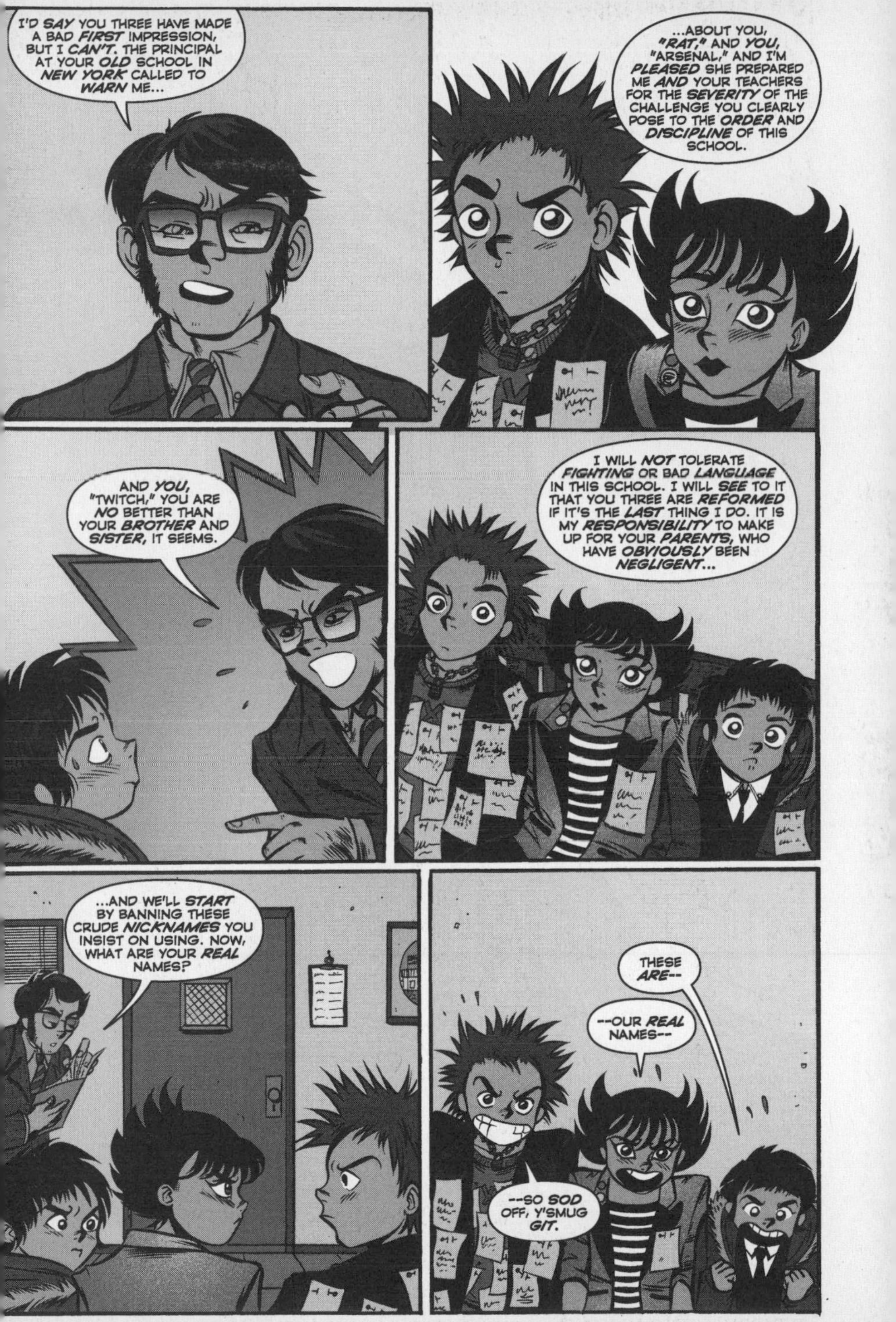
I'D SAY YOU THREE HAVE MADE A BAD FIRST IMPRESSION, BUT I CAN'T. THE PRINCIPAL AT YOUR OLD SCHOOL IN NEW YORK CALLED TO WARN ME...
...ABOUT YOU, "RAT," AND YOU, "ARSENAL," AND I'M PLEASED SHE PREPARED ME AND YOUR TEACHERS FOR THE SEVERITY OF THE CHALLENGE YOU CLEARLY POSE TO THE ORDER AND DISCIPLINE OF THIS SCHOOL.
AND YOU, "TWITCH," YOU ARE NO BETTER THAN YOUR BROTHER AND SISTER, IT SEEMS.
I WILL NOT TOLERATE FIGHTING OR BAD LANGUAGE IN THIS SCHOOL. I WILL SEE TO IT THAT YOU THREE ARE REFORMED IF IT'S THE LAST THING I DO. IT IS MY RESPONSIBILITY TO MAKE UP FOR YOUR PARENTS, WHO HAVE OBVIOUSLY BEEN NEGLIGENT...
...AND WE'LL START BY BANNING THESE CRUDE NICKNAMES YOU INSIST ON USING. NOW, WHAT ARE YOUR REAL NAMES?
THESE ARE--
--OUR REAL NAMES--
--SO SOD OFF, Y'SMUG GIT.

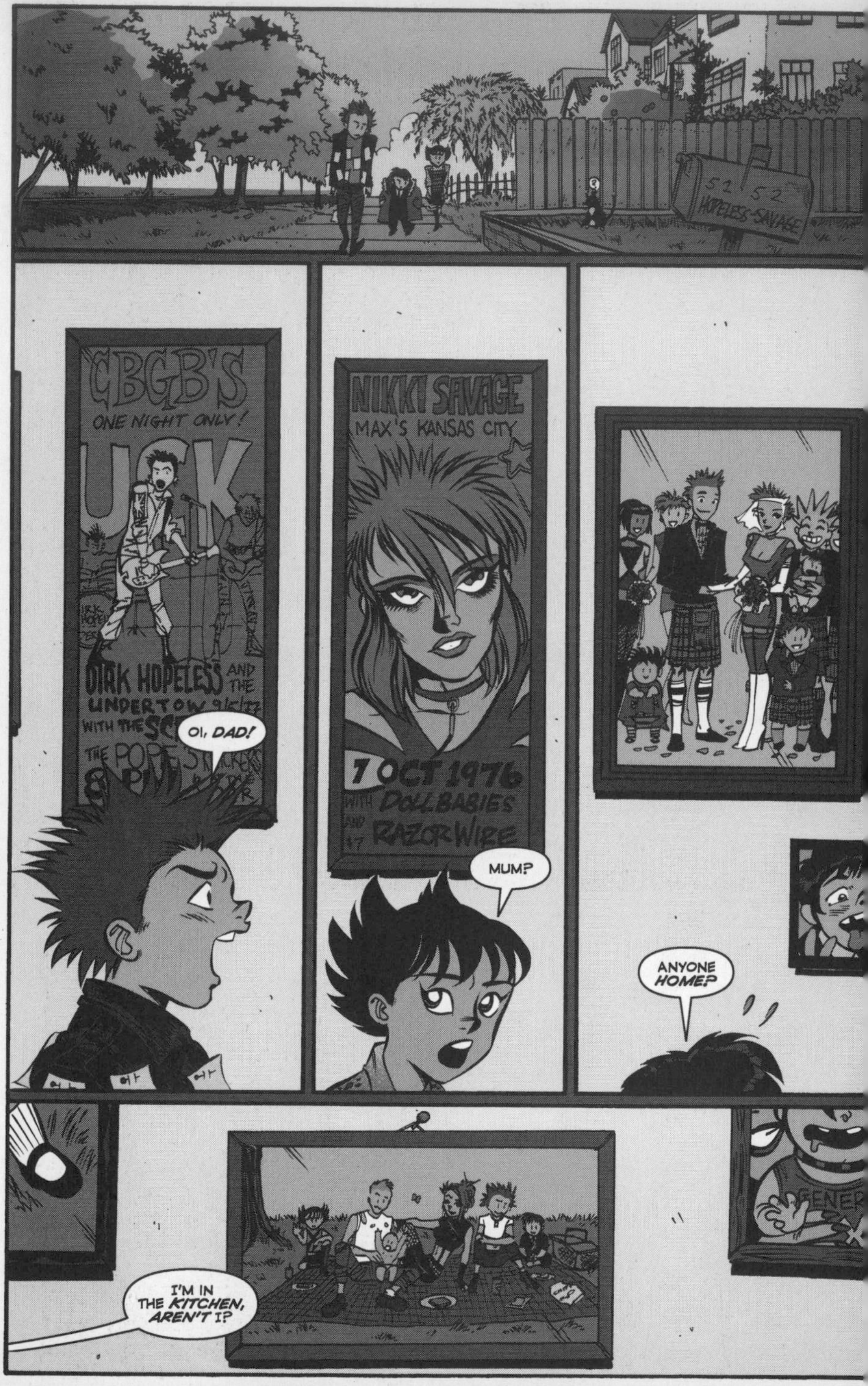
51 52
HOPELESS-SAVAGE
CBGB'S
ONE NIGHT ONLY!
DIRK HOPELESS AND THE UNDERTOW 9/5/77
OI, DAD!
NIKKI SAVAGE
MAX'S KANSAS CITY
7 OCT 1976
WITH DOLLBABIES AND 17 RAZOR WIRE
MUM?
ANYONE HOME?
I'M IN THE KITCHEN, AREN'T I?

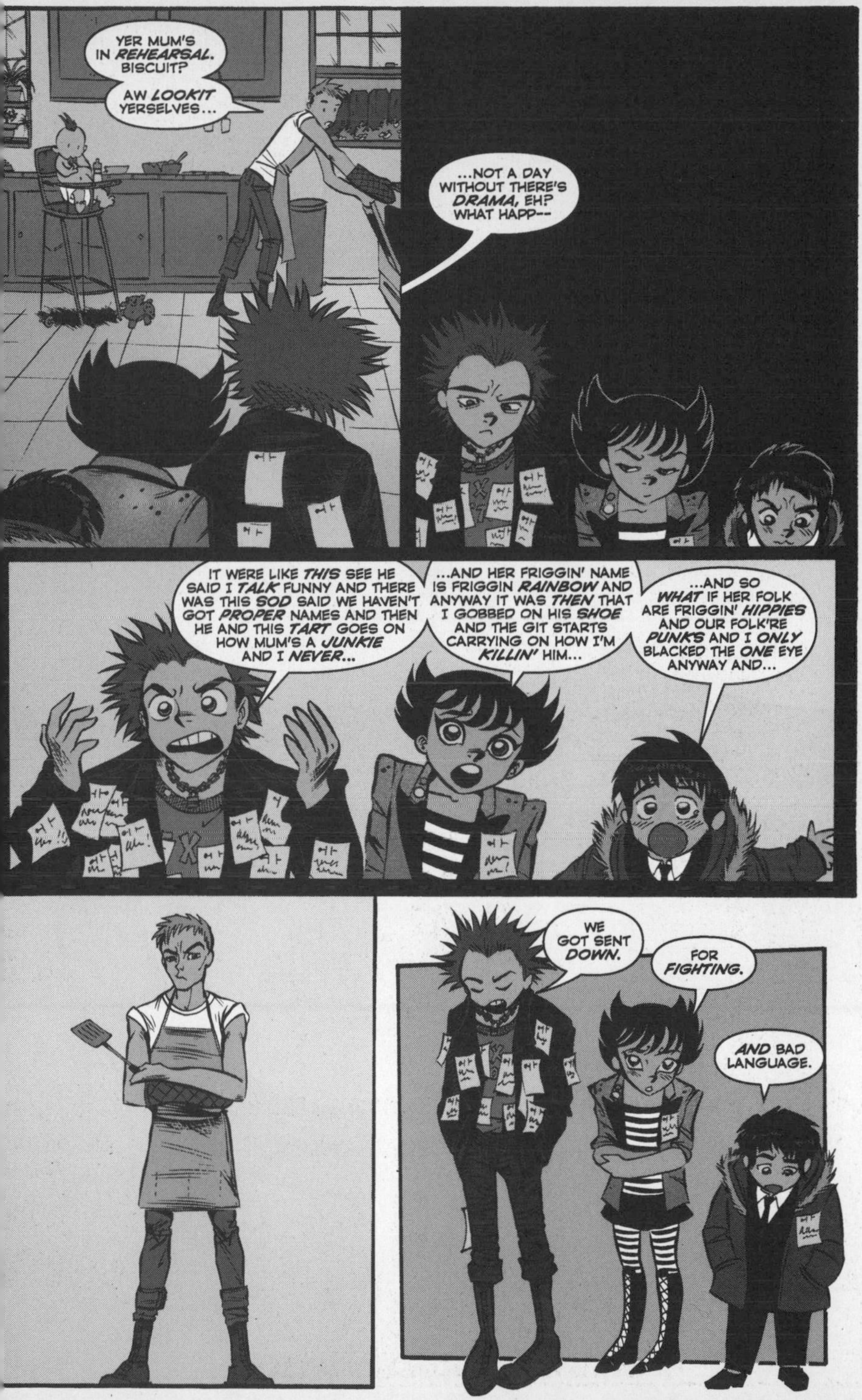
YER MUM'S IN *REHEARSAL.* BISCUIT?
AW *LOOKIT* YERSELVES...
...NOT A DAY WITHOUT THERE'S *DRAMA,* EH? WHAT HAPP--
IT WERE LIKE *THIS* SEE HE SAID I *TALK* FUNNY AND THERE WAS THIS *SOD* SAID WE HAVEN'T GOT *PROPER* NAMES AND THEN HE AND THIS *TART* GOES ON HOW MUM'S A *JUNKIE* AND I *NEVER*...
...AND HER FRIGGIN' NAME IS FRIGGIN *RAINBOW* AND ANYWAY IT WAS *THEN* THAT I GOBBED ON HIS *SHOE* AND THE GIT STARTS CARRYING ON HOW I'M *KILLIN'* HIM...
...AND SO *WHAT* IF HER FOLK ARE FRIGGIN' *HIPPIES* AND OUR FOLK'RE *PUNKS* AND I *ONLY* BLACKED THE *ONE* EYE ANYWAY AND...
WE GOT SENT *DOWN.*
FOR *FIGHTING.*
AND BAD LANGUAGE.

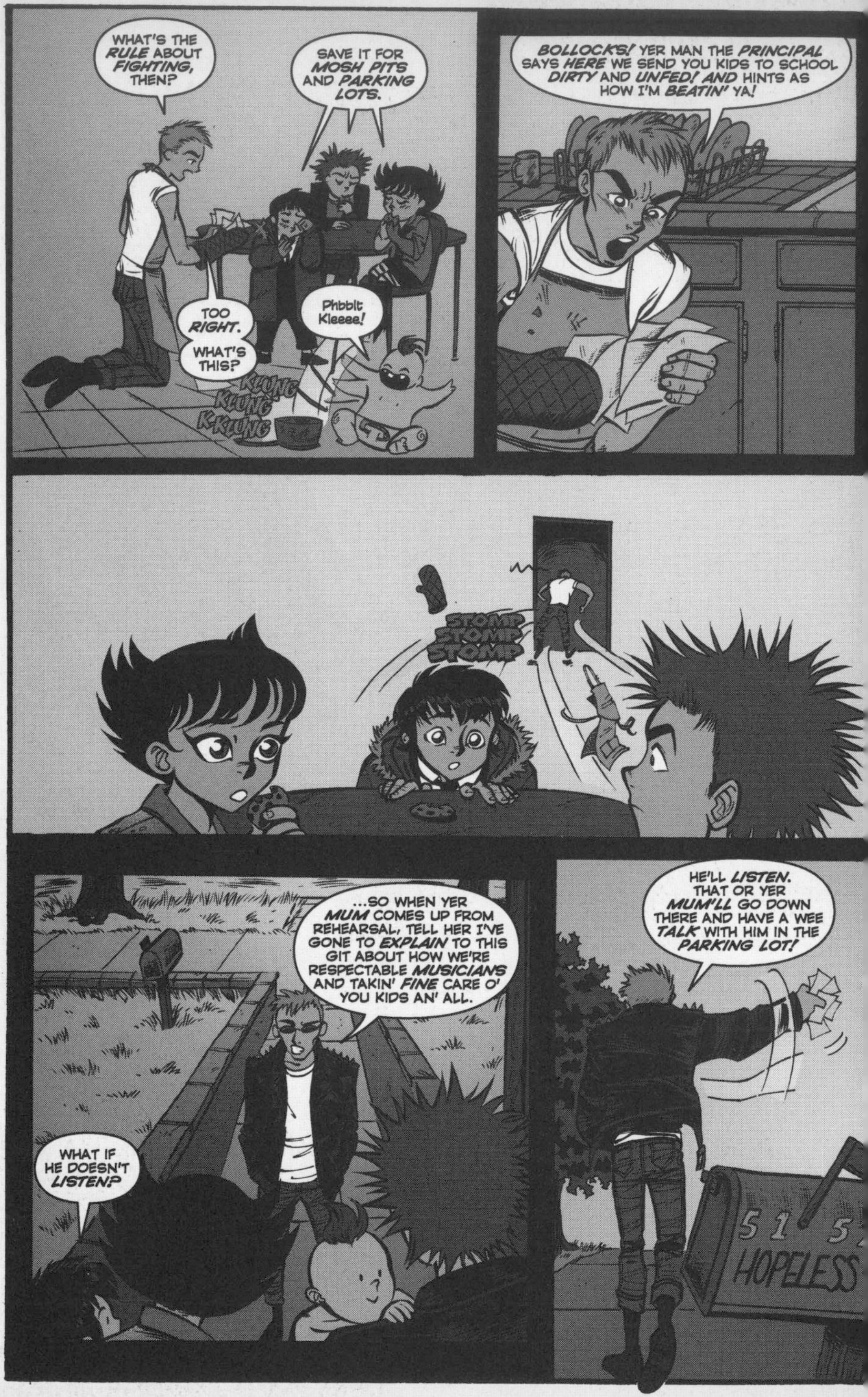

WHAT'S THE RULE ABOUT FIGHTING, THEN?
SAVE IT FOR MOSH PITS AND PARKING LOTS.
TOO RIGHT.
WHAT'S THIS?
Phbblt Kleeee!
KLUNG
KLUNG
K-KLUNG
BOLLOCKS! YER MAN THE PRINCIPAL SAYS HERE WE SEND YOU KIDS TO SCHOOL DIRTY AND UNFED! AND HINTS AS HOW I'M BEATIN' YA!
STOMP
STOMP
STOMP
...SO WHEN YER MUM COMES UP FROM REHEARSAL, TELL HER I'VE GONE TO EXPLAIN TO THIS GIT ABOUT HOW WE'RE RESPECTABLE MUSICIANS AND TAKIN' FINE CARE O' YOU KIDS AN' ALL.
WHAT IF HE DOESN'T LISTEN?
HE'LL LISTEN. THAT OR YER MUM'LL GO DOWN THERE AND HAVE A WEE TALK WITH HIM IN THE PARKING LOT!
HOPELESS

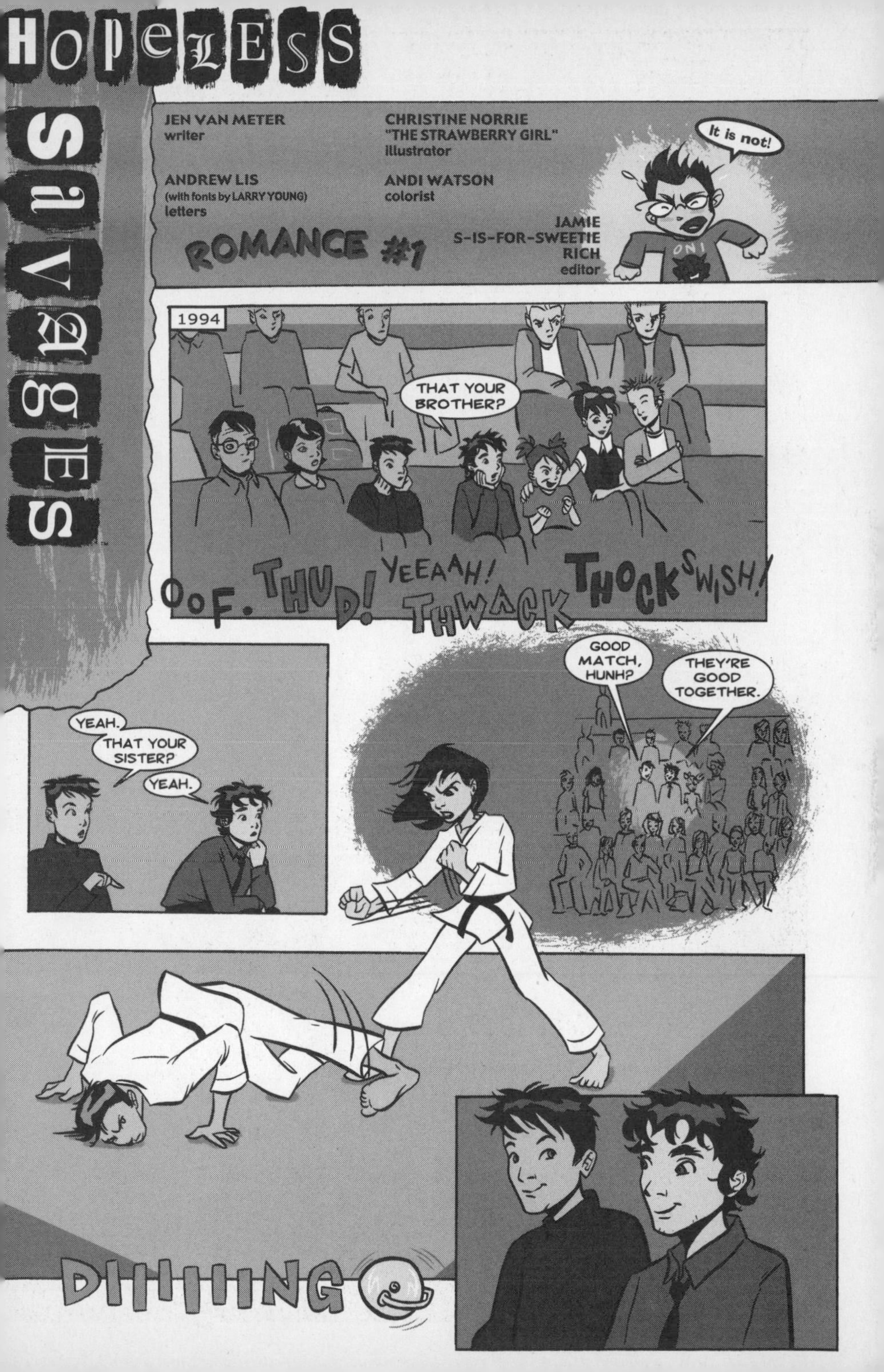

HOPELESS SAVAGES
JEN VAN METER
writer
CHRISTINE NORRIE
"THE STRAWBERRY GIRL"
illustrator
ANDREW LIS
(with fonts by LARRY YOUNG)
letters
ANDI WATSON
colorist
JAMIE
S-IS-FOR-SWEETIE
RICH
editor
ROMANCE #1
It is not!
1994
THAT YOUR BROTHER?
OOF. THUD! YEEAAH! THWACK THOCK SWISH!
YEAH.
THAT YOUR SISTER?
YEAH.
GOOD MATCH, HUNH?
THEY'RE GOOD TOGETHER.
DIIIIING

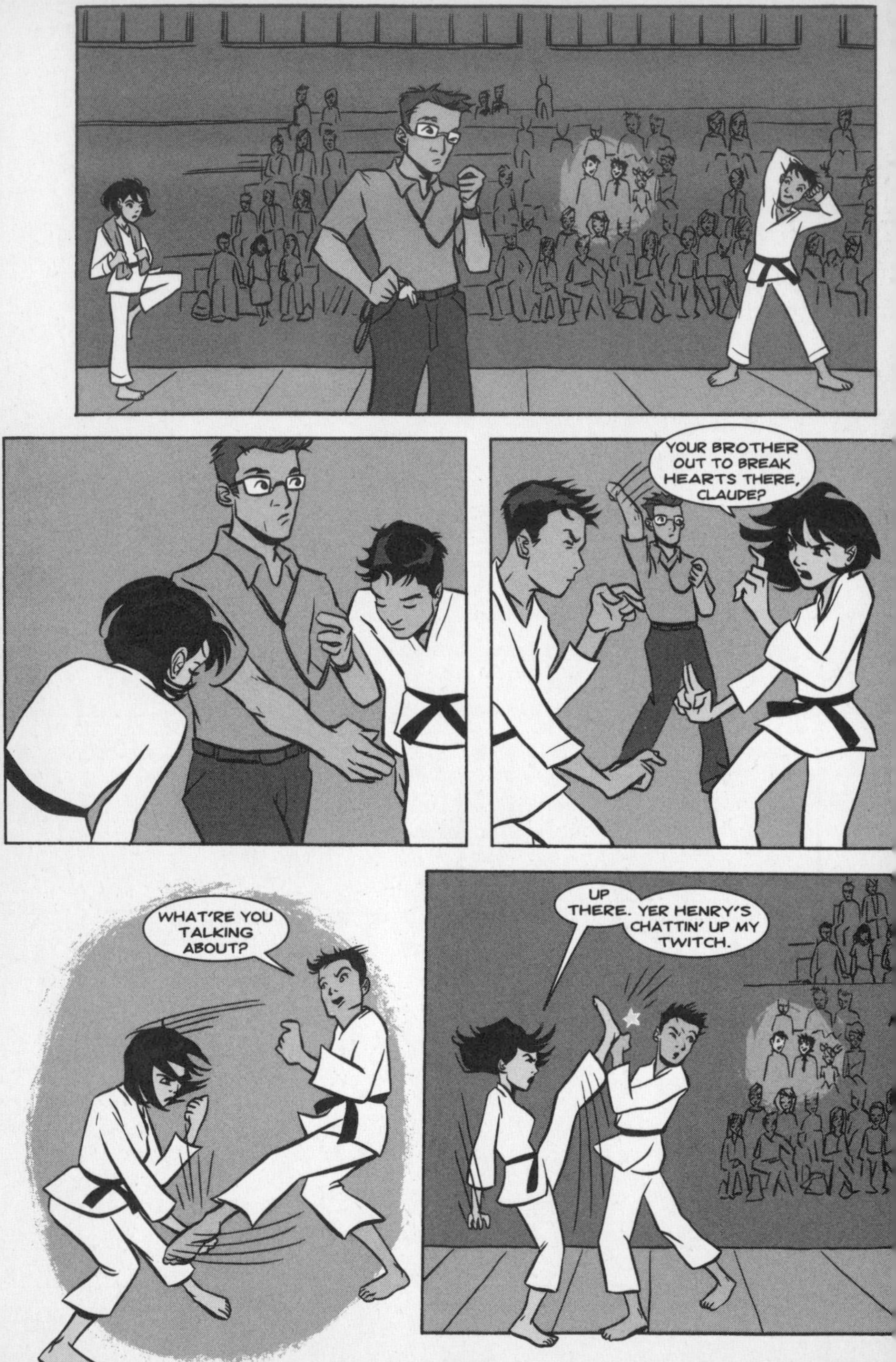
YOUR BROTHER OUT TO BREAK HEARTS THERE, CLAUDE?
WHAT'RE YOU TALKING ABOUT?
UP THERE. YER HENRY'S CHATTIN' UP MY TWITCH.

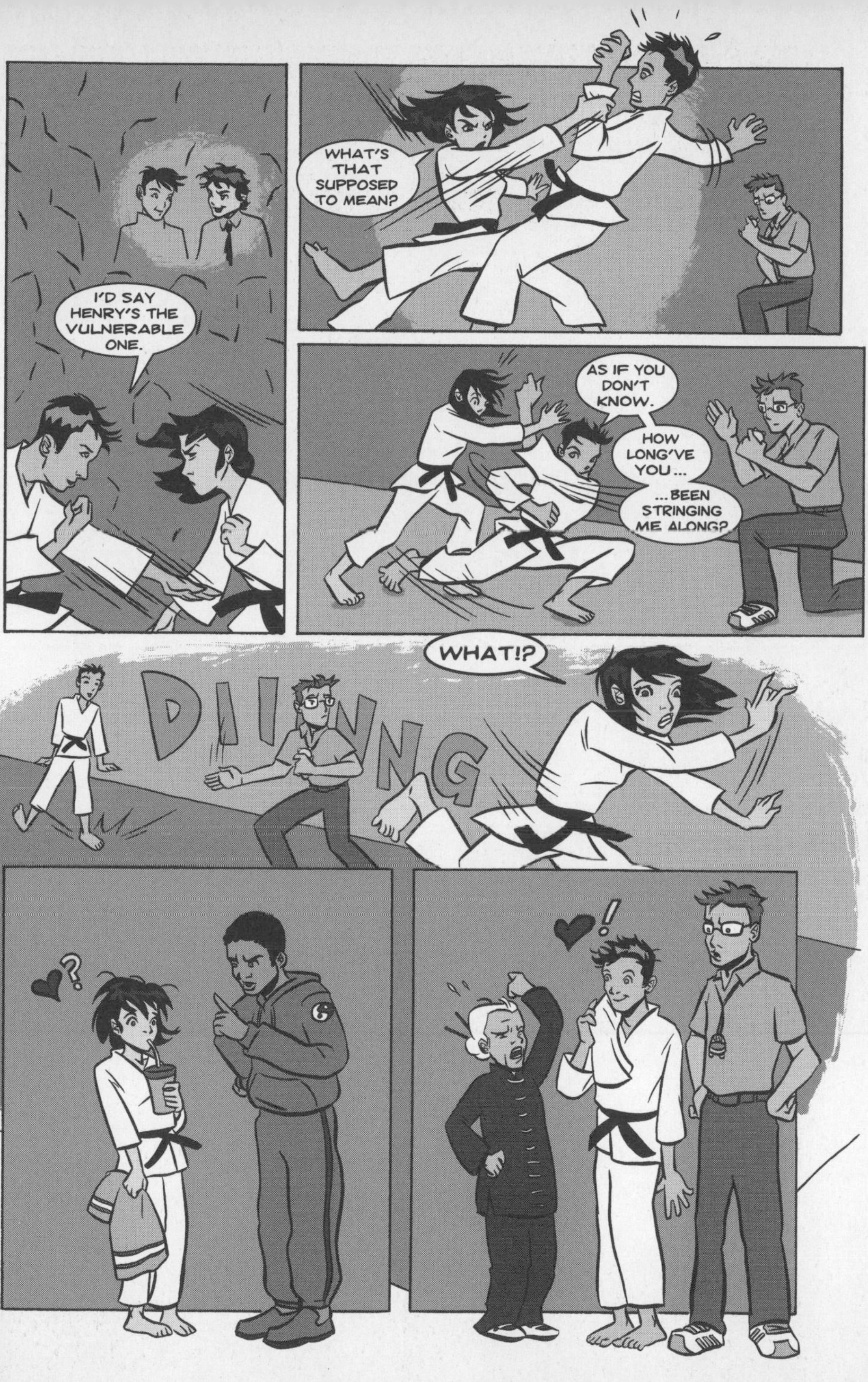
I'D SAY HENRY'S THE VULNERABLE ONE.
WHAT'S THAT SUPPOSED TO MEAN?
AS IF YOU DON'T KNOW.
HOW LONG'VE YOU...
...BEEN STRINGING ME ALONG?
WHAT!?
DIIING

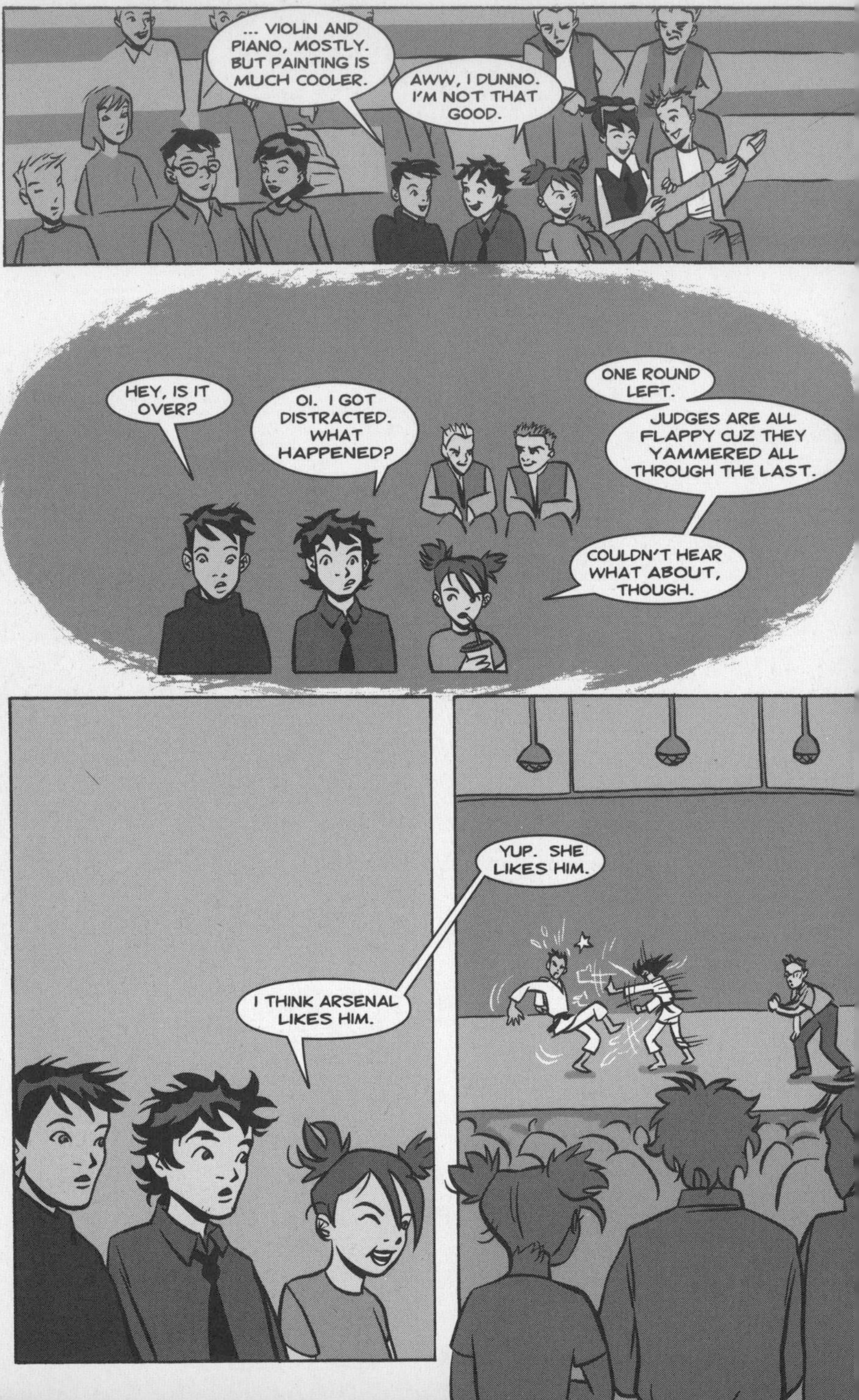
... VIOLIN AND PIANO, MOSTLY. BUT PAINTING IS MUCH COOLER.
AWW, I DUNNO. I'M NOT THAT GOOD.
HEY, IS IT OVER?
OI. I GOT DISTRACTED. WHAT HAPPENED?
ONE ROUND LEFT.
JUDGES ARE ALL FLAPPY CUZ THEY YAMMERED ALL THROUGH THE LAST.
COULDN'T HEAR WHAT ABOUT, THOUGH.
I THINK ARSENAL LIKES HIM.
YUP. SHE LIKES HIM.

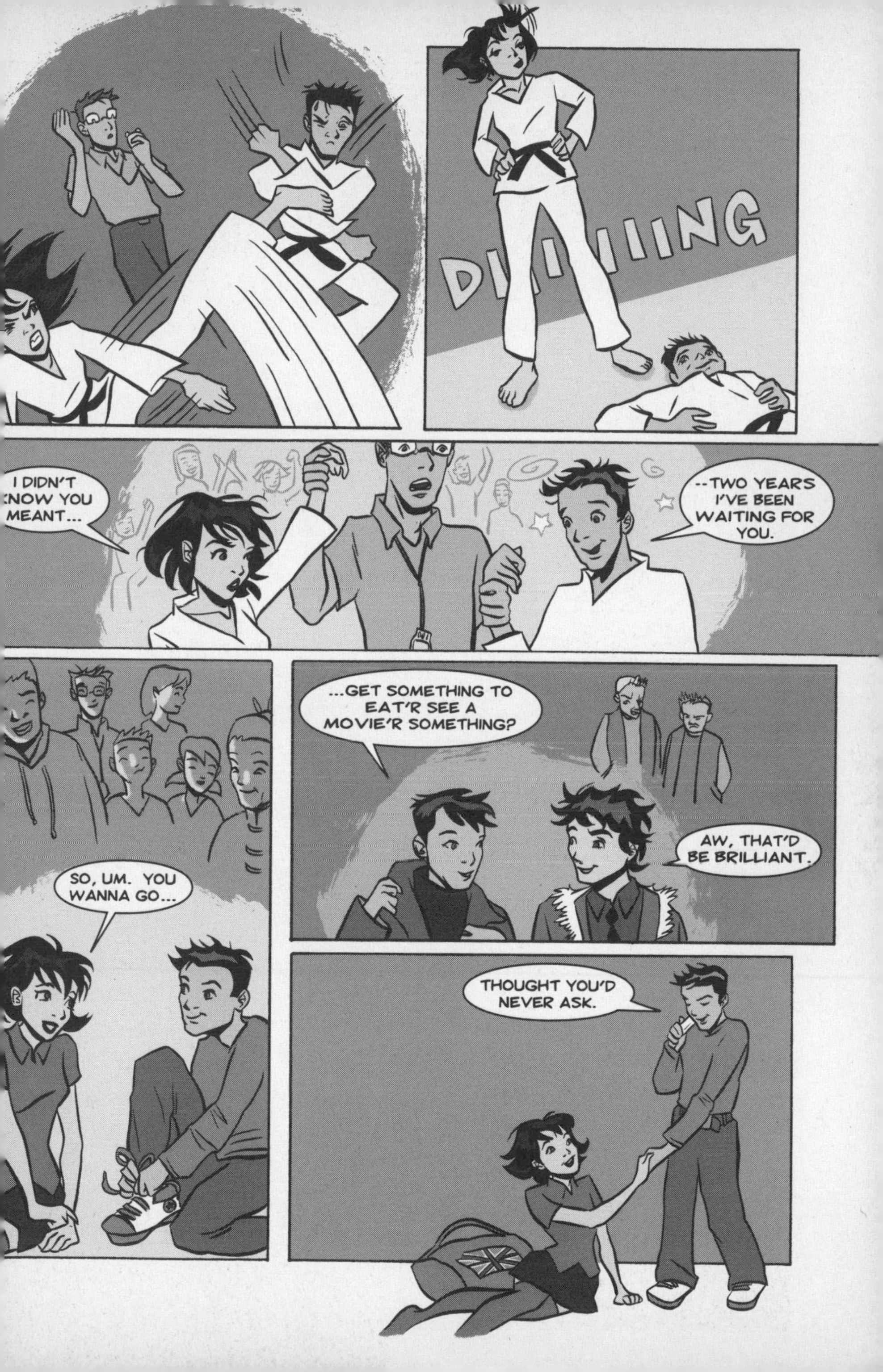
DIIIIIIING
I DIDN'T KNOW YOU MEANT...
--TWO YEARS I'VE BEEN WAITING FOR YOU.
SO, UM. YOU WANNA GO...
...GET SOMETHING TO EAT'R SEE A MOVIE'R SOMETHING?
AW, THAT'D BE BRILLIANT.
THOUGHT YOU'D NEVER ASK.

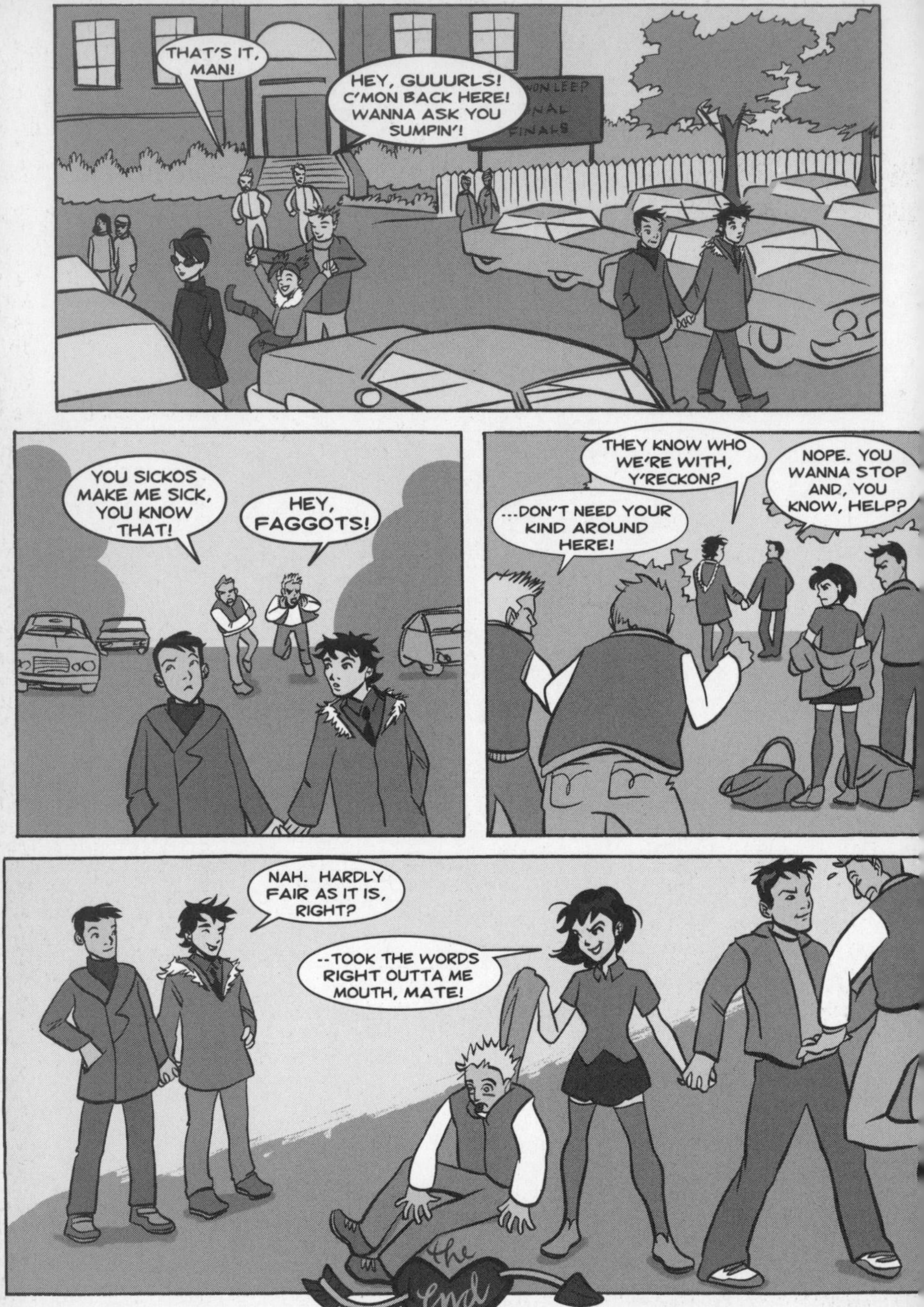
THAT'S IT, MAN!
HEY, GUUURLS! C'MON BACK HERE! WANNA ASK YOU SUMPIN'!
YOU SICKOS MAKE ME SICK, YOU KNOW THAT!
HEY, FAGGOTS!
THEY KNOW WHO WE'RE WITH, Y'RECKON?
...DON'T NEED YOUR KIND AROUND HERE!
NOPE. YOU WANNA STOP AND, YOU KNOW, HELP?
NAH. HARDLY FAIR AS IT IS, RIGHT?
--TOOK THE WORDS RIGHT OUTTA ME MOUTH, MATE!
the end

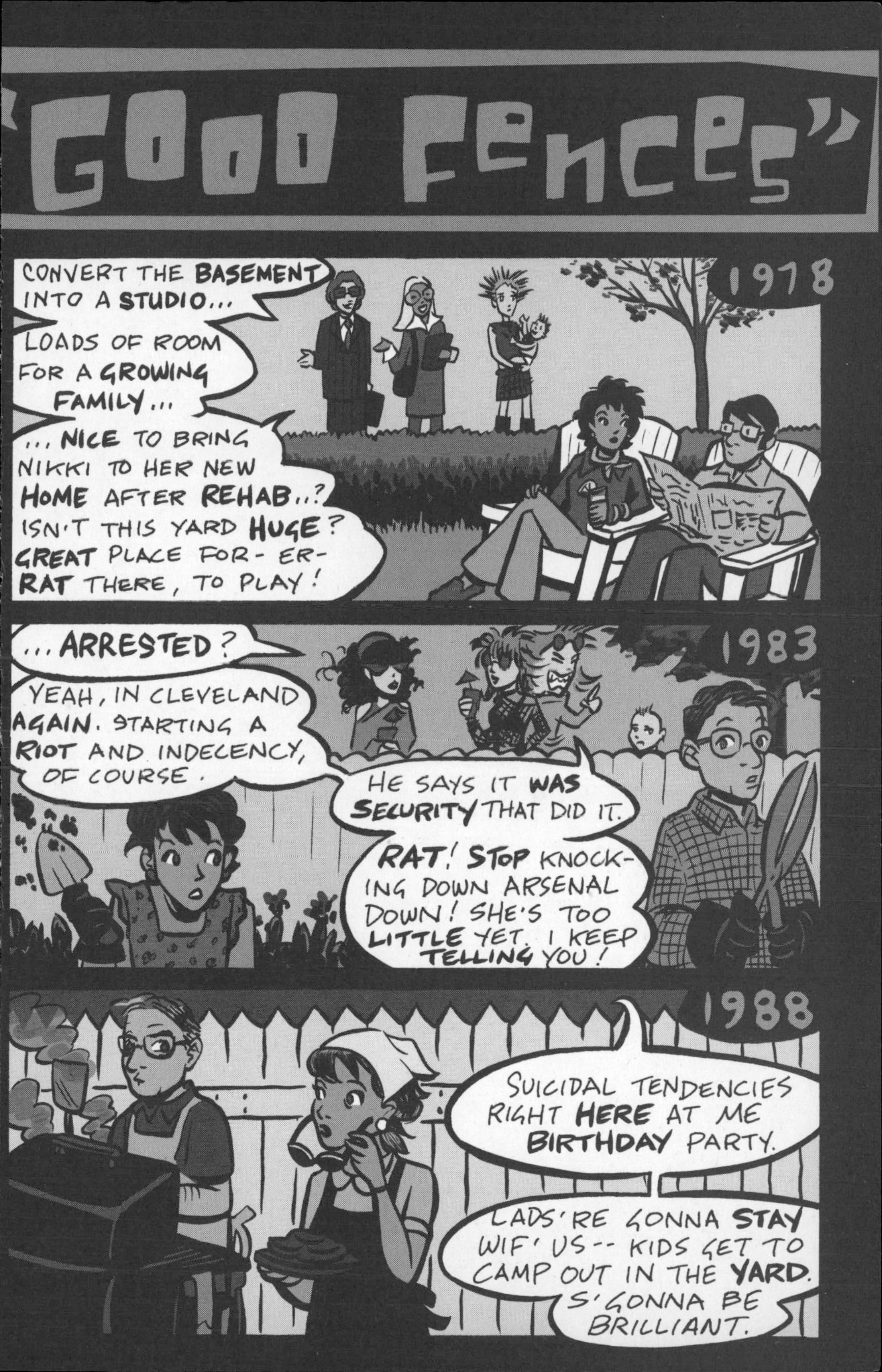
"GOOD FENCES"
1978
CONVERT THE BASEMENT INTO A STUDIO...
LOADS OF ROOM FOR A GROWING FAMILY...
...NICE TO BRING NIKKI TO HER NEW HOME AFTER REHAB..? ISN'T THIS YARD HUGE? GREAT PLACE FOR- ER- RAT THERE, TO PLAY!
1983
...ARRESTED?
YEAH, IN CLEVELAND AGAIN. STARTING A RIOT AND INDECENCY, OF COURSE.
HE SAYS IT WAS SECURITY THAT DID IT.
RAT! STOP KNOCKING DOWN ARSENAL DOWN! SHE'S TOO LITTLE YET. I KEEP TELLING YOU!
1988
SUICIDAL TENDENCIES RIGHT HERE AT ME BIRTHDAY PARTY.
LADS'RE GONNA STAY WIF' US-- KIDS GET TO CAMP OUT IN THE YARD. S'GONNA BE BRILLIANT.

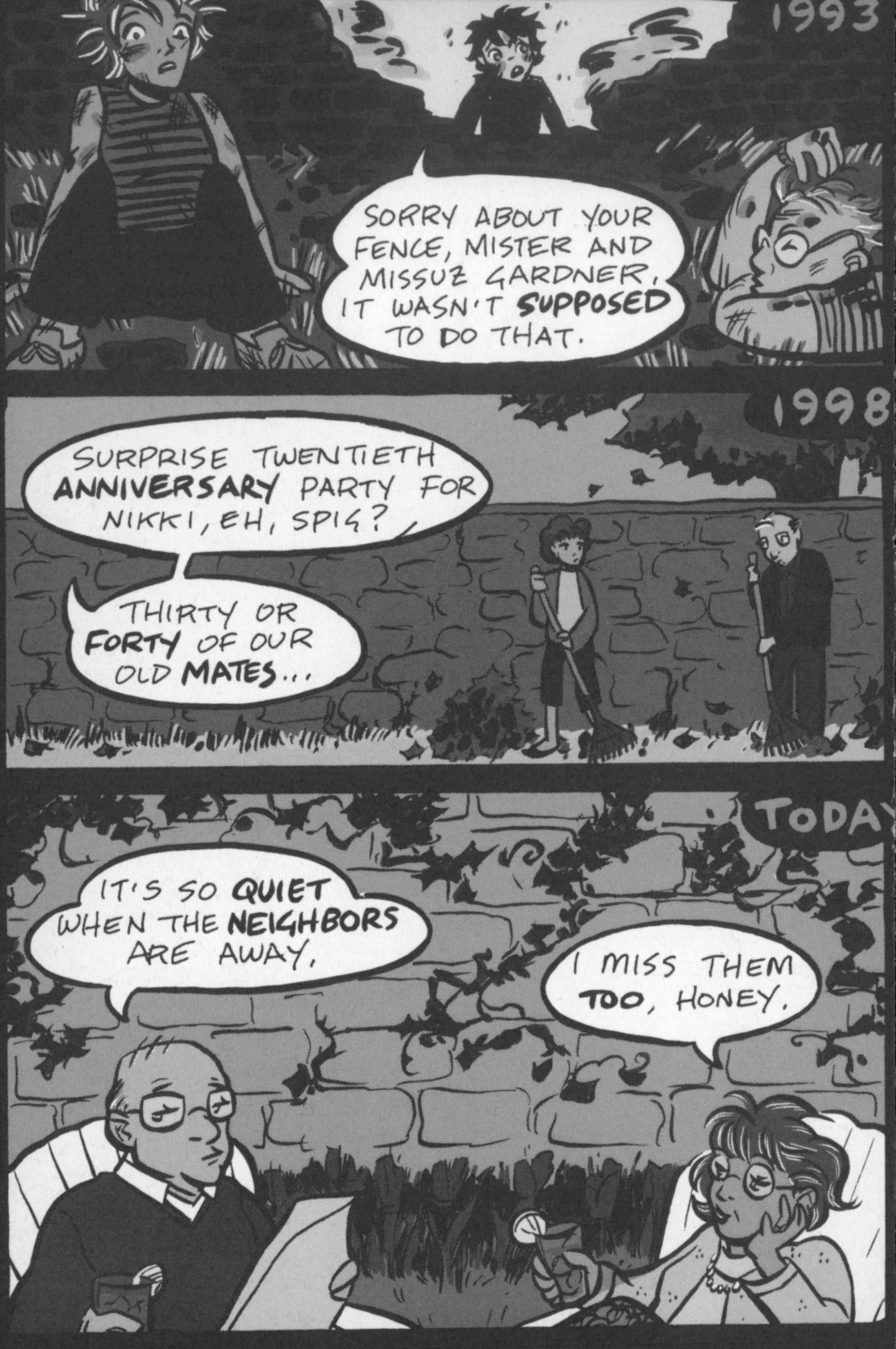
1993
SORRY ABOUT YOUR FENCE, MISTER AND MISSUZ GARDNER, IT WASN'T **SUPPOSED** TO DO THAT.
1998
SURPRISE TWENTIETH **ANNIVERSARY** PARTY FOR NIKKI, EH, SPIG?
THIRTY OR **FORTY** OF OUR OLD **MATES**...
TODAY
IT'S SO **QUIET** WHEN THE **NEIGHBORS** ARE AWAY.
I MISS THEM **TOO**, HONEY.

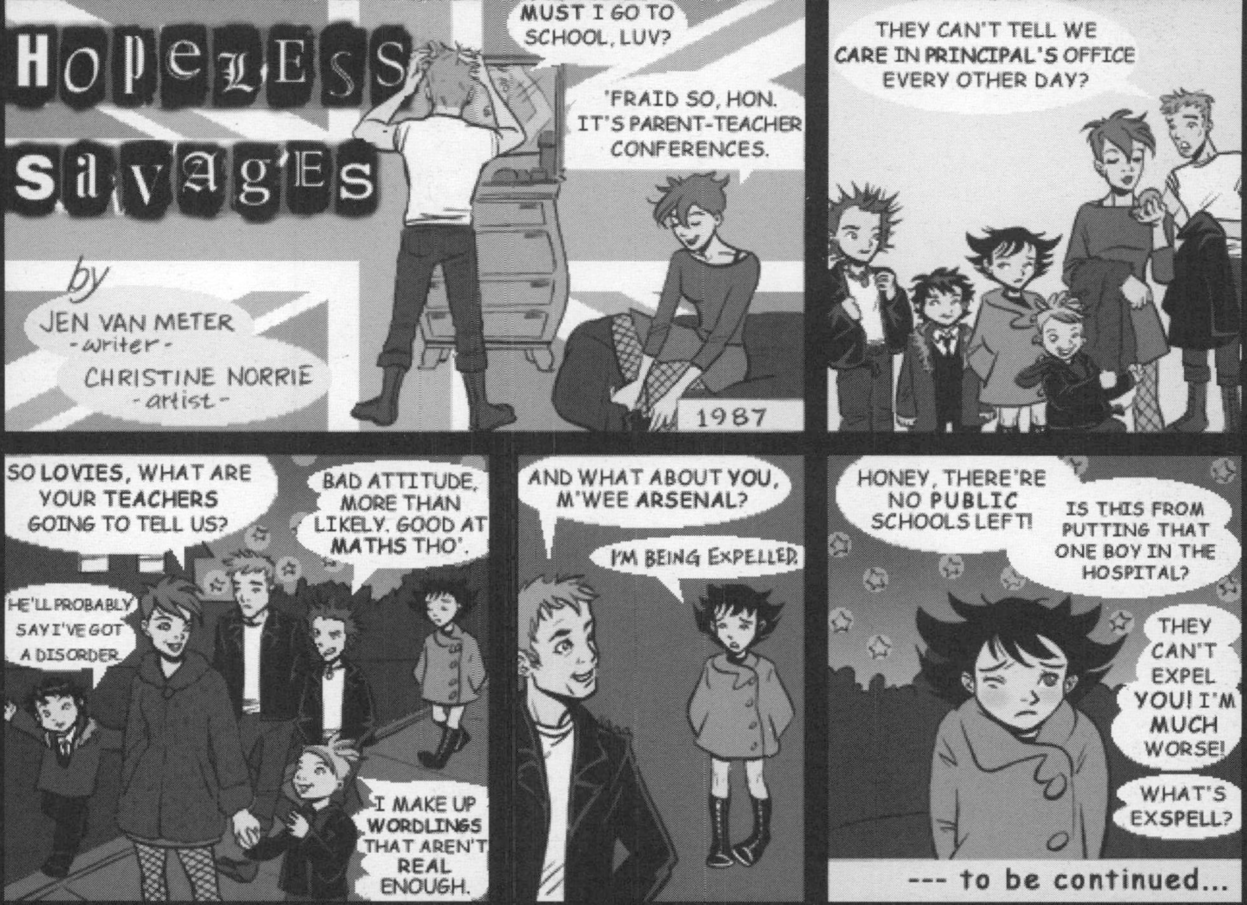
HOPELESS SAVAGES
by
JEN VAN METER -writer-
CHRISTINE NORRIE -artist-
MUST I GO TO SCHOOL, LUV?
'FRAID SO, HON. IT'S PARENT-TEACHER CONFERENCES.
1987
THEY CAN'T TELL WE CARE IN PRINCIPAL'S OFFICE EVERY OTHER DAY?
SO LOVIES, WHAT ARE YOUR TEACHERS GOING TO TELL US?
BAD ATTITUDE, MORE THAN LIKELY. GOOD AT MATHS THO'.
HE'LL PROBABLY SAY I'VE GOT A DISORDER.
I MAKE UP WORDLINGS THAT AREN'T REAL ENOUGH.
AND WHAT ABOUT YOU, M'WEE ARSENAL?
I'M BEING EXPELLED.
HONEY, THERE'RE NO PUBLIC SCHOOLS LEFT!
IS THIS FROM PUTTING THAT ONE BOY IN THE HOSPITAL?
THEY CAN'T EXPEL YOU! I'M MUCH WORSE!
WHAT'S EXSPELL?
--- to be continued...

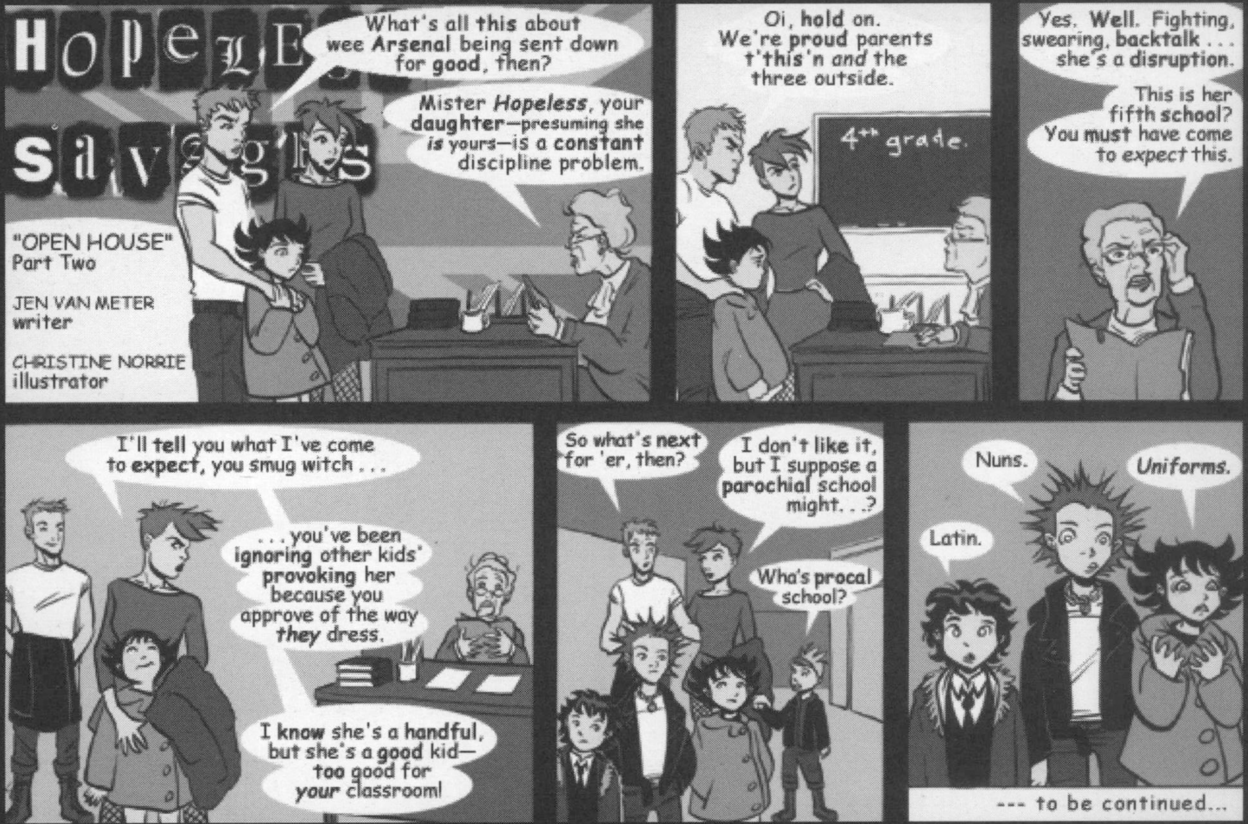
Hopeless Savages
"OPEN HOUSE"
Part Two
JEN VAN METER
writer
CHRISTINE NORRIE
illustrator
What's all this about wee Arsenal being sent down for good, then?
Mister Hopeless, your daughter—presuming she is yours—is a constant discipline problem.
Oi, hold on. We're proud parents t'this'n and the three outside.
4th grade.
Yes. Well. Fighting, swearing, backtalk . . . she's a disruption.
This is her fifth school? You must have come to expect this.
I'll tell you what I've come to expect, you smug witch . . .
. . . you've been ignoring other kids' provoking her because you approve of the way they dress.
I know she's a handful, but she's a good kid—too good for your classroom!
So what's next for 'er, then?
I don't like it, but I suppose a parochial school might. . .?
Wha's procal school?
Nuns.
Uniforms.
Latin.
--- to be continued...

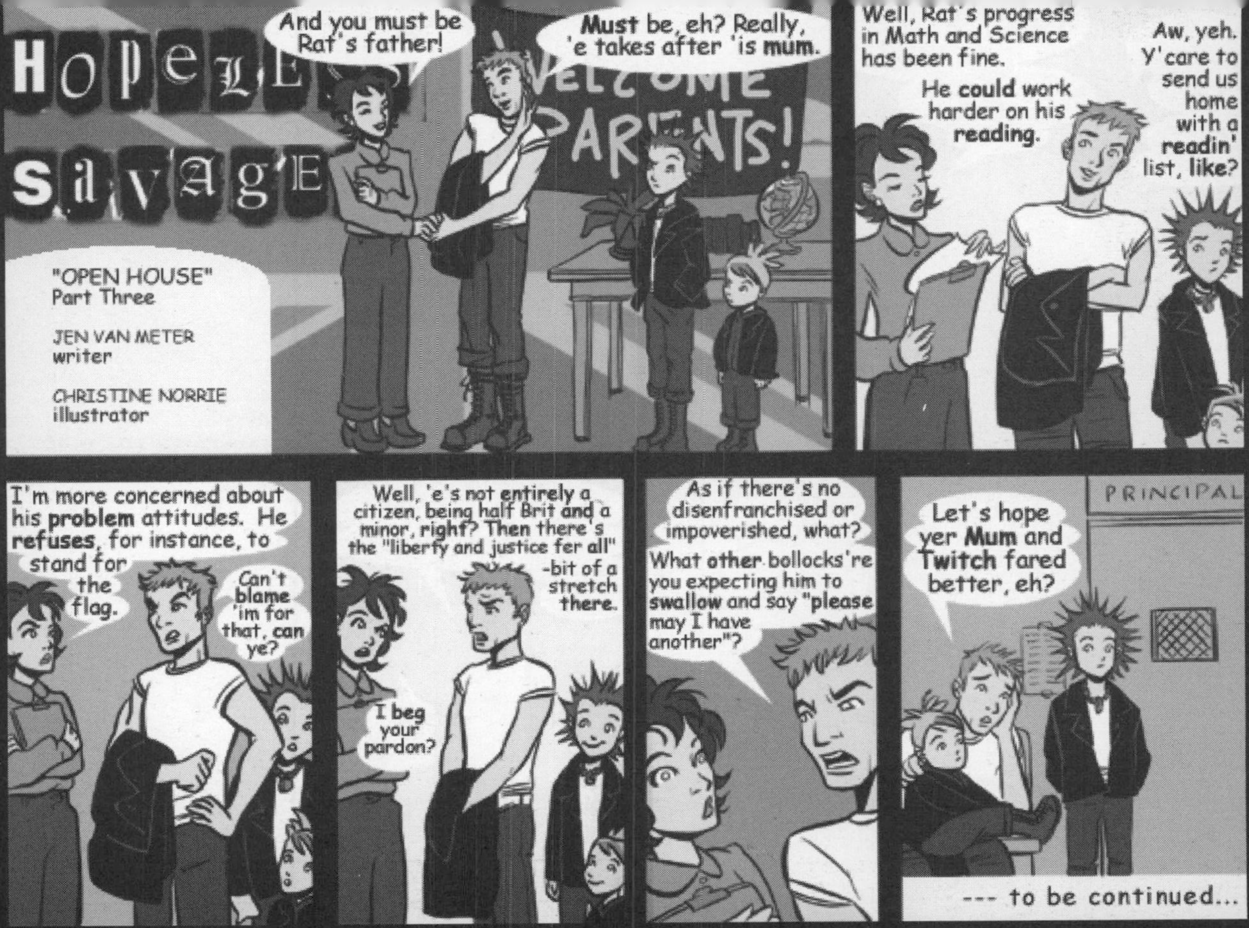
HOPELESS SAVAGE
"OPEN HOUSE"
Part Three
JEN VAN METER
writer
CHRISTINE NORRIE
illustrator
And you must be Rat's father!
Must be, eh? Really, 'e takes after 'is mum.
WELCOME PARENTS!
Well, Rat's progress in Math and Science has been fine.
He could work harder on his reading.
Aw, yeh. Y'care to send us home with a readin' list, like?
I'm more concerned about his problem attitudes. He refuses, for instance, to stand for the flag.
Can't blame 'im for that, can ye?
Well, 'e's not entirely a citizen, being half Brit and a minor, right? Then there's the "liberty and justice fer all" -bit of a stretch there.
I beg your pardon?
As if there's no disenfranchised or impoverished, what?
What other bollocks're you expecting him to swallow and say "please may I have another"?
PRINCIPAL
Let's hope yer Mum and Twitch fared better, eh?
--- to be continued...

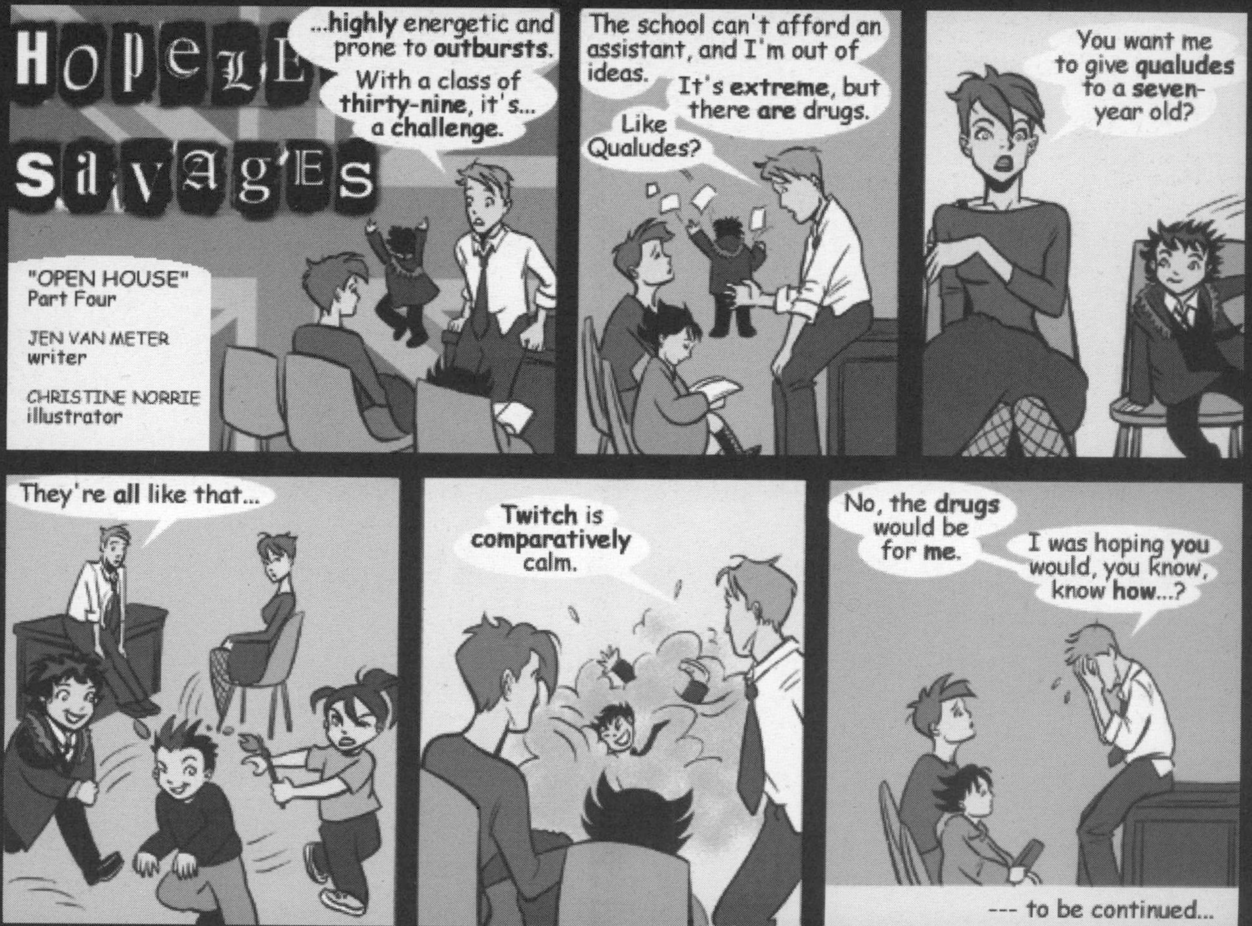
HOPELESS SAVAGES
...highly energetic and prone to outbursts.
With a class of thirty-nine, it's... a challenge.
"OPEN HOUSE" Part Four
JEN VAN METER writer
CHRISTINE NORRIE illustrator
The school can't afford an assistant, and I'm out of ideas.
It's extreme, but there are drugs.
Like Qualudes?
You want me to give qualudes to a seven-year old?
They're all like that...
Twitch is comparatively calm.
No, the drugs would be for me.
I was hoping you would, you know, know how...?
--- to be continued...

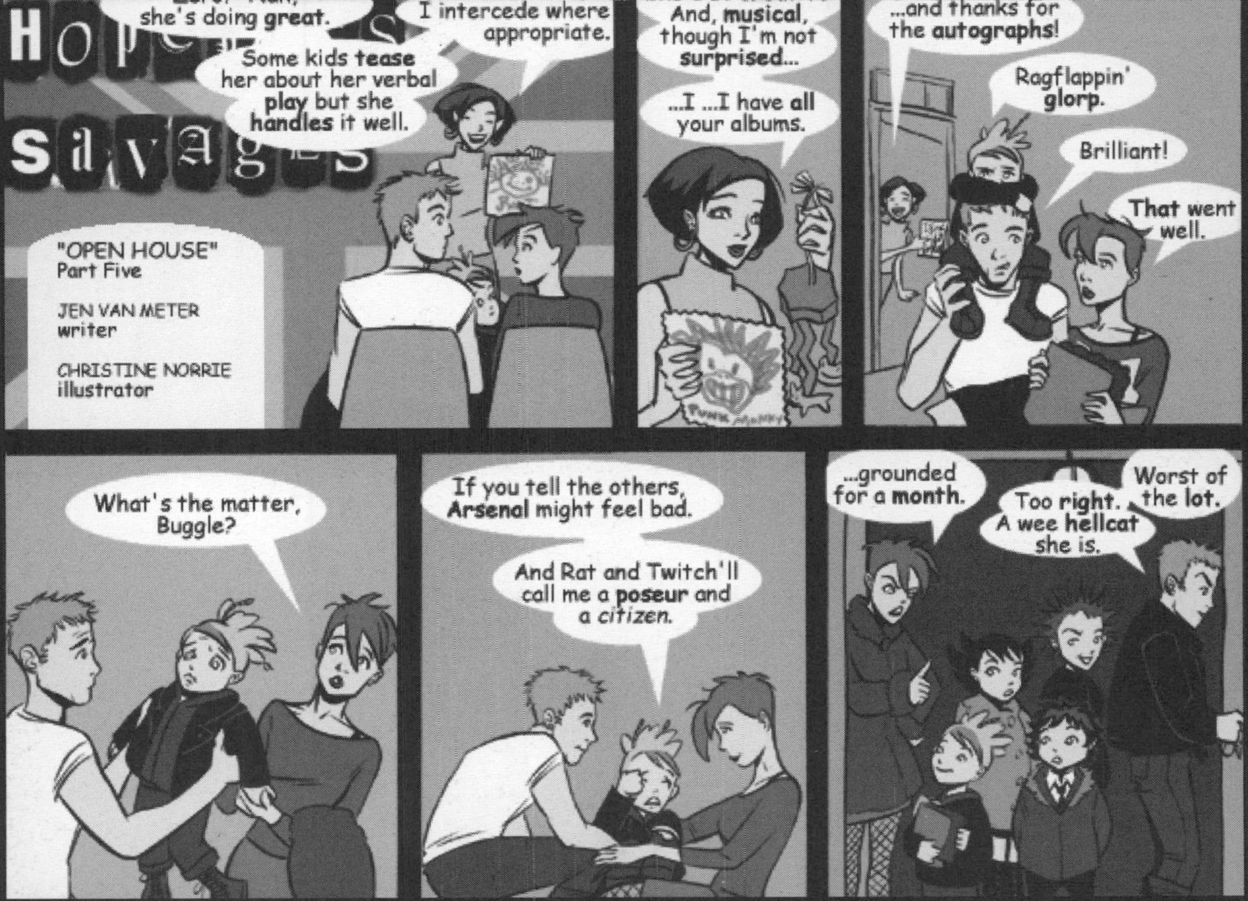
she's doing great.
Some kids tease her about her verbal play but she handles it well.
I intercede where appropriate.
"OPEN HOUSE" Part Five
JEN VAN METER writer
CHRISTINE NORRIE illustrator
And, musical, though I'm not surprised...
...I ...I have all your albums.
...and thanks for the autographs!
Ragflappin' glorp.
Brilliant!
That went well.
What's the matter, Buggle?
If you tell the others, Arsenal might feel bad.
And Rat and Twitch'll call me a poseur and a citizen.
...grounded for a month.
Too right. A wee hellcat she is.
Worst of the lot.

JEN VAN METER made her comic book debut alongside Buffy the Vampire Slayer, scripting that character's first-ever comic book story for the *Dark Horse Presents Annual 1998*. She followed it up with a collaboration with Frank Quitely in Vertigo's horror anthology *Flinch*, a script for DC's *Gotham Knights*, a segment of Marvel's *Captain America* #50, and the licensed comic book tie-in *The Blair Witch Project*, the best-selling single issue in Oni Press' history. *Hopeless Savages* is her first creator-owned work (if you don't count her son, Elliot), and its first series was nominated for an Eisner in 2002. She has followed it with two more series, *Ground Zero* and the currently in progress *Too Much Hopeless Savages!* Her latest work for DC includes a *Batman* Elseworlds book called *Golden Streets of Gotham* and the current *Cinnamon: El Ciclo* miniseries. She recently had her second child.

Born in West Germany, CHRISTINE NORRIE has lived many places but fondly claims St.Louis as her hometown, the place she grew to love comic books. She moved to New York in the late nineties, worked in the business end of comic book publishing for DC Comics, and later became a freelance illustrator. Since the debut of the first *Hopeless Savages* series, she's been nominated for many awards including the prestigious Eisner Award, the Russ Manning Award, and was a recipient of the New York City Comic Book Museum's Award for Breakout Artist of 2002. Christine Norrie is the comic artist for *Redbook* magazine's *Q&A with John Gray: You and Him* and *Spy Kids* for Disney, and just published her first graphic novel, *Cheat*. She is currently at work on the third *Hopeless Savages* series and is pencilling *Bad Girls* for DC comics, while also preparing to do illustrations for the new edition of Sarah Grace McCandless' young adult novel *Grosse Pointe Girl* (coming June 2004 from Simon & Shuster). She resides in the historic North Shore of Staten Island in a menagerie of animals that includes a parakeet, rabbit, three cats, and the ever-marvelous dog, Orwell.

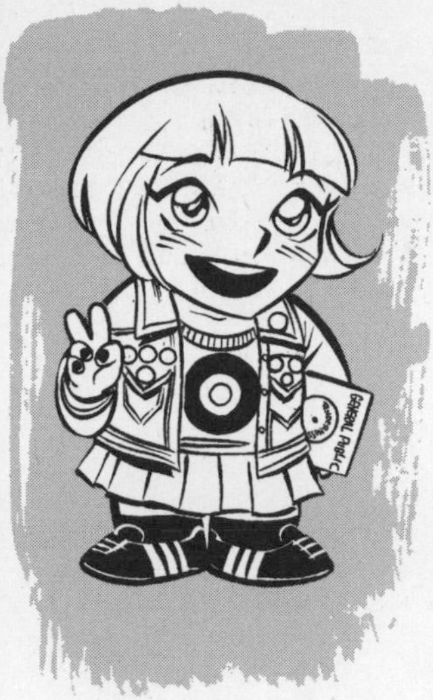

CHYNNA CLUGSTON-MAJOR is the talented cartoonist behind the award-nominated series, *Blue Monday*—available in three trade paperbacks, *The Kids are Alright*, *Absolute Beginners*, and *Inbetween Days*. She has also done work for Dark Horse's *Buffy the Vampire Slayer* comics, Paul Dini's *Jingle Belle*, Mike Allred's *The Atomics: Spaced Out & Grounded in Snap City*, Jamie S. Rich's novel *Cut My Hair*, and Marvel's *Ultimate Marvel Team-Up*. When not drawing, she is usually shouting at neighborhood children from her studio window or cooking up the best tacos known to man. She is currently midway through her six-issue miniseries *Scooter Girl* and will be returning to *Blue Monday* in 2004.

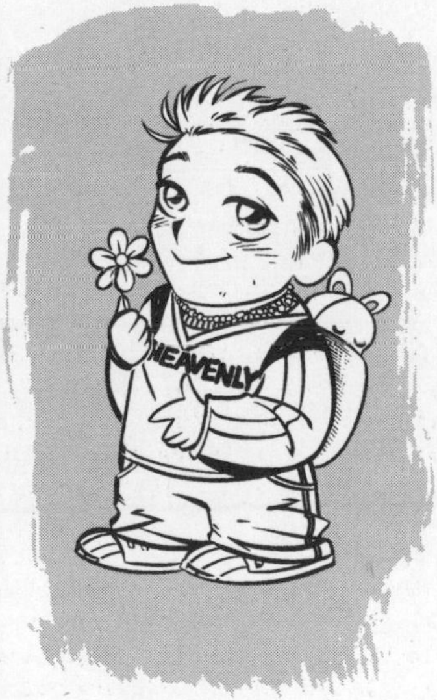
HEAVENLY

ANDI WATSON is the creator of *Skeleton Key*, *Geisha*, *Slow News Day*, *Dumped*, and *Breakfast After Noon*. He also scripted the *Buffy the Vampire Slayer* comics for two years, has optioned *Skeleton Key* for a cartoon series, designed animated advent calendars for AOL.co.uk, written books like *Namor* and *15-Love* for Marvel Comics, and had one of his cover images appear fleetingly in the background of teen flick *Coyote Ugly*. In the year 2001, Andi and *Breakfast After Noon* were nominated for an Eisner Award for Best Limited Series, the second nomination for the artist (he previously received notice for the collection of *Geisha* in 2000). He is currently hard at work on a brand-new series, *Love Fights*, for Oni Press, who have also released an expanded edition of *Geisha*. Similarly, Slave Labor has returned his first ever series, *Samurai Jam*, back to the shelves in a 10th anniversary edition. Despite his brushes with fame, he remains remarkably down to earth.

Illustrations this page by Chynna Clugston-Major; previous page: Van Meter drawing is by Christine Norrie, and Norrie is by Daniel Krall

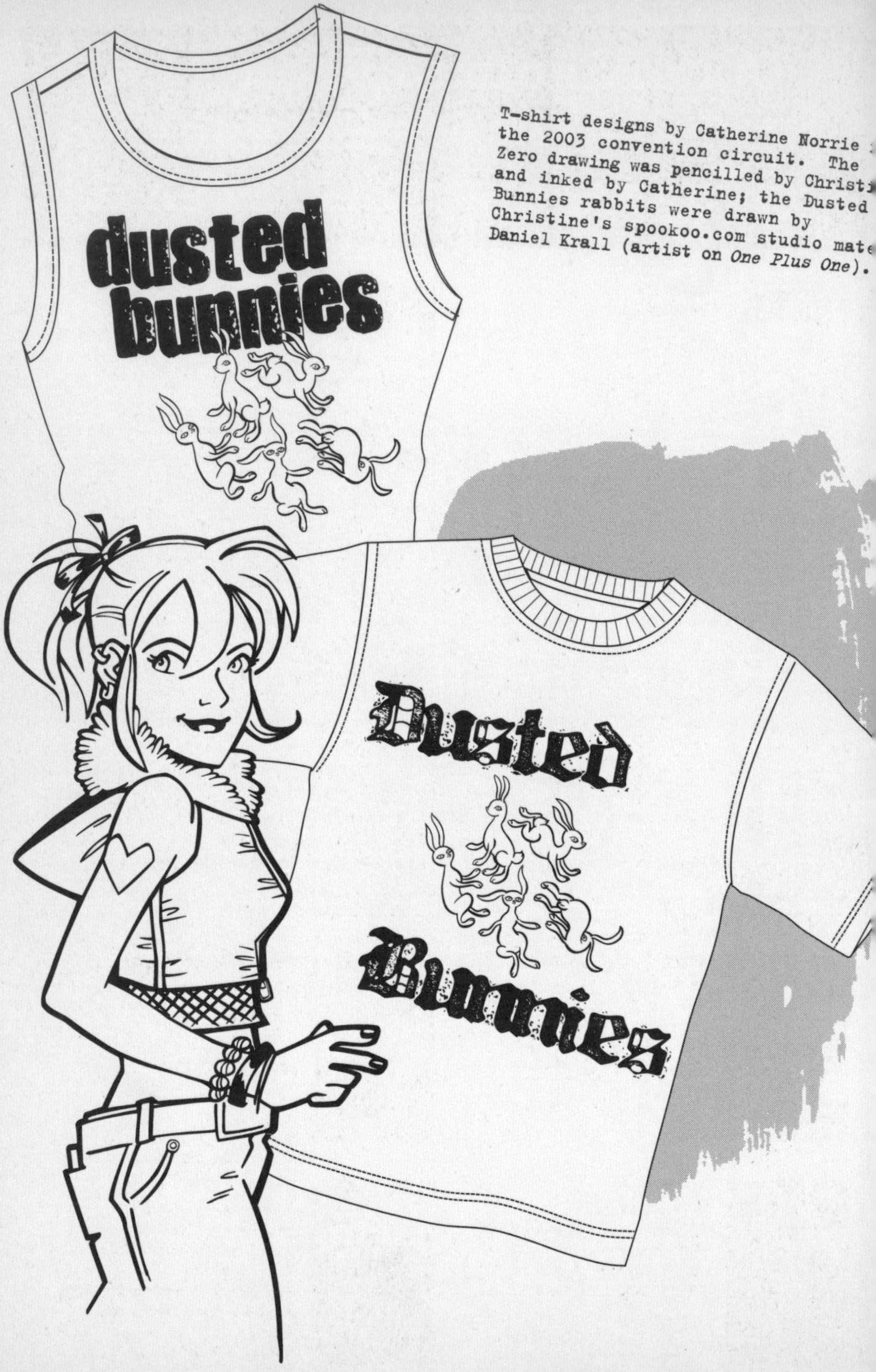
dusted
bunnies
Dusted
Bunnies

T-shirt designs by Catherine Norrie
the 2003 convention circuit. The
Zero drawing was pencilled by Christi
and inked by Catherine; the Dusted
Bunnies rabbits were drawn by
Christine's spookoo.com studio mate
Daniel Krall (artist on *One Plus One*).

Other books from the creators of *Hopeless Savages* and Oni Press...

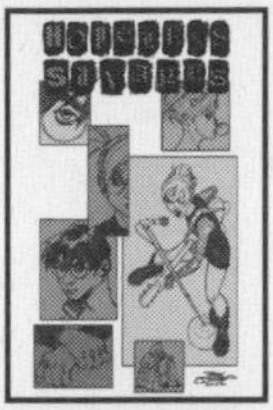

HOPELESS SAVAGES, Vol 2: GROUND ZERO™
by Jen Van Meter & Bryan O'Malley w/ Clugston-Major, Norrie, & Watson
128 pages,
black-and-white interiors
$11.95 US
ISBN: 1-929998-52-X

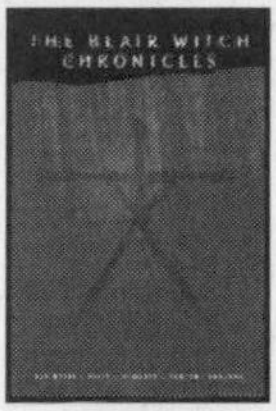
THE BLAIR WITCH CHRONICLES

THE BLAIR WITCH CHRONICLES
by Van Meter, Edwards, Mireault, Davis, & Fowler
120 pages,
black-and-white interiors
$15.95 US
ISBN: 1-929998-04-X

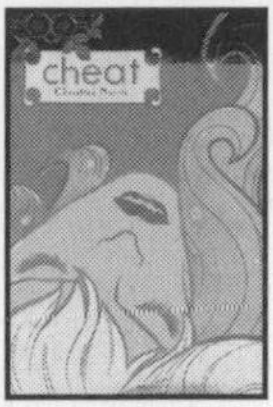
cheat

CHEAT™
by Christine Norrie
72 pages,
black-and-white interiors
$5.95 US
ISBN 1929998-47-3

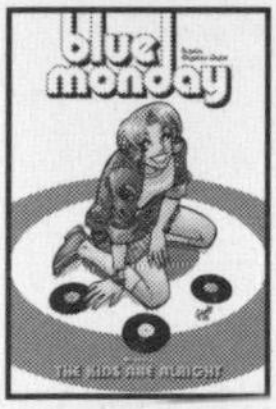
blue monday

BLUE MONDAY, Vol. 1: THE KIDS ARE ALRIGHT™
by Chynna Clugston-Major
136 pages,
black-and-white interiors
$10.95 US
ISBN: 1-929998-62-7

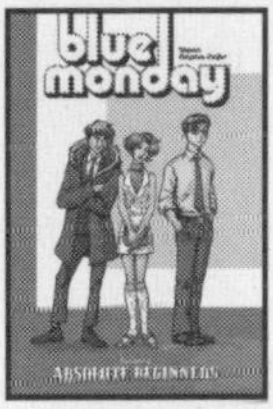
blue monday

BLUE MONDAY, Vol. 2: ABSOLUTE BEGINNERS™
by Chynna Clugston-Major
128 pages, black-and-white interiors
$11.95 US
ISBN 1-929998-17-1

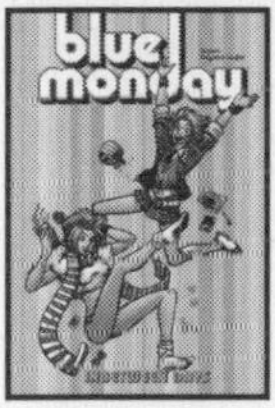
blue monday

BLUE MONDAY, Vol. 3: INBETWEEN DAYS™
by Chynna Clugston-Major
120 pages, black-and-white interiors
$9.95 US
ISBN: 1-929998-66-X

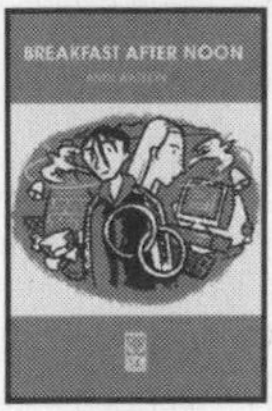
BREAKFAST AFTER NOON

BREAKFAST AFTER NOON™
by Andi Watson
208 pages, black-and-white interiors
$19.95 US, $30.95 CAN
ISBN: 1-929998-14-7

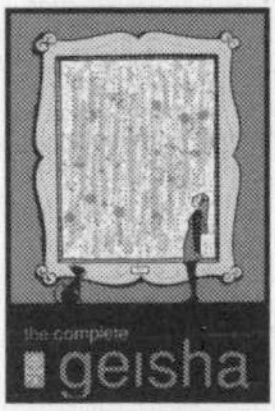
the complete
geisha

THE COMPLETE GEISHA™
by Andi Watson
152 pages, black-and-white interiors
$15.95 US
ISBN: 1929998-51-1

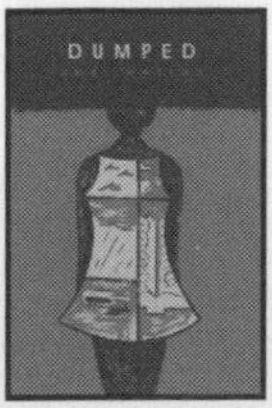
DUMPED

DUMPED™
by Andi Watson
56 pages, black-and-white interiors
$5.95 US, $8.95 CAN
ISBN: 1-929998-41-4

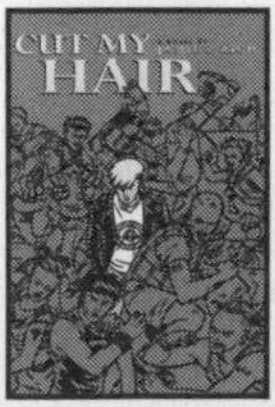
CUT MY HAIR

CUT MY HAIR™
by Jamie S. Rich
w/ Chynna Clugston-Major, Scott Morse, Judd Winick, & Andi Watson
236 pages, black-and-white text with illustrations
$15.95 US
ISBN: 0-9700387-0-4

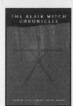

OTHER BOOKS AVAILABLE FROM ONI PRESS...

*THE ATOMICS: SPACED OUT AND
GROUNDED IN SNAP CITY™*
by Allred, Bone, Clugston-
Major, Marvit, & Ontiveros
112 pages,
full-color interiors
$12.95 US
ISBN 1-929998-67-8
Available October 2003.

*COURTNEY CRUMRIN &
THE NIGHT THINGS™ Vol. 1*
by Ted Naifeh
128 pages,
black-and-white interiors
$11.95 US
ISBN: 1-929998-60-0

JINGLE BELLE'S COOL YULE™
by Paul Dini, Chynna Clugston-
Major, Jeff Smith,
Jill Thompson, etc.
132 pages black & white,
8 pages color
$13.95 US
ISBN: 1-929998-36-8

LOST AT SEA™
by Bryan Lee O'Malley
160 pages,
black-and-white interiors
$11.95 US
ISBN 1929998-71-6
Available October 2003!

MARIA'S WEDDING™
by Nunzio DeFilippis,
Christina Weir, &
Jose Garibaldi
88 pages,
black-and-white interiors
$10.95 US
ISBN 1929998-57-0

ONE BAD DAY™
by Steve Rolston
120 pages,
green-and-white interiors
$9.95 US
ISBN: 1-929998-50-3

ONE PLUS ONE™
By Neal Shaffer & Daniel Krall
152 pages,
black-and-white interiors
$14.95 US
ISBN: 1-929998-65-1

POUNDED™
by Brian Wood & Steve Rolston
96 pages,
black-and-white interiors
$8.95 US
ISBN 1929998-37-6

*SIDEKICKS, Vol. 1
THE TRANSFER STUDENT™*
by J. Torres & Takeshi Miyazawa
144 pages,
black-and-white interiors
$11.95 US
ISBN: 1-929998-76-7
New edition October 2003!

VISITATIONS™
by Scott Morse
88 pages,
black-and-white interiors
$8.95 US
ISBN 1-929998-34-1